FLY LOW
FLY FAST

ALSO BY ROBERT GANDT

Season of Storms: The Siege of Hong Kong 1941
China Clipper: The Age of the Great Flying Boats
Skygods: The Fall of Pan Am
Bogeys and Bandits: The Making of a Fighter Pilot

FLY LOW

FLY FAST

INSIDE THE RENO

AIR RACES

ROBERT GANDT

VIKING BOOKS

VIKING
Published by the Penguin Group
Penguin Putnam Inc., 375 Hudson Street,
New York, New York 10014, U.S.A.
Penguin Books Ltd, 27 Wrights Lane,
London W8 5TZ, England
Penguin Books Australia Ltd, Ringwood,
Victoria, Australia
Penguin Books Canada Ltd, 10 Alcorn Avenue,
Toronto, Ontario, Canada M4V 3B2
Penguin Books (N.Z.) Ltd, 182–190 Wairau Road,
Auckland 10, New Zealand

Penguin Books Ltd, Registered Offices:
Harmondsworth, Middlesex, England

First published in 1999 by Viking Penguin,
a member of Penguin Putnam Inc.

1   3   5   7   9   10   8   6   4   2

LIBRARY OF CONGRESS CATALOGING-IN-PUBLICATION DATA

Gandt, Robert L.
Fly Low, Fly Fast : the Reno Air Races : a season at speed /
by Robert Gandt.
p.   cm.
ISBN 0-670-88451-0
1. National Championship Air Races.   I. Title.
GV759.2.N37G36   1999
797.5'2'0979355—dc21   99–24512

This book is printed on acid-free paper.
∞

Printed in the United States of America
Set in New Aster
Designed by Mia Risberg

For pretty Pia
who makes me proud

You love a lot of things if you live around them, but there isn't any woman and there isn't any horse, nor any before nor any after, that is as lovely as a great airplane, and men who love them are faithful to them even though they leave them for others. A man has only one virginity to lose in fighters, and if it is a lovely plane he loses it to, there his heart will ever be.

—Ernest Hemingway

Contents

CONTENTS

PART TWO
The Road to Reno

PART THREE
The Young Turks

Acknowledgments

This is a true story. The events, thoughts, dialogue, and impressions in this book are construed from multiple, sometimes conflicting points of view. Any errors of transcription or interpretation are my own.

To all the members of the air-racing community who admitted me to their inner circle, I owe sincere thanks. In particular, I am indebted to intrepid race pilots Bill "Tiger" Destefani, Lyle Shelton, Skip Holm, Howard Pardue, Bruce Lockwood, Bill Rheinschild, Bob "Hurricane" Hannah, Robert "Hoot" Gibson, and Curt Brown for sharing personal information and anecdotes. Master crew chief Bill Kerchenfaut cheerfully shared his thirty-some years' racing experience as well as his unstinting good humor.

Thanks to the Reno Air Racing Association for giving me ingress to the Room of Hard Benches, and special gratitude to friend and fighter pilot Jack Thomas, Reno Air Boss, who opened the right doors. To writer and historian John Tegler, for sharing his encyclopedic knowledge of the sport of air racing, I am particularly indebted.

Thanks, again, go to my literary agent, Alice Martell, of the Martell Agency, and to Hal Fessenden, my editor at Viking Penguin, for staying the course.

RG
Spring 1999

PART ONE

The Brethren

Two and a half football fields every second . . .
If that doesn't get your stuff working,
then your stuff's not gonna work.
                    —race pilot Alan Preston

Prologue

It was damned peculiar, he thought. Bill "Tiger" Destefani had never heard this particular noise before. Here he was, ripping across the floor of the desert at nearly 500 miles per hour, and suddenly there was this . . . *silence*.

But it wasn't really silence. The big, throbbing sound of the Rolls-Royce Merlin engine had been replaced by a kind of shriek. It sounded like a howling banshee. It took Destefani several seconds to realize what he was hearing: the high-pitched screech of the airstream slipping over *Strega's* aluminum skin at nearly supersonic speed. The sound had always been there, of course, but it was usually drowned out by that baritone bellow of the Merlin engine cranking out 3000 horsepower.

The Merlin was one of the most goose-bump-inducing engine noises on the planet, ranking somewhere between the space shuttle and the Harley-Davidson in charismatic sound effects. Anyone who had ever been in the vicinity of a low-flying Mustang or Spitfire fighter never forgot the sound.

3

The Rolls-Royce Merlin engines, race pilots said, were like high-strung mistresses. When they were good, they were *really* good. They could transport you to a state of ecstasy. When they were bad, they could spit flame and oil and molten metal like screaming furies from hell. Of all the racing airplanes out there at Reno, the Merlin-powered Mustangs were the most temperamental. Over the years Mustangs had made more spectacular returns to the earth at Reno than any other type of race plane.

It wasn't hard to understand why. Inside the cowling (which in layman's terms means "under the hood") of a Mustang was a scene of unimaginable violence: twenty-one thousand high-compression explosions each minute, three thousand hunks of sizzling metal alloy flailing, rotating, gyrating, in unison, sucking in an exotic high-octane, compressed air-fuel vapor with the explosive property of nitroglycerin. What was even more unimaginable was that all this violence stayed somehow contained within the fragile metal shell of the engine compartment.

Of course, sometimes it didn't.

In his secret heart every Mustang pilot knew that if he flew long enough behind a Merlin, a certain day would come. That sweet-sounding, contented purr of the Merlin would be replaced by a cacophony of metallic violence. Or a flash of god-awful orange flame. Or a sheet of superheated oil blackening the windshield.

Or the ghastly silence of a stopped engine.

Everyone who raced Mustangs knew that such a day might come. The bitch-mistress Merlin would turn on him. The big, throbbing rumble would become a hideous shriek. For Tiger Destefani, that day was today.

Destefani was the reigning world's Unlimited Air Racing champion. He had already won this event, held annually at Stead Field in Reno, Nevada, five times; this year he intended to make it six. But first, before they began the heat races and then the final trophy race on the upcoming Sunday, everyone had to go out on the course and post a qualifying time.

Strega, Destefani's *very* tricked-out Mustang, with clipped wings and a hugely overstretched engine, was humming nicely. The Merlin sounded like a happy animal mounted up there in the Mustang's long, graceful nose. In its original World War II version, the Merlin cranked out 1,475 horsepower, which gave the Mustang enough clout to eat up anything the Luftwaffe could put in the sky.

That was then. *Strega*'s engine had been modified, stretched, and stroked so that it was capable of an incredible 3,800 horsepower! Of course, Destefani wasn't pushing it that hard, at least not today. All that high-end, unrestrained, eyeball-popping torque he intended to save for Sunday, the day of the Unlimited Gold race. Then he'd use it all if necessary—whatever it took to be in front of the pack when they waved the checkered flag.

Yes, things were humming nicely—as far as Tiger knew. But what he didn't know was that certain events were transpiring inside the cowling that would change his day.

It was Monday afternoon, nearly five o'clock, and Tiger had *Strega*'s nose pointed down the chute. Except for an hour-long test flight and then the ferry flight over the mountains from Bakersfield, this newly installed engine had not been worked hard. Tiger was taking it easy. For his first lap around the course he nudged the throttle up to sixty inches of manifold pressure—less than half of *Strega*'s full power.

All okay. The early-evening air was smooth, and *Strega* was handling well. Destefani was rounding the pylons on a counter-clockwise circuit, staying level, not wasting energy by letting the Mustang climb in the turn, then descending back to the straight-away. This kind of flying was a treat, zipping around the course without the presence of other racers to challenge and harass him. His only rival out here today was the clock. All he had to do was fly fast and post the best qualification time. Then he could take the next three days off until the first heat races.

Strega was ready, and so was Destefani. No need to waste fuel or engine life. Approaching the home pylon, he radioed, "Race Seven, on the clock."

He pushed the throttle up. The throb of the Merlin deepened. Tiger felt himself nudged back in the seat as the Mustang accelerated.

Strega was moving now, approaching 500 miles per hour on the straightaway. Coming up on pylon 8, Destefani rolled the Mustang up on its left wing, pulling four and a quarter Gs as he entered the turn. Under the force of over four times his normal weight, he felt himself squashed down in the seat. Little streams of perspiration squirted down from beneath his helmet. Coming around the pylon, he was aimed down the home stretch, the last leg of the course, past the grandstands and the pits and the ramp area. For Destefani, this was a familiar scenario.

Meanwhile, the *other* scenario—the one being played out just beyond the periphery of Destefani's awareness—was reaching a climax.

At some point since its installation, the flange of the Merlin engine's rear-left exhaust stack had become warped, causing it to be imperfectly mated to the engine's exhaust port. Through the tiny leak between the exhaust port and the stack, a jet of white-hot exhaust gas was spewing against the aluminum cowling. And now that the engine was being revved up to very high power—nearly twice its original design limit—the heated gas was melting away the cowling frame that separated the hot engine compartment from the ignition magnetos.

Something had to give. And, in the space of the next three seconds, it did. A sequence of events brought the two scenarios—the one in Destefani's cockpit and the one beneath the cowling—into chaotic union.

The jet of hot exhaust reached the vital P-leads, the two main cables from the magnetos to the Merlin's twenty-four spark plugs . . .

Zzzzzssst! The P-leads melted, followed by . . .

A cessation of electricity from the magnetos to the spark plugs, causing . . .

All twenty-four spark plugs to stop firing, resulting in . . .

Silence—a quietness so profound and ghastly that it triggered a surge of adrenaline in Tiger Destefani powerful enough to jolt a mule.

Destefani's happiness vanished in a heartbeat. Here he was, at 500 miles per hour, a hundred feet over the desert floor, in full charge toward the home pylon. And his 3,800-horsepower engine was putting out this sudden, utter, ghastly *nothing*. He could hear just this *shriek*.

The most peculiar thing about it was that he couldn't hear a sound from the freaking engine. Not a growl, not even a croaking groan. It was as though every spark of life had been removed from the damned thing.

But the strangest noise was that goddamned *shrieking* sound. Shit, that was *really* weird, hearing all that air noise *without* the accompanying roar of a healthy, full-throated Merlin engine.

He had practiced this scene a hundred times in his head. That had always been Destefani's training technique, to play over and again such events in his imagination, going through each phase of the emergency procedure when things suddenly went to hell. It was the same visualization technique professional athletes used to rehearse their games. Destefani would rehearse each sequence in his mind until he could see himself handling it without a mistake.

But that was all in his imagination. This was the real thing.

Destefani hauled the nose of *Strega* upward, converting the nearly 500 miles per hour of kinetic energy to lifesaving altitude. The more the better.

"Race Seven, Mayday!" he called on the operations frequency.

"Roger, Tiger," came the calm voice of Jack Thomas, the operations director up in his open-air tower. "The airport's yours. Wind one-three-zero at ten knots. Which runway do you want?"

"Zero-eight."

"You're cleared to land, runway zero-eight."

Cleared to land. That sounded like a joke, except that no one was laughing. You were always supposed to get clearance before you landed. In this case *Strega* was going to land in exactly ninety seconds, clearance or not. The only question was whether it would be on concrete or dirt.

Up, up, high above the desert the engineless fighter soared. At four thousand feet Destefani nosed over. The Mustang was indicating 170 knots of airspeed, the optimum speed for an engine-out descent.

Now *Strega* was a glider. But unlike a *real* glider, the stubby-winged, nine-thousand-pound Mustang fighter had all the gliding characteristics of a descending dump truck.

Down he came. Below he could see the sprawl of Stead Field, with its three connected runways, all looking pitifully short and narrow. And he could see the surrounding terrain—rocks and dwarf trees and serrated ridges. It looked like the surface of an asteroid.

Tiger knew the procedure by heart. This would be a dead-stick landing—the pilots' term for an arrival in an airplane without power. Not only had he practiced it a hundred times in his head; he'd already lived through a dozen such experiences, most of them here at Reno.

Tiger was acting out all the moves he'd rehearsed in his visualization drills: Fly abeam the landing end of the runway at no less than two thousand feet. Keep the thing turning toward the runway. *Don't land short!* Landing short was ugly. It meant gullies and boulders and explosions. Landing short trashed your million-dollar airplane and turned you into a crispy critter. Aim a third of the way down the runway. That gave you some room for error. Get the gear down, then wait on the landing flaps. Use only a few degrees of flaps at first, just what you need. Flaps were high-drag items, meaning they increased your sink rate, shortened your glide, put your butt in the sagebrush. Save full flaps until you had the runway made.

It was working. Destefani brought *Strega* around the base leg of the approach, turning all the way, lining up with runway 08. He had the Mustang's gear down. He could tell that on this descent path he would land nearly halfway down the runway.

Good. Time to lower some more flaps, steepen the glide path. That would shorten the glide and land him only about a third down the runway.

The end of runway 08 swept beneath him. He lowered the flaps to full, letting the Mustang slow to landing speed.

Chirp! Chirp! The wheels of the main landing gear stroked the concrete. Tiger let the Mustang roll out, gently lowering the tail wheel to the runway.

From the pit area, *Strega*'s worried ground crew watched the drama play itself out. They had heard the engine go dead as the racer was roaring down the home stretch, seen Destefani pull up, held their collective breath while he executed the dead-stick approach and landing.

It was over. *Strega* and Destefani were safe. They could breathe again. However, like Destefani, they still had no clue as to what had gone wrong.

While *Strega* was still rolling out, Bill Kerchenfaut, the team's crew chief, called on the radio. In the high drama of the moment, no one seemed to notice the pointlessness of his question: "Can you make it on your own power, or do you need a tug?"

For several seconds, no one said anything. The Mustang rolled to a stop on the runway. *Strega*'s big four-bladed propeller was motionless. The Merlin engine was as silent as a tomb.

Destefani said, deadpan, "Better bring the tug."

⊱ 1 ⊰

The Room of Hard Benches

Brown. That's all you saw in any direction—a sprawling, unfertile desertscape as bleak and barren as the Kalahari. Someone back in the last century had named this place Truckee Meadow, which all the race pilots figured had to be a joke. How could a sun-fried plateau like this ever have been a *meadow?* Truckee looked like one of those boulder-strewn landscapes photographed on the surface of Mars. Nothing could live out there except roadrunners and rattlesnakes.

Which made it a suitable place for the National Championship Races. Out here in the high desert, in Reno, Nevada, pilots came every September to race these tweaked-out, temperamental ex-warbirds.

The briefing room had the look and feel of an old wartime facility, the kind you saw in *Twelve O'Clock High* and *Baa Baa Black Sheep*. It had that bare, no-nonsense ambience to it—corrugated metal walls, ubiquitous chalkboard on the front wall, rows of hard, butt-breaking wooden benches. You could imagine the squadron commander clearing his throat, pointing to the map on the wall: "Gentlemen, our target today is this ball-bearing factory at . . ."

In fact, this room once *was* a military facility, belonging to the former Stead Air Force Base and, later, the Nevada Air National Guard. Stead Field sprawled out over a high desert plateau, fourteen miles north of Reno.

The Brethren—the elite little coterie of pilots who flew Unlimited race planes—started trickling in at a quarter to ten. The rookies always showed up first. This being their first year of racing, they wanted to make a good impression. Keep their mouths shut and act deferential to the old-timers and the celebrity pilots. Show that they were taking this stuff seriously. A couple of minutes before ten, the older hands—Destefani, Howard Pardue, Lloyd Hamilton—would stroll in and take their seats toward the front of the room.

Prerace briefings at Reno were a big deal, and attendance was mandatory. The rule was inflexible: If you didn't show at the briefing, you didn't race. No brief, no fly. No exceptions.

As usual, the Brethren had organized themselves into a distinct pecking order. In the front row sat the old hands: gravel-voiced Lloyd Hamilton, who headed the race pilots' standards committee and could be counted on to deliver an ass chewing to whoever screwed up qualifying the day before; the two Sanders brothers, Dennis and Brian, whose family had been racing the big R-4360-powered Sea Fury, *Dreadnought,* for the past fourteen years; Destefani, reigning champion and top wisecracker of the Unlimited Class; Howard Pardue, veteran air racer and patriarch of the warbird community.

In concentric rows around these luminaries sat an equally rarefied group, the hired guns: Skip Holm, for-hire race pilot, two-time Unlimited champion and rival of Destefani's in sheer volume of wisecracks; Alan Preston, an athletic-looking young guy who had flown most of the top warbirds; Steve Hinton, who won the Gold race in 1978 with the *Red Baron* and in 1985 in *Super Corsair* and who now flew the T-33 pace plane.

The benches had been there for years, since long before air racing came to Reno. They had etchings and carvings—pilots' initials, cartoons, tracings of airplanes—the kind of things bored kids carved with pocketknives on wooden desks. One bench had an exaggerated depiction of the now-extinct twin-engined *Pond Racer*. Another bore a carved likeness of a P-51, with the caption SPONSORED BY MUSTANG RANCH (a local brothel). Some contained the initials of pilots who were no longer alive.

Waiting for the briefing to begin, the pilots joked and kidded each other. That was part of the prerace ritual, the wisecracking and friendly insults. It was the way you were expected to conduct yourself at these race briefings—acting lighthearted and casual about that which you knew could get you—or someone in this room—killed that very day. It was a form of high-stakes whistling in the dark. It was the same studied insouciance you saw in combat aviators, race-car drivers, matadors.

Beneath the surface, under the layer of frivolity and the briefing-room jokes, lay something else. It was a tension—an invisible current crackling in the air above their heads.

This space, the Room of Hard Benches, was filled with the ghosts of pilots they had all known, racers who had experienced Maydays—just like the scenarios they were discussing here at this briefing. For reasons not always understood, they had perished out there on the high desert. They were guys just like the ones who were sitting here today, joking, chewing furiously on wads of gum, carving their initials in the benches like unruly sixth-graders. Then they went out and got killed.

They were supposed to sit here and be lectured about course rules and why they shouldn't pass on the inside and how to handle a Mayday. As if the thought had never occurred to them: Me? Have a Mayday? Lose an engine? It was the very thought that haunted them like a bad dream.

Almost all Maydays during an air race stemmed from an engine problem. Race-plane power plants were, by definition, temperamental, tweaked-out, overstressed devices that could suddenly turn on you like a crazed rottweiler. You would be cruising down the straight-away, carving the *perfect* line around the pylons, thinking you were bulletproof, when—*whang!*—that big 3,000-horsepower behemoth on the nose of your airplane would suddenly self-destruct. How you handled yourself in the next ninety seconds meant everything—win or lose, land or crash, live or die. Your entire life's experience suddenly condensed to this little flashpoint in time. It was the race pilot's moment of truth.

Every pilot who raced at Reno for a few years experienced his own moment of truth. In most cases, *many* such moments. It was simply a matter of statistical probability: If you flew in enough races, *something* was going to happen. Someday, while you were sitting in the cockpit of your thundering, overtuned warbird, something godawful was going to go wrong, thrusting you right up to the precipitous edge of the Great Abyss. You could count on it.

In some previous season, each of those missing pilots had sat there on the wooden benches, trading jibes and insults, gnawing on a wad of gum, and carving schoolboy cartoons on the benches. Like everyone else, they knew that what they were doing was *very* dangerous. But like most race pilots, they believed that the bad things—the *really* ugly mishaps that ended in a smoking hole—would happen to someone else. They carried that notion around in their heads, like a secret talisman, that *they*, unique among all the creatures on the planet, were exceptionally blessed.

Yeah, bad things *did* happen out there. But not to them.

Each of the four Reno racing classes—Unlimiteds, AT-6s, biplanes, and the Formula Ones (100 horsepower homebuilts)—had its own "class president." The class president was responsible for his racers' prerace briefings and for their adherence to the racing association's rigid rules of safety.

John Penney, a studious-looking, bespectacled young man who

flew *Rare Bear* as Lyle Shelton's backup pilot, was president of the Unlimited Class. Penney took his duties very seriously. Every morning at ten o'clock during race week, he convened his class there in the Room of Hard Benches. The briefing covered subjects like schedules, the previous day's problems, rules infractions, and, mostly, not getting killed.

The pilots had heard this part of the briefing before. It was the same briefing every year, like a hymn from the same old choir book. It sounded so rudimentary: "Remember, if your engine quits, pull up overhead the airport. Turn *toward* the field, not away. Fly at the best glide speed for your type aircraft. Aim to land one-third of the way down the runway, on target speed."

Well, sure. Wasn't that what you were *supposed* to do? That part should be a no-brainer. It was the same thing they were taught back when each of them was a student pilot learning to fly puddle jumpers.

Penney was pointing at the schematic of the airport that was projected onto the wall screen. "Aim long. Don't land short." His pointer tapped on the empty white areas off the end of each runway. Every pilot knew what those empty white areas contained. They were not empty at all, but were the pocked, boulder-strewn moonscape of the high desert where, if you were unlucky or unwitting enough to land there—*KerrrrWhooom!*—the chances were more than even that you would become a Reno statistic.

But why would anyone land short? When you had a choice of three nice, long concrete runways just beneath you, why would anyone wind up plunking down on the lunar surface of the Nevada desert? It was something that just shouldn't happen.

The only thing was, it *did* happen. Pilots experiencing their first emergencies commonly reported a feeling of *denial*. That deathly clanking noise—the unearthly silence of a stopped engine, the sickening lurch of a loss of power from your racer—*wasn't real*. For the first few precious seconds of time, a pilot would sit there in an adrenaline-charged stupor, waiting for the bad dream to end. By the time the grim reality of his predicament sank in, his options were few. Lifesaving altitude and airspeed had been squandered.

"Pick your runway," Penney was saying. "Stay with it. Save your gear and flaps until you have the runway made. Stay calm."

Stay calm. Ah, now there was some really useful advice. Every pilot had to gnaw a little harder on his gum at that one. What an easy thing to say, sitting there in the hard-benched safety of the briefing room. It was a vital piece of information you were supposed to take with you in the cockpit, as if it were an item on a checklist: *Gear down. Flaps down. Boost pump on. And the last item— Oh, yeah: Stay calm.*

No problem. Consider me calm. Checklist complete.

Over the past few years nearly a score of pilots had dumped their airplanes in those empty white areas off the runway at Reno. In all four classes of racing, ten pilots had lost their lives. Most of the pilots in this room had known them. They were guys just like them; they, too, had sat through briefings just like this one, gnawing on the wads of gum, carving initials into the benches, believing the same self-deluding falsehoods: *Naaah, it won't happen. Not to me.*

⊁ 2 ⊁

That Old Feeling

With all the lights flooding the ramp, *Strega*'s pit area looked like a space-shuttle launch site. Crew members were perched on ladders and work stands, laboring on the exposed engine compartment of the Mustang.

All the other race pits were deserted. It was past ten o'clock, and everyone—race teams, fans, officials—had long ago headed for town and were now bellied up to the Pylon Bar down at the Hilton. All except Team *Strega*. Kerchenfaut and the *Strega* crew would be working until dawn.

The good news was that *Strega*'s engine itself had suffered no real damage when it shut down on Destefani. But the cowling—the external housing of the engine compartment—was a mess. It was deformed with bulges and ripples from the exhaust leak. A new former—the inside frame of the cowling—would have to be fabricated from raw sheet metal. And the faulty exhaust stack—the original culprit in this day's drama—would have to be resurfaced and fitted to the engine. The melted P-leads to the magnetos would have to be replaced.

The team's crew base and maintenance facility was a big red eighteen-wheel trailer. An attached awning formed the hangar enclosure for *Strega,* and an adjoining motor home served as the administrative and lounging space. In the trailer was a shop with sophisticated welding and metallurgy equipment, a high-tech avionics facility with real-time telemetry linking of vital engine and performance data between *Strega* and the ground base, and a storehouse of parts, including spare engines. Atop the trailer was a miniature control tower from which the ground team communicated directly with *Strega* in flight.

Bill Kerchenfaut was not your typical race-team crew chief. Most aviation maintenance professionals dwelled in their own little arcane world of tools and technology. They possessed business and managerial skills in inverse proportion to their mechanical talent. They were lousy organization men.

Team *Strega's* crew chief was different. Kerchenfaut was an organizational whiz. In real life he worked in Silicon Valley, in the aviation department at Hewlett-Packard. He was a fifty-something-year-old bachelor, and it was a joke around the pits that he was married to *Strega.* And there was some truth to it. Kerchenfaut was a guy with a passion for high-performance, intricately engineered contraptions—automobiles, stereos, airplanes. In the capricious, cold-metal heart of *Strega,* he had found the nearest thing to a soul mate.

Kerchenfaut was a congenial gnome, short and compactly built, filled with a demonic energy. His bald head was ringed with a fringe of white. And he loved to talk; he would talk your ear off, especially if the subject was airplanes or racing.

Around the pit area, he was in constant motion—in the shops, under the cowling, yakking with Destefani or a mechanic or a race fan or whoever felt like talking. He could juggle sixteen balls without dropping any of them. When things got slow or Kerchenfaut was bored, he would call a meeting of the race team. He ran his team like a corporate board. *Everyone*—pilot, mechanics, avionics guys, wrench gofers—was required to attend his meetings, which he held every morning. Like a mission controller, Kerchenfaut would go over the previous day's screwups, demanding accountability, soliciting input, assigning tasks.

Kerchenfaut had been involved with *Strega* since its first racing days. By now he understood every nuance of the sleek Mustang's personality. He knew how to tweak one more mile per hour out of its airframe. He could listen to the staccato bark of the Merlin engine and tell you whether something—fouled plug, sticky valve, bad timing—wasn't right. Over the years it was Kerchenfaut, more than anyone else, who had made *Strega* a winner.

Destefani understood the importance of keeping a guy like Kerchenfaut. The difference between first place and something in the back of the pack, or not finishing at all due to a failed engine, sometimes amounted to nothing more than an infinitesimal performance advantage. It was something you got only from the most nitpicking attention to detail. Kerchenfaut was a world-class picker of nits.

Destefani also knew that race teams sometimes came unraveled because of personalities. A winning race pilot, brimming with inflated ego ("We're all prima donnas, you know"), would clash with his crew chief over some petty issue—a difference of opinion about maintenance or a criticism of technique—and the crew chief (also a bona fide prima donna) would slam the lid on his tool chest and storm away. The crew chief would be replaced, but the team would never be the same. For no easily explained reason, the racer would stop winning.

In the opinion of several racers, that was what happened to Lyle Shelton. "Ol' Lyle had a good crew chief," said a veteran racer. "They were winning everything, setting records left and right. Then something happened. He got crossways with his crew chief. Since then the Bear's never gotten close to the speed record it set a few years back."

For eleven years Destefani and Kerchenfaut had been together, and though they sometimes clashed, usually over the care and handling of *Strega,* the team somehow managed to stay intact. And they kept winning.

It was Monday night, and Kerchenfaut had his crew working overtime. The inside of the trailer sounded like a blacksmith shop. A mechanic, Randy Foster, was whanging away on a piece of metal that would become the new cowling former. Dwight Thorn, the master engine builder whose power plants had won more Reno races than any other, was surfacing the exhaust stack. Kerchenfaut himself was cranking up the welder, preparing to fabricate the new cowling former.

They worked until dawn. That afternoon, Destefani was airborne again in *Strega.* After a practice lap, he reported that the engine was running perfectly. He called for the clock. In 70.8 seconds, *Strega* completed her qualifying lap, an elapsed time that translated to 464 miles per hour.

It was the fastest qualifying speed at Reno. So far.

Destefani liked to break racing down into three phases. "First, you gotta get there," he always said. This sounded basic, but it could get complicated. Not only did the airplane have to be ready; so did the parts and people that went into the team. You had to get your airplane over the High Sierra from California to Nevada. All your people and all the rolling and flying stock had to be sitting there on the ramp at Stead Field by Sunday, the first day of the race week.

"The second thing you gotta do is *qualify.*" You had three days—until Wednesday—to post a lap qualifying time. If something was wrong with your racer, you had to fix it. Only twenty-four airplanes—

the *fastest* twenty-four qualifying times—would be in the lineup when the first racing heats started Thursday. No matter how hard you'd worked that winter, how well rehearsed your crew, how refined your airplane, if you didn't push the thing around the course in a time that put you in the top twenty-four, you could fold your tent and go home.

"The last thing you gotta do, of course, is win the race. That's all. Just stay cool and win the damn race. That means you can't go *banzai*, do something stupid and blow it. There's no such thing as a sure thing."

In last year's Unlimited Gold race, Destefani followed his own advice. He had found himself in a head-to-head battle with *Dago Red*, a Mustang that he once co-owned and that had served as the model for *Strega*. Both fighters had rolled out of Destefani's raceworks back in Bakersfield. Each had almost the same clipped wings and were powered by nearly identical Dwight Thorn–built Merlin engines. They were so close in performance that it was impossible to say which was faster.

And that was how it turned out in the 1996 championship race. *Dago Red*, flown by her owner, David Price, traded the lead position with *Strega* for the first five laps. And then, hammering along in *Dago Red*'s wake, trailing by fewer than three seconds, Destefani witnessed an event of immense value to him: *Dago Red cut a pylon!*

Did the judges see it? Destefani could only pray that they did. A pylon cut meant a penalty assessment of two seconds per lap. Sixteen seconds! That amounted to a spread of a quarter of a lap. Between such identically matched racers, that was a gargantuan advantage. It meant that Destefani, armed with this secret knowledge that neither the fans in the grandstand nor, probably, Price himself shared, could loaf along in a comfortable spot well behind *Dago Red* without flogging the hell out of his delicate Merlin engine. And he would still win!

And that's what he did. He throttled back, crossing the finish line in second place but already knowing that the judges would penalize Price for the cut and bump him back to second.

The fans, of course, were pissed. There was a lot booing and hissing. This wasn't the kind of blood-stirring finish that they had come to see. They thought they were seeing some kind of mano a mano between rivals when all along, Destefani—that sneaky little shit!— was *dogging it! Pretending* to be challenging the leader when he was actually just coddling his damned engine! Playing it safe! The fans felt cheated.

Destefani, for his part, couldn't care less. He walked up to the victory circle gnawing a wad of Skoal, looking just as cocky and full of himself as always. Hell, winning was what it was all about, right? Gamesmanship counted for everything in racing. First place was first place, at least as long as the prize check cleared the bank.

That was 1996, and *Dago Red* was not in the lineup this year. No one would say exactly why. It was rumored that Price had found a buyer for *Dago* and was skipping this year's races. With *Dago Red* out of the picture, *Strega's* only real competition for the 1997 Gold was its perennial rival, a gold-and-white-painted Bearcat named *Rare Bear*. Over the years, Lyle Shelton's Bearcat had won the Reno race more times than any single airplane. During the past couple of years *Rare Bear*—and Shelton himself—had been plagued with troubles, both mechanical and personal.

Shelton had been out of the game for the past three years because he lacked one critical credential: He lacked a pilot's license because his medical certificate had been yanked by the Federal Aviation Administration (FAA). This came about because of a DUI arrest, an offense that costs you not only your driver's license but, these days, your ticket to fly airplanes.

Shelton had already beseeched the FAA to grant him a temporary certificate so that he could race *Rare Bear* at Reno. In 1995 his crew had even drafted a petition and gathered signatures imploring the

FAA to reconsider. It was all futile, of course. Persuading the FAA to reverse a license suspension was as likely as changing the orbit of Mars.

Thus was John Penney, the alternate pilot, drafted to fly *Rare Bear.* Penney was a classic airplane-head: He learned to fly as a kid, graduated from the Air Force Academy, flew 140 combat missions in Southeast Asia, worked as an engineer and test pilot on the experimental Lear Fan 2100, and was now an airline pilot and, on the side, test-flew exotic jets like the MiG-15 and MiG-17.

Penney started flying *Rare Bear* in 1994—when Shelton's troubles with the FAA began—and won his first race that year at Phoenix. In 1995, after setting a new qualifying-speed record, he came in second behind Destefani in *Strega.* The next year, 1996, with Shelton still getting no sympathy from the FAA, Penney was again *Rare Bear*'s primary pilot. After only two laps, the Bearcat came down with calamitous engine problems, and Penney nursed it back to the runway.

Now it was 1997, and Shelton was back, license in hand. And he wanted to win. He *needed* to win, because time and money were running out on him. Unlike other race teams, Shelton didn't have seriously big bucks behind him. He was a now-retired airline pilot with only his pension and a minuscule navy retirement fund. With each of the last several years here at Reno, he had gone deeper in the hole, borrowing against his retirement money to finance *Rare Bear*'s voracious appetite for parts and maintenance. True, he had several small sponsorships, the most generous one from Shell Oil, but none of this came close to matching the deficit he racked up every year.

For Shelton and *Rare Bear,* this was a make-it-or-break-it year. He needed a victory. Most of all, he needed the victor's prize money. All he had to do was beat that damned Destefani.

10 September 1997

It was ten minutes before six o'clock, and Shelton was pushing up the throttle on *Rare Bear*. No one else would have time to fly another qualifying lap before the deadline. Now, whatever speed he posted, he could be sure that Destefani wasn't going to come along and top it by one lousy mile per hour and steal the pole slot that Shelton was shooting for.

That old feeling was coming back. Shelton could feel the rhythmic *whum whum whum*—a harmonic vibration from the propeller at a little over two cycles per second—coming up through the airframe, transmitted to his body through the seat. His hand tingled from the vibration on the control stick. His feet were getting a high-frequency massage through the rudder pedals.

It was all a matter of gamesmanship. Shelton knew that better than anyone. Hell, he had *invented* most of the tricky little games they played out there on the pylons. Gamesmanship was at least as important as having the fastest airplane or the coolest pair of hands. It was how Destefani won in 1996, dogging along in second place, ensuring the survival of his engine, *knowing* he had the prize locked in.

And it was exactly what Shelton was doing now—waiting until the last minute on Wednesday evening to *really* let out all the stops and post the fastest qualifying time. The idea was to qualify as fast as you could and get the pole position. That gave you an automatic leg up on the rest of the pack. Anyone who wanted to pass you had to do it on the outside of your path around the pylons, going wide and covering more real estate.

But once you'd posted a qualifying speed and captured the pole position, then it naturally became the target for everyone else to shoot at. You were allowed to come back and requalify, trying to up your official time, but the last official qualifying opportunity was Wednesday at six o'clock. Then all the times were locked in, and that would determine the official order of starting.

Three years. Three humiliating, ego-grinding, earth-dwelling years

24

he'd been grounded by the FAA. And during that time Shelton's problems had been aired for the whole world to see—all the ugly stuff about drinking and driving and being arrested and whether or not he was a bona-fide alcoholic. A few Shelton haters had even suggested that, considering his reputation, it would be better for the sport if he were no longer associated with it.

Well, none of that mattered now. He was back, and the only thing that mattered was how he flew. And how *Rare Bear* performed. Winning was all that mattered.

You get rusty, being out of the cockpit that long. And Shelton was no longer a kid fighter pilot who could make up with nerve and superior reflexes what he lacked in recent experience. He was sixty-three, an age when most men thought about slowing down.

But Shelton wasn't slowing down. Instead, he was going 480 miles per hour downhill, adding the power to *Rare Bear*. It was all coming back now, but he knew he wasn't as sharp as he used to be or as he would be after he'd done this a few more times.

He was adding the power incrementally, nudging the throttle and the rpm (revolutions per minute of the propeller) up, balancing the two settings, until he had full power—3,200 rpm and seventy inches of manifold pressure. This was supposed to deliver 3,800 horsepower. But *Rare Bear* had even more available. By injecting nitrous oxide into the engine ("going on drugs," the engine builders called it), the horsepower jumped up to 4,200. It was like kicking in the afterburner of a jet.

And the controls—they were getting stiff! This always happened, he remembered now, at about 375 miles per hour; then they got stiffer the faster the Bearcat flew.

Then he noticed something else he'd forgotten: It was hotter than hell inside this damned cockpit! At race power, inside this little Plexiglas bubble canopy, ripping through the air at this speed, the temperature built up until it was like a sauna in the tiny Bearcat cockpit.

Coming around the first pylon, he remembered something else.

For reasons he and Penney had never figured out, the nose of the Bear slewed way off to the right when he rolled into the turn. He had to literally *stand* on the left rudder to keep the fighter's nose straight.

But now there was something new that he hadn't observed before: At high speed, he was having to hold forward stick—maintaining downward pressure on his control stick—to keep *Rare Bear*'s nose from pitching up. A *lot* of forward stick. Why? He felt grossly uncomfortable, and not just because of the strain of holding the damned stick forward; he couldn't help thinking what would happen if the nose *did* pitch violently up at nearly 500 miles per hour. It would probably rip the wings off.

It was a serious problem. What the hell was causing it? An aft center of gravity? That would mean that the airplane, for whatever reason, was out of balance. It had too much weight in the tail, which was causing the nose to pitch upward. But nothing had been added or subtracted from the Bearcat's airframe to alter its center of gravity. Or had it? During the past year of overhaul and maintenance, was something modified on the airframe that they hadn't accounted for? Or was it something to do with the trim—the way the elevator surfaces were exposed to the airstream? Was the elevator—the control surface on the tail that raised and lowered the airplane's nose—somehow causing the nose to pitch up? Shelton decided it was a problem that would have to be solved, one way or another, before the championship race.

What about the engine? It was running smoothly enough. Those little *whum-whum-whums* meant that things were normal up there. But something was missing: It didn't seem to be putting out as much as it should. As if it were short a few hundred horses. Shelton had flown behind these engines—Wright R-3350 radials—for so many thousand hours, he knew their every little nuance. He could *feel* when they weren't putting out.

This one felt *anemic.*

He knew that *Rare Bear,* in favorable circumstances, was capable of a speed in excess of 500 miles per hour. No one had yet posted a 500-mile-per-hour qualifying speed at Reno, but several racers were nibbling at the edge, including *Strega* and *Rare Bear*. It was mostly a matter of how much you wanted to hold back, spare your engine, before the *real* racing began.

Two years ago, in 1995, Penney had set a new qualifying-speed record with the Bearcat, turning a lap speed of 489 miles per hour. That was within spitting distance of the elusive 500 miles per hour. But during the Unlimited Gold championship race that same week, the Bear's R-3350 engine developed its mysterious infirmity and came up short. Penney trailed Destefani across the finish line by two miles per hour, turning in a speed of only 465 miles per hour.

In 1996 the mysterious infirmity was back, lurking like a gremlin under *Rare Bear*'s cowling. Except this time it swelled into a full-fledged power outage, causing Penney to drop out after two laps.

Now it was Shelton who had to confront the gremlin. And he could tell that it was still there. Despite all the disassembly, reassembly, tweaking and tuning, cursing and head scratching, the engine was *still* losing power. It was damned frustrating.

This was Shelton's last chance to beat Destefani's qualifying time of 464 miles per hour. In five more minutes the books would be closed.

Shelton called for the clock.

Around the pylons he went, holding forward stick, still wondering *why* the Bear was so tail-heavy, coaxing as much as he could from the big radical engine. It was hard to tell, having been away from the game that long, how he was doing. How fast was the Bear? Was it fast enough to beat *Strega*?

Pulling up from the course, powering back on the engine, he got the answer on the radio from his ground crew, who had been timing the lap from atop their headquarters trailer: His qualifying speed was 461 miles per hour. Three miles per hour slower than *Strega*.

That damned Destefani. He had the pole position again.

⊱ 3 ⊰

Shelton

Lyle Shelton was a dinosaur. He'd been around the racing business longer than any of them, and by now he had developed his own unique style. Shelton was on the opposite end of the personality spectrum from Tiger Destefani.

Ol' Lyle was in his early sixties, still fairly trim, but you could see by the eye pouches and the softened jawline that he wasn't the studly young fighter jock he'd been when he first came to Reno. He was happy to leave all the swaggering and loose-hipped gunfighting to that cocky little pissant Destefani, who was only fifty-three.

Shelton's style was more laconic. Laid back and cool. When asked if he thought *Rare Bear* had a chance against *Strega* this year, Ol' Lyle would pull at his earlobe and gaze for a few seconds out at the nothingness in the desert and then utter something profound. Something like "Yup."

And that was *his* act, of course—Shelton's take on the Gary Cooper aw-shucks-ma'am-just-a-flesh-wound *High Noon* technique.

He had it down to perfection, and it was just as cool and practiced as Destefani's hardball-gunfighter act.

Before all his troubles, Shelton used to tell the story about how he got into racing.

It was in 1964, and he was on a thirty-day leave from his assignment as a navy flight instructor. After a rambling party at Hamilton Air Force Base, where he'd gone to hitch a ride on an air force transport to Hawaii, he woke up the next morning in a flower patch. His head throbbed, and his mouth tasted like the Red Army had bivouacked in it. He had the mother of all hangovers. And he'd missed his free ride to Hawaii.

Shelton found his way back to the base and reassessed his vacation plans. Where to go now? He'd read something in a magazine about an air race of some sort out in Reno, which sounded interesting. Maybe he'd go out there and take a look.

He found a ride to Reno on an Air National Guard airplane. What he saw parked on the ramp sent a jolt of revitalizing energy through him: a row of gorgeously painted, long-snouted Mustang and Bearcat fighters, lined up like birds of prey, waiting to do combat out there on the racecourse.

Shelton was like a kid at his first circus. He studied the airplanes up close. He introduced himself to the pilots. He offered to join the ground crew of a pilot named Clay Lacy, who was there to race his own P-51 Mustang. As Shelton stood there on the ramp, transfixed, watching the races, listening to the lovely staccato growl of the Merlin engines, something clicked. This was it! It was all making perfect sense, coming together like the pieces of an elegant mosaic.

Thus did Lyle Shelton's life take one of those fortuitous detours from which he never turned back. After he said good-bye to his new acquaintances at Reno, he went home to rearrange his situation. He requested a transfer to the West Coast, where he could be closer to the air-racing community. The navy obliged by assigning him as the catapult and arresting gear officer aboard the USS *Kearsarge,* which was home-ported in Long Beach.

During the next year he hung out at California airports like Chino and Santa Paula and Van Nuys, where the warbirds were based. He telephoned the owners of the resident Mustangs, offering to split the expenses and income if they would let him race their airplane at Reno. Finally, an owner named Richard Vartanian took him up on his offer. Shelton would be flying one of Vartanian's three P-51 Mustangs.

Shelton's next problem, which would persist for the next thirty years, was the matter of expenses. At the urging of another navy pilot and air racer named Walt Ohlrich, Shelton flew up to the high desert town of Tonopah, in upstate Nevada, looking for sponsorship from the local businesses. The idea was that he would advertise the name of the town on the nose of his Mustang in exchange for contributions from local businesses.

Arriving overhead in Vartanian's P-51, he decided to soften up the locals with a little impromptu buzz job, including an inverted pass down Main Street. Just as he hoped, the townsfolk *loved* it. When Shelton arrived from the airport, they opened up their establishments—and their wallets. Shelton worked his way down the main drag, shaking hands and accepting donations and drinks. By the time he'd reached the far end of town, he'd collected support from nearly every legitimate business establishment in Tonopah— and some not so legitimate. Shelton acknowledged all his new supporters—including his biggest contributor—by painting "Tonopah Miss" on the nose of the P-51.

Though he had not yet flown his first race, Lyle Shelton could claim a new distinction: He was the first race pilot ever to be subsidized by a whorehouse.

Shelton didn't win in 1965. Or in 1966, when he flew a borrowed Sea Fury at Reno. (He was penalized for cutting a pylon.) And then he sat out the next couple of seasons because he was unable to borrow anyone's warbird. By then Shelton had reached a decision: Screw this routine of trying to borrow another guy's airplane. Somehow he would own his own race plane.

The problem was, few naval officers with the rank of lieutenant could afford an exotic warbird. Most were lucky to afford automobiles. In 1966, Shelton left the military and commenced a new career as a junior airline pilot with TWA. And though, initially, the new job didn't do anything to improve his financial status, it gave him time to hunt for affordable airplanes.

In an Indiana cornfield he found something he could afford. It was a forlorn-looking derelict—a 1946 World War II F8F-2 Bearcat—that had been abandoned after a crash in the early sixties. All that remained was the fuselage, wing center section, landing gear, and one wing panel. The fighter was a wreck, almost beyond repair. He bought the derelict Bearcat for twenty-five hundred dollars.

Shelton was suffering the perennial problem of all working-class warbird owners: He was broke. The Bearcat project was gnawing through his meager bank account like a voracious beast. For parts and labor he depended on loans, handouts, and the expert help of friends who were mechanics.

By the 1969 race he had the Bearcat ready to fly. Instead of the originally installed R-2800 engine, Shelton mounted a gargantuan Wright R-3350—the same big radial engine he had flown for a couple of thousand hours in navy A-1 Skyraiders. Stuck out there on the nose of the Bearcat, the Wright looked like a corncob on a toy airplane. In its first race at Reno, Shelton's Bearcat came in fifth.

And then he started winning. In 1972, Shelton broke the world's time-to-climb record, going to three thousand meters in 91.9 seconds. He won races at Miami, Mojave, and then, finally, the big one—the Unlimited Championship at Reno in 1973. The next year, he again led the pack across the finish line, but was penalized for a technicality (not having observed a pull-up altitude—a race rule that was deleted the next year). In 1975 he came back to win the Unlimited Gold Trophy. Shelton's Bearcat, now bearing the official name *Rare Bear,* became the winningest racer ever to compete at Reno. Flown by Shelton, *Rare Bear* racked up six first-place finishes (not counting the disqualified win in 1974) and then won again in 1994, flown by John Penney.

For the next few years Penney, an ex–air force pilot and a trained test pilot, did all the racing with *Rare Bear,* and did it well. Shelton was sidelined by the FAA with troubles so complicated that everyone figured they'd seen the last of him at Reno.

Once again they were wrong about Ol' Lyle. Here it was 1997. He was back.

But it wasn't the old Lyle. Shelton was sitting by himself at the pre-race briefing, at the far edge of the room. It was his first race after a four-year layoff, and Lyle, everyone was saying, had changed. He had gotten grumpy these last few years, no longer laughing and cutting up as he used to. And he sure as hell wasn't hanging out at places like the Pylon Bar over at the Hilton with the other guys.

He was the last to arrive, showing up just as the scheduled briefing began. As soon as it was over, Shelton was headed for the door, skipping all the banter and pilot talk. Between Shelton and some of the other pilots you now could sense a distinct *coolness.* Of course, they all knew about the DUI arrests and his grounding by the FAA. In the opinion of some, Shelton had made a mess of his life, and now it was reflecting badly on the rest of them. It gave the racing community a bad image.

Others could care less. They shrugged and figured, What the hell, they were all here to fly, not to serve as role models for the Boy Scouts. Image? Since when were air racers known for a saintly image? Over the years, well-known pilots had been busted for misdeeds ranging from larceny to drug hauling to money laundering. A few had served hard time and then come back to racing. Air racing had nothing to do with saintliness.

Everyone figured this was Shelton's last race. Sixty-something was long in the tooth for a G-pulling sport like Unlimited racing, and even if he *wanted* to persevere in the game, that seemed unlikely after he confronted yet another unsmiling Nevada judge. Shelton was facing yet another DUI charge. If convicted, it would likely be the end of his flying ticket.

So here was Ol' Lyle, sitting again on the hard bench, looking pouchy and grim. The year 1997 would be his last hurrah. Anyone with a memory knew that despite the layoff and the softening at the jawline, Shelton was there for one solitary purpose: to take the Gold Trophy *and* the prize money. Most still had this image locked into their memories of Shelton and his Bearcat appearing over their shoulder, roaring from behind to pass them and snatch the Gold Trophy.

You didn't have to approve of Ol' Lyle or his lifestyle. But every race pilot knew that if Shelton was in the race, you had better look over your shoulder.

⊱ 4 ⊱

Mustang Mystique

Mustang is a tough,
good name for a bad, tough, husky, angry plane.
—*Ernest Hemingway*

It was the most charismatic sound in aviation. Hearing it from a distance, you stopped, looked up, tilted your head. You *had* to look up because what you were hearing was simply the most compelling noise in the sky—the lovely, swelling, deep-throated crackle of an oncoming Mustang fighter.

Charisma was a word seldom applied to soulless, cold metal machines. But it fit precisely the persona of the P-51 Mustang. Here it was, over half a century since its inception, and the mighty Mustang still reigned—king of the prop-driven fighters. The trim, futuristic design of the fighter had been validated in wartime and then proved year after year as slicked-up incarnations of the Mustang ripped through the skies, setting world speed records and winning Unlimited racing trophies.

You couldn't be ambivalent about the Mustang. If you lusted after warbirds, you were one of those pilots who would trade a body part to own a Mustang. You were someone who fantasized about shoving the throttle up and aiming that sexy long nose down a strip of concrete. Or else you were one of those incomparably blessed individuals who already owned one.

There were the others, of course: those who owned or flew fighters like the Grumman Bearcat or the Hawker Sea Fury or the graceful gull-winged Chance-Vought Corsair or the twin-boomed P-38 Lightning. These warbirds, in their own way, were also charismatic. They were beautiful and deadly and swift. But they were like supporting actors in a show that had a single superstar.

Like Spam and the Jeep, the Mustang was one of those fortuitous accidents of war. It was the spring of 1940. Panzer divisions were slicing like a cleaver through France. The survival of Great Britain hinged on the strength of the Royal Air Force. They were down to little more than a thousand fighters, and the Battle of Britain was about to begin.

A British purchasing commission, headed by Sir Henry Self, arrived in the United States to arrange for the immediate export of American-built fighter aircraft. The only acceptable fighters being produced in America were the Bell P-39 Airacobra and the Curtiss P-40 Tomahawk. And "acceptable" was stretching a point. What neither the British nor the Americans were willing to say, at least not out loud, was that both these fighters were dogs.

The P-40 *looked* as if it ought to be a hellish killing machine. Every schoolboy could draw the Tomahawk's sexy lines—the rakish nose with the shark's-teeth design, made famous by Claire Chennault's American Volunteer Group, the Flying Tigers. But as sexy as the P-40 looked, it had serious deficiencies. It was slow. And ponderous, at least when matched against its opponents, the Japanese Zero and the German Messerschmitt 109. The P-40 Tomahawk was like an overage prizefighter who still looked good but couldn't beat the tough young contenders.

The P-39 Airacobra was equally doggy, with its anemic Allison engine mounted aft in the fuselage, driving a long propeller shaft that extended forward between the pilot's legs. For Army Air Corps duty, the P-39 had already been relegated to training fields and for export to America's allies.

But to the desperate RAF it didn't matter. They needed combat-ready fighters. The British purchasing commission placed an immediate order for 675 Airacobras and 560 P-40s.

Then the Curtiss corporation balked. They already had a huge backlog in their delivery schedule. The commission turned to North American Aviation of Inglewood, California: Could North American build the Curtiss fighters, under license, for immediate delivery to the RAF?

North American was a fast-growing company with a resident corps of hotshot engineers, whose average age was somewhere around thirty. The notion of replicating a fleet of obsolete P-40s, designed in someone else's shop, made none of them happy. Thus did the engineers come up with a counterproposal: Suppose they built a *better* fighter than the P-40? What if they put together an altogether new warplane that would blow Zeros, Messerschmitts—anyone's fighter—out of the sky?

It was bold talk, of course. Particularly since the upstart company's experience so far was in the production of lumbering air-dog training planes. The war-weary British were interested but skeptical. How long would it take to produce the hot new fighter?

It had already been established that it would take 120 days to put the California plant facilities into production status for the P-40 program. Using the same time frame, the North American team made a rash promise: They would design and build a prototype of an all-new fighter in 120 days.

Which was an outrageous promise. It wasn't the way modern warplanes were produced. A minimum of three years normally went into the development of a new fighter.

But these were not normal times. Sir Henry Self, representing the

British Purchasing Commission, signed a letter of intent with J. H. "Dutch" Kindelberger, the head of North American. North American's preliminary design was approved by the British, and following the British custom of assigning airplanes names rather than numerical designations, the new fighter would be called Mustang.

That America's most famous fighter would be commissioned by the British was not the Mustang's only paradox. The fighter that would destroy so many German fighters was designed by a German. Edgar Schmued, chief design engineer assigned to the NA-73 (Mustang prototype) project, was born in Hornbach, Bavaria. Trained and educated in Germany, he arrived in the United States in the 1930s and went to work for the young North American Aircraft Corporation. The very Americanized engineer would forever be linked to the distinctive design of the North American P-51.

Rather than mounting one of the big, barrel-shaped radial engines built by Pratt & Whitney or Wright, Schmued and his crew intended to power the Mustang with an in-line, liquid-cooled V-12 engine in order to maintain its sleek, narrow-nosed design. The only such power plant in America was the Allison V-1710, which, in 1940, powered all America's front-line fighters—the P-40, P-39 Airacobra and the P-38 Lightning.

But liquid-cooled engines, though they eliminated the blunt-nosed shape of radial-powered fighters, also extracted an aerodynamic penalty: Somewhere you had to install a large air intake for a coolant radiator. In the P-40, the radiator was mounted in the front, beneath the nose, giving the P-40 its distinctive "chin" scoop and providing a suitable place for painting the ubiquitous shark's mouth. The scoop also amounted to a huge speed brake, contributing to the P-40's plodding dogginess.

It was Schmued's idea to locate the Mustang's air scoop aft of the wing section, mounted in the belly of the fighter. Experiments had already been conducted with what they called "zero drag" air scoops. The idea was that ram air—the raw, outside blast of the airstream—could be used to accelerate the warmed, coolant air through the radiator and out the exit door in the back of the scoop. In this way the narrow, sleek lines of the Mustang's nose would be preserved without paying a penalty for the coolant air scoop.

Another revolutionary idea for the new fighter was its laminar-flow wing. "Laminar flow" was the name for an idea in airfoil design that, so far, had only been tested on racing planes of the thirties. The laminar-flow wing possessed a nearly symmetrical airfoil. It had almost the same curvature on the top as on the bottom of the wing. The wing was relatively thin at the leading edge, widening much farther aft than on normal airfoils. The theory was that the airflow would adhere to the surface of the wing all the way up to nearly supersonic velocity, thus greatly reducing the drag associated with conventional wings. Such a wing design was still considered highly experimental and had never been implemented on production warplanes.

The North American engineers kept their word. The NA-73X, as the prototype Mustang was designated, rolled out of the North American hangar three days ahead of the 120-day deadline stipulated by the British. On the afternoon of 26 October 1940, the Mustang leaped off the runway at North American's California facility, flown by test pilot Vance Breese. The new fighter validated all of the engineer's pet theories, including the critical laminar-flow wing.

The British had placed an additional order for three hundred more Mustangs. By late 1941, a year after its first test flight, the first Mustangs were arriving in England. The new fighter was an instant success, surprising the British—and the Luftwaffe—with its low-altitude, high-speed attack capability.

By the time the Mustang entered service with the RAF, the U.S. Army Air Corps was awakening to the fact that an air-superiority weapon was being produced, right under their nose, for the British. During 1941, the army moved to procure experimental models of the Mustang, dubbed the XP-51, and these were flight-tested and found to be superior to anything in the inventory.

Then came 7 December 1941. The United States went to war. Belatedly, the P-51 Mustang was summoned into service.

The first use of the Mustang was not as a fighter but as a ground-attack aircraft. A specially fitted model, designated the A-36, was equipped with wing-mounted speed brakes and bomb racks to permit nearly vertical dive-bombing. In North Africa, and then during the Italian campaigns, the A-36 earned a reputation as a battle-tough fighter-bomber. Because of the Mustang's long-range capability, it was also pressed into service as an escort for the waves of B-25 and B-26 bombers.

An upgraded Allison engine, the V-1710-81, was introduced to the Mustang. With this engine, the Mustang could climb—and fight—at altitudes in excess of twenty thousand feet. Designated the P-51A, the new fighter rolled off the assembly lines and went directly to combat in Africa and southern Europe.

But the Allison-powered Mustang, for all its superior performance, was still at its best in the low-altitude regime. That meant air to mud, not the more glorious stratosphere, where the *real* air battles were being fought. That was still the province of the Spitfire and the Hurricane and their enemies, the Me-109 and Focke-Wulf 190. What the Allison-powered Mustang lacked was a highly supercharged, upper-altitude engine.

The British had already put their indelible stamp on the North American fighter, placing the original design order for the airplane and then naming it Mustang. And then they went one step further: They installed the power plant that would transform the Mustang from an acceptable fighter to the world's most deadly air-superiority weapon.

Rolls-Royce was a name synonymous with sophistication. Already famous for its auto engines, the company had been developing a V-12 aircraft engine since the early years of World War I. The "Eagle" engine, delivering 360 horsepower, was used in a dozen British warplanes during the Great War. The Vickers Vimy bomber, flown by Sir

John Alcock and Sir Arthur Whitten-Brown on the first transatlantic flight in 1919, was powered by Rolls-Royce Eagle engines.

Thereafter came a succession of Rolls-Royce aircraft engines. The "Hawk" engine was followed by the "Falcon," then the "Condor." In 1930 the "Kestrel" engine broke new ground, using four valves per cylinder, with an enclosed-overhead-valve operating mechanism. With a slick new supercharging system, the engine produced nearly 800 horsepower. The Kestrel was then enlarged to a more powerful version called the "Buzzard."

For the famous Schneider Trophy floatplane races of the thirties, Rolls-Royce developed an enhanced version of the Buzzard—the "R" racing engine—to be mounted in the sleekly beautiful British racer, the Supermarine S.6 floatplane.

With its Rolls-Royce racing engine, the S.6 was unbeatable. In the 1929 races, the Rolls-Royce "R" engine delivered an astonishing 1,900 horsepower. The S.6 ran away with the trophy, winning the Schneider at a speed of 328 miles per hour. Two days later, the S.6 set a new world speed record of 357 miles per hour.

In 1931 the S.6 returned to the Schneider competition, this time without government sponsorship. With private funding, design teams from Supermarine and Rolls-Royce produced a faster, more powerful racing machine—the modified "R" engine now putting out an awesome 2,350 horsepower. The S.6 again beat the field, winning the Schneider Trophy with a speed of 341 miles per hour. Later, with a strengthened and overboosted "R" engine, the S.6 shattered the world record with a top speed of 407.5 miles per hour.

As a racing engine, the Rolls-Royce "R" engine was a winner. It would now metamorphose into the most famous fighter engine in the world.

It would always be assumed that the Merlin took its name from the sorcerer of King Arthur's court. The truth was that the Merlin, like all its predecessor aircraft engines at Rolls-Royce, was named after a bird of prey—a small European falcon called a merlin.

But the true derivation of the name was lost in the hoopla around the new engine. Of course it was named after a sorcerer! It was perfect—*Merlin*—conjuring up notions of magic and wizardry and impossible feats. No other engine in aviation history seemed as capable of sorcery as the mighty Merlin.

By 1940, at the height of the Battle of Britain, the progression of Merlin models had reached Mark 60 (sixtieth iteration). Fitted with a sophisticated two-speed supercharger, the Merlin was delivering an altitude capability that exceeded that of any other engine in the world—Axis or Allied.

Until then, U.S. Army fighters depended on derivatives of the Allison V-12 engine, which were generally stronger and more durable than the Merlin. But in terms of raw horsepower, particularly at altitude, the Allison couldn't touch the Merlin. Rolls-Royce's long military heritage had brought about refinements that made the Merlin the ultimate in-line, liquid-cooled fighter power plant. The difference between the two V-12s lay in the Merlin's superior metal alloys, its use of exhaust-gas discharge, and more sophisticated supercharging.

Both V-12 engines were liquid-cooled, mounting the cylinders in two 6-cylinder banks, separated by 60 degrees of angle. The Merlin displaced 1,650 cubic inches (hence the designation: V-1650), while the American-built Allison displaced 1,710 cubic inches. The compression ratios of engines were nearly identical. With both engines turning at the same 3,000 rpm, the Merlin V-1650-7 delivered 1,695 horsepower versus the Allison V-1710-81's 1,330 horsepower.

The secret ingredient in the Merlin was its two-stage supercharger. The supercharger was, in effect, an engine-driven centrifugal compressor that increased the density of the air charge fed to the engine. By processing a greater fuel-air volume, the engine produced more torque and at higher altitudes, where the air thinned, maintained its power. Rolls-Royce had pioneered supercharger technology beginning back in the twenties and raised it to an art in the Merlin engine.

Thus came a decision that ran against the grain of downhome American engine manufacturers: *Build the Merlin in the United States.* The Packard Motor Company of Detroit was licensed to begin manufacturing a variant of the Merlin for the Army Air Corps, with the designation V-1650-1.

Meanwhile, out in Inglewood, North American began testing a Merlin-powered version of the Mustang. They couldn't believe what they were seeing.

The airplane looked the same, still possessing that rakish, pointy-snouted engine housing. But the service ceiling of the Mustang, with the new engine, had just jumped by more than *ten thousand feet.* The top speed increased by over 50 miles per hour. This new Mustang, which they were calling the P-51B, possessed more power at twenty-six thousand feet than the Allison-driven P-51A could deliver on a sea-level takeoff. What they had on their hands now was a fighter that could go head-to-head—at *any* altitude—with any fighter on the planet!

Shiploads of the new Mustangs began arriving in England and went into immediate bomber-escort duty. With external drop tanks, the enhanced Mustang was able, for the first time, to provide fighter cover for the heavy bombers of the Eighth Air Force all the way to their targets in Germany.

By 21 January 1944, the 354th Fighter Group claimed the hundredth confirmed kill of an enemy aircraft by the Mustang. A total of forty-five squadrons of Mustangs would be based in England, and by war's end the Mustang would kill over five thousand enemy aircraft. The Mustang became the Luftwaffe's worst nightmare. Never had the world seen such a cruelly efficient aerial killing machine.

Back in California, and in Texas, where an additional North American plant had been established to build Mustangs, one more item of wartime technology was being installed on the P-51: the all-Plexiglas bubble canopy. This was the final modernization of the

P-51, giving it the sleek, omnidirectional vision capability that would be standard on the coming generation of jets. With its bubble canopy, the P-51D was the ultimate Mustang, and it would be produced in the greatest numbers.

For the rest of the war the Mustang ruled the skies over Europe. Only the Luftwaffe's Me-262 twin-jet could fly faster than the P-51, and the German jet failed for two reasons: Germany's supply of experienced fighter pilots was already depleted and outclassed by its Allied enemies; and the Me-262, instead of being deployed as a terrifyingly fast fighter-interceptor, was assigned to a ground-attack mission in a desperate last-hour effort to stop the advancing Allied armies. It was an egregious blunder, reportedly ordered by Hitler himself.

By war's end, 15,582 Mustangs had been produced. Though the fighter had spent less time in war service than the others, it had the longest production run. It would continue in service with the U.S. Air Force throughout the forties, go into retirement, then be summoned again to serve in Korea. The Mustang was the last piston-engined fighter to serve in the U.S. Air Force. It would be assigned to Air National Guard squadrons and would eventually join the air forces of countries around the world.

After the war it seemed a sure bet that the world's hottest fighter—the P-51 Mustang—would also be the world's hottest air racer. But it didn't happen. The Mustang didn't win the Thompson in 1946. Or in 1947.

Though it was undeniably sleek and fast, the Mustang was proving itself to be a prima donna. The problem was always the same: the temperamental Merlin. The Merlin-powered Mustang fighter was designed as an upper-altitude fighter; the cold, thin atmosphere allowed the engine to run at full power without self-destructing. Down low, around the racing pylons, the Merlin, driven at full power, tended to overheat and shed parts.

Unlike the liquid-cooled Merlin, the tough, air-cooled radial engines mounted on the Bearcat, Corsair, and later, the Sea Fury, were
built to run at maximum power down in the thick, hot air close to
the earth. In the hard-charging slugfest around the pylons, insensi-
tive and rugged machines like the F2G Super Corsair, driven by the
brute force of its gigantic 28-cylinder R-4360 corncob radial engine,
could run at full throttle lap after lap and not disintegrate.

In its stock version, the Merlin delivered less than 2,000 horsepower—far less than the brute torque of the big radial engines. It
meant that transforming the Mustang fighter into a winning Unlimited racer required tweaking. Although such tweaking—water injection, exotic fuels, increasing the rpm to as much as 3,400–3,600
rpm—dramatically increased the power, it also virtually guaranteed
that the engine would fail. Or, worse, destruct in a stomach-turning
shower of molten parts.

Transforming a reliable stock fighter into a hypertuned racing
machine invoked an old engineering aphorism: *There ain't no such
thing as a free lunch.* It meant, in the case of racing engines, that no
improvement came without a price.

So it was with the Merlin. Standard Merlins turned at 3,000 rpm,
and the engine's reduction gearing allowed the propeller to turn
at slightly less than half the engine speed. But as racing versions
of the Merlin were pushed closer to 4,000 rpm, propeller velocities,
even with the stock reduction gears, were going supersonic. The
propeller was biting into a wall of granite-hard air. It became necessary to custom-build new gearing, going to lower ratios to keep the
propeller-tip speeds in an efficient range.

The engine builders were up against a law of physics: Horsepower produced heat. The more you boosted the horsepower of a
racing engine, the more heat you produced. The stock Mustang's
puny belly-radiator cooling system was unable to cope with the
blazingly high temperatures produced by the exotic racing engines.

A Lockheed engineer named Pete Law perfected a system called spray-bar cooling, which became a standard item on almost every Unlimited racer. With Law's spray-bar system, a fine mist of water and glycol was sprayed directly onto the hot surfaces of the belly-mounted radiators. At high power settings, the spray turned to steam, leaving a contrail-like trail of vapor behind the fast-moving Mustang.

Another power enhancement came from the use of water injection, or ADI (antidetonant injection), which increased the available power from the normal sixty-seven inches of manifold pressure to between eighty and ninety inches.

The enhancement of last resort was the use of exotic fuels—alcohol, methanol, and specially blended racing fuels. And then came the ultimate enhancement: the addition of nitrous oxide to the fuel-air mixture, stretching the engine up to—and sometimes beyond—its explosive limit.

"If we could just keep the Merlin running for eight laps," said a frustrated crew chief, "we'd win every time."

Keep the Merlin running: It was easier said than done. As the brute torque of the Merlins kept increasing, things kept breaking. But then, in the 1980s, bright engine builders like Dwight Thorn, Mike Nixon, Dave Zeuschel, and Jack Hovey figured out how to build highly modified Merlins that produced over 3,000 horsepower. And they didn't explode, at least not with the same gut-wrenching frequency as in the old days.

The trick was in the connecting rods, the Merlin's most vulnerable component. The Rolls-Royce connecting rods, which joined the pistons to the engine's crankshaft, tended to fail under the stresses of high-speed racing. But engine builders like Thorn and Nixon managed to adapt the larger and stronger rods from the Allison V-1710 engine, which had an identical six-inch piston stroke, to the Merlin. The result was an engine that could deliver almost 4,000 horsepower—without exploding. Almost.

. . .

Throughout the Thompson Trophy years and into the revived period of racing at Reno, beginning in 1964, it was the same thing: The barrel-shaped Grumman Bearcat dominated the competition. Not until 1970 did the first Mustang, flown by Clay Lacy, manage to win a Gold Trophy. And though it was a sweet victory for the Mustang crowd, it was, in a sense, a reversal of fortunes, since both front-running Bearcats—Darryl Greenamyer's and Lyle Shelton's—had broken down and left the field wide open to the Mustangs.

And then in 1972, a P-51, powered by a highly tweaked Merlin, proved what the Mustang fanatics had always believed: A properly prepared Mustang, if it held together, could beat anything in the world. Gunther Balz's *Roto-Finish Special* held together, passing *both* Bearcats—Greenamyer's, flown by test pilot Richard Laidley, and Shelton's. Balz thundered past the finish line with a record speed of 416.16 miles per hour, surpassing Greenamyer's standing record by 3 miles per hour.

Balz was pioneering new territory. The Merlin in his Mustang was a mix-and-match hodgepodge of components from different en-gines, each bringing a special quality to the engine. Balz's engine used the heavier cylinder heads and banks from a Merlin 620 trans-port engine. He had replaced the reduction gearing, using a lower gear ratio, which allowed for a higher engine rpm without turning the propeller tips at supersonic speed.

It was a sweet moment for the Mustang mavens. In the years to come, Mustangs with names like *Red Baron, Jeannie, Dago Red,* and *Strega,* powered by beefed-up engines, would lay siege to Reno's Gold. Mustangs would again rule the skies.

⊱ 5 ⊱

Tale of the Tiger

There was something about Tiger Destefani. You saw it when he made the long walk across the ramp, out to where *Strega* was sitting on the concrete, waiting for him to come fly. You'd see him slip into a sort of swagger.

He'd be wearing the tailored Nomax fire-resistant flight suit. Destefani's flight suit had a special attachment—a hose connected at the hip that conducted cool air from the on-board air-conditioning unit into his suit while he was flying. It was an ingenious idea—borrowed from the NASCAR (National Association for Stock Car Auto Racing) crowd—that permitted him to stay cool while sealing all of *Strega's* vent holes and scoops and to gain a few more miles per hour of precious airspeed.

But from a distance, Destefani, strutting across the ramp, walking in that cocky, loose-hipped gait, the hose dangling like a holster at his hip, looked like something else. With that wiry build, the trim mustache, the wad of Skoal under his lip, he looked like nothing so much as a gunfighter.

And after a while you figured it out: That was how Destefani *wanted* to be seen: the gunfighter . . . out there on the sun-fried desert . . . heat waves shimmering in the distance, the archetypal, single-combat warrior. Solo. Taking on all comers.

And he talked the same way. When a reporter asked him how he thought the Unlimited Championship would go this year, Tiger gave the guy a typical Tigerism: "I'll tell you what you're gonna see out there: twenty-three losers—and me."

Destefani's real name, of course, wasn't "Tiger." He picked that up, at least according to the official story, back when he was five years old. A traveling salesman had come out to the Destefani farm, and while the salesman was demonstrating his pots and pans, the rambunctious kid kept interrupting his pitch and playing with the hardware. "Get out of the way, Tiger," said the salesman. The family loved it, and the kid had a new nickname.

Or so went the story. To those who had known Destefani for a while, it was conceivable that the name might have come from somewhere else. With Destefani you never knew, because he was a guy who loved to put people on, trying out preposterous stories on them just for effect. He could have made up the whole tale.

But now it didn't matter. The name had become stamped on Destefani's persona, an indelible label. *Tiger!* It defined how he lived and flew—and saw himself. He looked like a character from a thirties movie—pencil-line mustache, slicked back hair, wise-guy grin—with a steady delivery of one-liners. He loved telling—and playing—jokes.

In fact, with Destefani it was hard to tell when he *wasn't* joking. One minute he'd be the serious warbird pilot, talking about engine-parameter data linking and aerodynamic drag reduction; then, in the next moment, he'd be Farmer Bill from Bakersfield ("Y' know, flying these damn things isn't any different from gettin' on a farm tractor. You just put your ass in the seat and *go*").

When he was *really* getting into the Farmer Bill stuff, going on about baling hay or spreading cow shit over his alfalfa, you couldn't help noticing that there was always this little lump of something under his lip. Then he'd interrupt his delivery to lob a globule of Skoal—*splaat!*—six or eight feet across the hangar floor. Or the office floor, or *any* floor—it didn't matter. The Skoal was just one more of those habits he brought from the farm.

It was all role-playing, of course. But with Destefani it had a more calculated purpose.

What everyone recognized but no one mentioned out loud was an invisible but powerful class distinction among the Brethren of the racing fraternity. On one side of the spectrum you had civilian-trained pilots like Destefani—hardscrabble farm kids and crinkly-eyed crop sprayers and guys who learned to fly at civilian airports. On the opposite end resided the Blue Bloods—the coterie of military-trained astronauts and test pilots and pointy-nosed fighter jocks. The distinction was mostly indiscernible, but not always. At times during one of those heated exchanges between pilots over some abstruse aeronautical point, you could pick up just a whiff of condescension.

Which was why Destefani loved to do his "Farmer Bill from Bakersfield" act, lobbing the Skoal and deadpanning about the manure on his alfalfa. It was a form of reverse snobbism. Instead of deferring to the Blue Bloods, with their exotic pedigrees, he would just go out there on the racecourse and wax them at their own game. And while he was at it, he might just rub their faces in a little Bakersfield cow shit. "I'll tell you what you're gonna see out there: twenty-three losers—and me."

When he was about ten, Tiger started watching the crop sprayers working the fields on their farm. He loved those old Stearman biplanes, especially the sound of their engines. You could hear them coming from several miles away, because that big, old, round R-985 engine had an unmistakable growl, like distant, rolling thunder.

Out there in the fields, especially when the hay or the cotton had grown to three or more feet, you could hide. And you could position yourself and wait.

And that's what Tiger did. He waited in the tall hay for the ancient biplane filled with insecticide or weed killer or fertilizer or whatever chemical they were using that season. The sprayer would swoop down on the field, ticking its wheels along the top of the crop, working its way across the field in swaths.

It was wonderful! Part of the thrill was just being that close, having that round-motored, roaring behemoth thundering down on him—*Whaaarrrrooooom!*—the whirring propeller blade slicing the air a few inches over his head, feeling the downwash from the wings spill over him like a wave of warm surf.

It was dangerous as hell, of course. Sometimes sprayers got a little low, letting their wheels and propeller carve through the tops of the crop. But that was what made it so appealing to the kid. And the danger wasn't just from the crop sprayer thrashing over his head or the toxic chemicals spewing from the belly of the sprayer to kill the season's bugs or weeds. The other, more palpable danger was if he got caught. The old man would blister his butt.

Destefani's father was a first-generation immigrant whose only passion was work. In his judgment, airplanes were frivolous. A waste of time. Tiger was supposed to take over the Destefani farm, which encompassed nearly two thousand acres of cotton and alfalfa in the fertile San Joaquin valley. To the elder Destefani, farming was a full-time occupation. Forget the flying.

Thus, Tiger Destefani learned flying as he had almost everything in his life: the hard way. Not that learning to fly had been difficult or beyond his grasp. It was just that he missed out on the opportunity some of his fellow racers had—learning to fly high-performance, government-issue jets at the taxpayers' expense. Coming of age during the Vietnam War, he had gone directly from the farm to the navy, where he served as an enlisted sailor in a Seabee unit (construction battalion) building airfields and barracks and bridges in Vietnam. Not until he came back home to the farm in Bakersfield did he seriously begin learning to fly.

And still, he kept his flying a secret from his father.

When he was thirty, Destefani bought a 1947 Navion, an old, low-winged, slow-moving family airplane. He restored it himself, learning as he went. It was slow going. "Anything it needed, I just did it, like it was another piece of machinery on the farm."

He might have gone on like that for years, fixing up old airplanes, learning in tiny increments about flying, keeping the whole thing a secret from his father. But all that changed one morning in 1978. It was the closest thing to an epiphany that Destefani had ever experienced.

He was working out in the fields when he came down with a splitting headache. By noon he had lost almost all feeling in his body. They rushed him to the hospital, where he learned that he had spinal meningitis. For fifteen days he drifted in and out of consciousness, near death.

But he didn't die. He began to recover, but the experience had changed him. "People go through their lives saying, 'One of these days . . . ,' and then they die," he recalled later. Well, he had nearly died, and he had almost done it without ever acting out those secret dreams he'd had since he was a kid. He wasn't going to wait any longer.

Destefani went out and bought an airplane, but not an ordinary one. It was the world's most charismatic airplane, a World War II P-51 Mustang, which he began restoring. On its cowling he painted its name, *Mangia Pane*. It meant "Eats Bread," which was precisely what the thing did, gobbling up Destefani's hard-earned money like a gluttonous animal. It didn't matter. By now Destefani was living his dream, and he didn't give a damn what it cost. He wasn't ever again going to be caught dead, or even nearly dead, without having owned an airplane like this one.

He got *Mangia Pane* flying. Then he flew the hell out of it. He flew it every day, for nearly nine hundred hours.

His father had still never acknowledged Tiger's passion for airplanes. But the old man was getting on, nearing the end of his own career. One day he said, "I hear you bought a Mustang." Tiger had to admit that, yeah, he was messing around with this old fighter he had bought.

And that was it. His father let the subject drop. Nothing more needed to be said. It was his way of recognizing that a milestone had been reached in the relationship with his son. It meant that Tiger was his own man.

Owners of airplanes like the Mustang fell into two loose categories: the Dilettantes and the Killers. The Dilettantes were mostly well-to-do amateur pilots who had never flown in the military but were attracted by the aura of the old military gunfighters. They loved the leather-jacketed feel of the whole thing—the military flight suits with squadron patches and epaulets and a flag and burnished aviator's wings embroidered over the left breast. They liked to have their name painted beneath the cockpit of their warbird, usually prefixed with the honorific rank of "Colonel."

You could taxi around the local airport with the canopy back, wearing your flight suit with the patches and the hard hat with the oxygen mask dangling from the side, gazing flint-eyed over the long, gorgeous snout of your very own fighter. And *everyone* stopped to watch. It never failed. They would stand there, mouths agape, staring like serfs at a coronation, listening to the big V-12 engine chuffing and growling that unmistakable Merlin sound.

It was, in fact, exactly what you may have bought the airplane for—to wear the leather-jacketed mantle of the single-combat gunfighter with the sweet knowledge that all those covetous souls down there on the concrete staring wet-eyed and worshipful at you would, at that single moment, give *anything*—wife, mother, body part—to be *you*.

If you actually *flew* the airplane, then whenever you landed, the same kind of crowd would instantly gather to gaze in reverence at the shiny gunfighter. And, of course, at the intrepid fighter pilot. For most of the Dilettantes, that was enough. It was what they were there for—the patches and the aura and the wet-eyed reverence of the unprivileged masses. It was Walter Mitty Land.

None of this counted for the smaller group, the Killers. For them, all that crowd pleasing and the colonel stuff and the flight suits with the flags and wings were an embarrassment. To hell with Mitty Land.

For the most part, the Killers were guys who had gained entrance to the warbird club in quite a different way from the Dilettantes: They acquired their warbirds by hocking everything they had. First, they bought the airplane. After that, they found a suitable hangar. Then, if they had any money left, they found a place to live, which in some cases amounted to nothing more than a camper behind the hangar. It was a matter of priorities.

But the Killer/Dilettante distinction cut deeper than money and social status. It had more to do with attitude: Airplanes were meant to be flown, not employed as backdrops for self-aggrandizement.

The Killers tended to hang out with each other, disdaining the company of Dilettantes. When the air was slick and they could afford a tank of high-octane fuel, they would join up for some formation practice. Or they'd go one-on-one in a little hardball dogfighting. Or sometimes they'd just go do a little hotdogging by themselves, beating up the desert or doing some solo aerobatics. Hell, what was the point in having a high-performance fighter if you couldn't push the envelope just a little?

For some, even this grew tiresome. And risky. The FAA had a mean-spirited intolerance for 400-mile-an-hour buzz jobs. It was at that point, for a few of the Killers, that something else—something *really* interesting to do with their hot warbirds—caught their attention.

That's when they caught the racing fever.

· · ·

Destefani was never one of the Dilettantes. Almost from the beginning, he was pushing his new Mustang, taking off at daybreak from Minter Field, a few miles from his Bakersfield farm, climbing up high over the sprawling farmlands, wringing out the fighter. Destefani was still a low-time pilot, having fewer than a thousand total hours of flying experience. By aviation standards, that meant he was a neophyte. Going in one leap from the clunky old Navion to the air-splitting, fire-breathing Mustang fighter was something akin to stepping from a go-cart to a Grand Prix racer.

Destefani never saw it that way. He was still the farm kid who regarded any machine as just another variant of a John Deere tractor. "You just put your ass in the seat and drive the thing."

In daily increments, he learned. He learned about the Mustang and high-performance flying and aerobatics. And in the process he learned a few things about himself.

It didn't take long, fewer than a couple of years, before he was ready for something else. Something *really* interesting to do with his hot airplane. Like air racing. It was 1981, and he was hearing the siren song of Reno.

For *Mangia Pane*'s first race at Reno, Destefani recruited a race pilot named Ron Hevle. Hevle, a tall young man with sideburns and a drooping mustache, already had extensive experience flying high-performance warbirds. Though Destefani and his crew had enhanced the Mustang's engine to produce greater horsepower, *Mangia Pane* was otherwise a stock airplane, meaning that it had an unmodified airframe and wore replicated air force markings.

For a first outing, the team did well. Hevle drove the Mustang hard, crossing the finish line in the championship race in a respectable third place.

For Tiger Destefani, standing there in the pits and hearing the crowd cheering, watching his own airplane roar around the course, it was all very exciting. Very gratifying. It was neat to put together a fast plane and watch it race. And it made good sense, of course, that you put the most experienced pilot in the cockpit.

But good sense had its limits. Screw this, Destefani decided. It was the last damn year he was going to stand in the pits.

During the next twelve months, the lull time between the 1981 and the 1982 races at Reno, Destefani became seriously involved in the air-racing business. He and another California race aficionado named Frank Taylor formed a partnership to produce a new Reno racer. Destefani found the remains of a Mustang that had crashed in the early seventies. Taylor provided the labor and the technical expertise to rebuild the pieces into a competitive racer. The result was a gorgeous, highly modified racer named *Dago Red*. The pilot for the new racer's debut season would be Ron Hevle.

Which left *Mangia Pane,* Destefani's original love. And way back at the end of last year's race he had already decided who would be the next pilot for *Mangia Pane:* himself. Tiger would make his debut as a race pilot. Ron Hevle, already experienced at racing the pylons, would fly *Dago Red.*

They showed up as a team, with the two Mustangs and the two pilots, Destefani and Hevle, and their entourage from Bakersfield and Salinas, including engine wizard Mike Nixon and the engineering brain behind the project, Bruce Boland. When Hevle took *Dago Red* out on the course, it was the first time the engine had ever been pushed up beyond seventy-five inches of manifold pressure, which was far more power than had ever been previously demanded of the freshly assembled Merlin engine.

It was obvious to everyone that *Dago Red* was going to be hard to beat. It entered the record books by being the first highly modified racer to come to Reno and, on its first outing, top all qualifying speeds—a dazzling 440 miles per hour—then go on to win its first race ever. That Sunday, *Dago* swept the Unlimited Championship at a throttled-back speed of 409 miles per hour, far ahead of its lagging competition.

Destefani, the rookie racer, surprised everyone, including himself, by qualifying with the third-fastest time. Then he further astonished everyone by ripping around the course in the final heat of the

Unlimited Championship, passing the number-four racer and then, on the last lap, roaring past number three. Destefani managed to finish right on the heels of his teammate Hevle, who had run away with the championship in *Dago Red*.

It was almost a clean sweep, a one-two punch for Destefani's two-plane team. But as he climbed out of *Mangia Pane's* cockpit, he saw bad news walking toward him across the ramp. The glum-looking race judges reported that Destefani, in his eagerness, had made two pylon cuts—sliding inside the racecourse perimeter at the turn points—each of which would cost him sixteen seconds in penalty. *Mangia Pane* was bumped from second place to fifth.

Still, it was a *very* respectable finish for a rookie racer right off the farm. It galled Destefani that he had screwed up, and he made up his mind that he was finished with pylon cutting. Next year he would be back. And he was going to kick some ass.

The problem was, he needed yet another airplane. His partner, Frank Taylor, was so pleased with the success of *Dago Red* that he bought Destefani out, leaving Tiger to find yet another Mustang for his stable. Just as he had done with *Dago*, Destefani found another derelict warbird, this one in Australia. Though the old P-51 had logged only fifty-seven flying hours before the end of the war, it had been sitting in the open and had bullet holes from being used for target practice.

He called it *Strega*, which, in Italian, meant "Witch." Again, the new racer was barely complete by the next racing season. And again, Destefani tapped Ron Hevle to fly the experimental new mount while he again raced the reliable *Mangia Pane*.

Strega still had bugs to work out when the 1983 races started at Reno. Ironically, it was *Dago Red*, this time owned by another team and flown by an up-and-coming young pilot named Rick Brickert, that dominated the Unlimiteds. Destefani held his own with the trusty but not-so-hot *Mangia Pane*, hanging on to fourth place among the Gold finishers.

The other two Mustangs did not fare as well. Hevle was jockeying with the other hot Mustang, *Dago Red*, for second place, inching up on the front-runner, a Sea Fury called *Dreadnought*, when a glop of oil hit the windshield, then another, and it became obvious that an oil line had let go. "If you can't see, you can't race," he reasoned. He pulled up and out of the race, safely landing a couple of minutes later.

And then Brickert in *Dago Red*, who was now running away with the race, declared a Mayday and also pulled out. He had an unexplained vibration from up front that turned out to be not so serious—a broken propeller spinner. But with the two fast Mustangs out of the race, the way was clear for *Dreadnought*, the R-4360-powered Sea Fury, flown by test pilot Neil Anderson, to flash across the finish line in first place.

By 1985, Destefani felt ready to take over the flying duties in *Strega*. Mechanical problems plagued the Mustang that year and again in 1986. Then, in 1987, Tiger Destefani stuck his name for the first time on the list of Unlimited champions. He took the Gold Trophy at a speed of 452 miles per hour. It was the beginning of a legend.

❯ 6 ❯

Collision

9 September 1997

With his towering figure, bald pate, and beaklike nose, Howard Pardue looked like an amiable ostrich. He had been around the air-racing business for a long time. In normal circumstances, good ol' Howard—the laid-back, ex-marine fighter jock who liked to swap flying stories with anyone who came by—was an easy guy to talk to.

It was Pardue's second time on the course today. As usual, he had showed up at Reno with *both* his racing planes—the pristine F8F-1 Bearcat, decked out in its authentic navy blue paint scheme, and his latest acquisition, the big camouflage-painted Sea Fury named *Fury*.

For Pardue, flying the Bearcat was an affair of the heart. It was a relationship that went back nearly twenty years, when he made his first takeoff in the agile little fighter. He could still remember: He shoved the throttle forward, got the tail up and the fighter rolling on its main landing gear, nudged the stick back, and—*Hot damn!*—the fighter was screaming skyward like a homesick angel.

It was love at first flight. The Bearcat was a fighter that *begged* to be flown, quick and nimble as a hawk, powered by the big, round Pratt & Whitney R-2800. Pardue took the Bearcat to air shows around the country, putting on an aerobatic routine and showing off the hot little ex–navy fighter.

And, of course, he took it to Reno, where it competed satisfactorily but would never finish in the big money. Pardue's Bearcat was a stock fighter, right down to its insignia and paint detailing, just as when it rolled out of the Grumman factory in Long Island. And that's the way Pardue wanted it. He had no intention of cutting metal or swapping out the engine for a more humongous power plant as Lyle Shelton had done with *Rare Bear*. Pardue's Bearcat would remain pristine but slow.

That's why he had the Sea Fury. He had bought the big British-built navy fighter, then had master mechanic Nelson Ezell replace the sliding-valve Olympus engine with the big Wright R-3350 corn-cob radial, the same basic engine Shelton was running in *Rare Bear*.

Pardue's Sea Fury was fast enough—on a good day it could turn a lap at well over 400 miles per hour—but still wasn't as blazingly quick as *Rare Bear* or *Strega*. And that was okay with Pardue. To get into Gold Trophy contention, which meant speeds upwards of 460, he knew you had to make serious modifications to your airplane: Clip wings and inject nitrous into the induction system and scale down the canopy—alterations that converted a fast and predictable warbird into a *very* fast and appallingly unpredictable winged monstrosity. Pardue hated nasty surprises like blown engines and oil-blackened windscreens and orange flames licking from cowlings. And he didn't need, thank you, that ghastly silence when an engine lunched itself altogether and your powerless fighter descended to the desert like a falling crowbar. He had a solid, predictable mount with *Fury*, and that was the way he wanted it.

It was Tuesday, and the racers were flying their qualifying laps. The speed at which you qualified determined which heats—Gold, Silver, or Bronze—you would compete in when the action started on

Thursday. The idea was to turn the fastest time you could and get the most favorable starting slot in your heat race *without* trashing your temperamental racing engine. Not until Sunday, the day of the championship races, did you pull out all the stops. Then, engines be damned. Winning was everything.

All Pardue wanted was to get a decent qualifying time. He'd already qualified the Bearcat at a sedate 374 miles per hour, which he knew would be good enough to race in the Bronze heats. Now he needed to qualify the Sea Fury in something over 400—fast enough for the Silver and, if he beat a few guys in the heat races, sufficient to move up to the Gold.

Pardue wondered for a moment if anyone else was on the course. Hadn't he heard another racer calling "on the clock," meaning that he was being timed for qualification? He looked up ahead, toward the next pylon. No one in sight.

That was what he didn't like about these qualifying laps. If you were a rookie or felt uncomfortable not having flown low and fast over the sagebrush in a while, they let you fly practice laps on the course, getting used to the high Gs around the pylons, seeing the brown moonscape blurring past you like a video game. But the trouble was, the slow practice flyers got in the way of the faster racers trying to qualify in the best time.

Other pilots had complained about it, too. It was one thing to come down the starting chute in an official race, all the planes in your heat stretched out, line abreast, where you could see them. The fastest racers would jump ahead of you, and the slow ones would fall back. You had a good idea where everybody was. But in these damned qualifying laps, they sent people out there by themselves, like kids on a playground. Fast ones, slow ones, sometimes with speed differences of a hundred miles per hour, passing each other like Corvettes overtaking Volkswagens.

Pardue was ready for the timer. He'd had enough practice. Practice was for rookies, and anyway, he'd been out there once today in the Bearcat.

He bent the Sea Fury around the last pylon and keyed his microphone: "Race Sixty-six, on the clock." This was the signal to the official timers that his speed over the next two laps would be his official qualifying time.

Jack Thomas, up in the tower, answered: "Roger, Race Sixty-six, on the clock."

Now on his third lap, Sam Richardson was on the clock, too. He was a tall, freshly retired United States Airlines captain with a thatch of gray hair and a neat mustache. Richardson wasn't a rookie, at least by strict definition. This was his second year at Reno. He'd bought the Czechoslovakian-built Yak from another airline pilot, a Delta captain who had flown it in the air shows and named the fighter *Czech Ride,* an allusion to the dreaded check flights airline pilots take to keep their jobs.

As he turned the corner, flying along the northernmost leg of the course, Richardson thought he heard someone else calling on the course. He missed the call sign. Who was it? What kind of airplane? Ahead or behind? And then he stopped wondering. He was busy, and he had other things to think about.

Technically, the Yak-11 wasn't a competitive racer. Out there on the course with the bigger Sea Furies and American warbirds, the Yak looked like a gnat. It was small and nimble, a World War II–era Soviet fighter-trainer, with a Pratt & Whitney R-2000 mounted in place of the original Russian power plant. The Yak could manage only about 330 miles per hour on the course, making it more than a hundred miles an hour slower than the front-runners.

Richardson was still getting used to the Yak. Since he'd owned the racer for a little over a year now, he'd been fixing problems: oil leaks, carburetor troubles, a rough-running engine. But now he and his crew had gotten the Yak running smoothly. Here he was, hammering around the course again at Reno and not doing too badly at it.

Except that he was having trouble picking up the next pylon. Where the hell was it? Number 5 pylon . . . up there somewhere in the shimmering brown terrain . . . Shit! There it was . . . inside his line. He was going wide around the damned thing. . . . He had to cut back hard . . . get tighter on the next pylon, number 6. Going wide was bad because it lengthened your distance around the course, and each extra second getting around the course diminished your qualifying speed by just a hair. The Yak was barely fast enough, in any case, to be one of the twenty-four qualifying airplanes for the heat races. Every second counted.

Now. Cut hard left, aim straight for pylon 6. Go for it.

Pardue got a glimpse of the airplane ahead. It looked like a distant flea speck, a mile, maybe two miles, barely distinguishable against the bleak, molten landscape. What was it? A Sea Fury, he figured, judging by its shape and size. It was obviously no problem.

Pardue was barreling down the straightaway, headed for pylon 5. He was on the clock, flying a tight line, pushing the Sea Fury hard. He needed good speed—something well in excess of 400 miles per hour—to qualify in the top rung. Then he could park his two airplanes and take a day off while he waited for the first heat races on Thursday.

He was gaining on the airplane ahead. The racer—it *still* looked like a Sea Fury—was just rounding pylon 5. And going wide! Now Pardue knew he would be passing somewhere between pylons 5 and 6. And if the guy ahead was going to fly such a loose, wide line, then all Pardue had to do was bend it tight around pylon 5, then make a beeline straight for the sixth pylon. Pass him on the left.

By strict interpretation of the rules, you couldn't pass *inside*—to the left—of another racer while turning around a pylon. Race planes rounded each pylon in a nearly vertical bank, bellies to the outside of their turn. With his right wing pointed skyward, each pilot was totally blinded to the traffic on his right, *outside* his turn. Thus, the rule: You passed only on the right, and it was your responsibility to keep the traffic inside your turn in sight.

But there was a certain slack in the way the passing rule was enforced. If a racer went sashaying way out around a pylon as though he were on a scenic tour of Nevada, then it was considered prudent to go ahead and pass to his left. It came down to judgment: Was there room? Was it safe and prudent?

Pardue didn't think about it for more than a nanosecond. He'd been in the racing game for . . . how long? More than ten years, now? He knew about safe and prudent, and he knew he sure as hell wasn't going to trash his qualifying time getting stuck behind a greenhorn in a stock warbird muddling around the course like Miss Pringle at a garden party.

Pardue rounded pylon 5 in a steep bank. The guy who was way out there on the right—*out of sight now*—would be way outside his line to pylon 6. No problem.

Wham! The impact came from somewhere behind. Richardson felt the Yak lurch to the left. The airframe was buffeting and shaking. The nose of the racer was trying to yaw off to the left.

It was the moment every pilot wondered about: What will I do when it happens? After all the years of rehearsal, of training, of mental preparation, that was the unanswered question: Will I be cool? Will I do the right thing? For Sam Richardson, that moment had come.

He stepped on the rudder. It felt strange, unresponsive. The Yak was still trying to yaw left. He fed in some right aileron. He eased back on the stick, gently raising the fighter's nose.

The question flashed through his mind: What the hell happened? *The other airplane!* He hadn't seen anything, but somehow they must have come together. Where was he now? At the bottom of a smoking hole out there?

It didn't matter, at least at the moment. What mattered to Richardson was that he get the hell out of there, up and out of the goddamned sagebrush and the rocks and the rattlesnakes. Climb! When shit really happened, a race pilot's only hope was altitude. High enough to dead-stick it—make a power-off landing—or if things got *really* grim, to go over the side and use the parachute.

The Yak was soaring upward, through a thousand feet, still climbing. The engine was running. So far, so good. Richardson keyed the mike and, for the first time in his thirty-some-year flying career, used the international emergency call: "Mayday! Race Twenty-nine, Mayday!"

"Roger, Twenty-nine," answered Jack Thomas. "The wind is two twenty degrees, twelve knots. The field's yours. You're cleared to land."

Richardson wondered, How badly is this thing damaged? He craned his neck to look backward through the Plexiglas canopy and—Shit! The rudder! The thing was half-gone! The rudder was the aft fin on the tail that gave the airplane directional control. It was chopped away! Little pieces of the Yak's tail were fluttering and spewing out in the breeze like chaff in a hurricane.

But the Yak was still flying. As long as the thing was still controllable, he'd stay with it. He was flying directly over the airport, setting up for a left-hand approach to runway 14, into the southerly wind.

He rolled onto the long concrete surface, then taxied down the ramp, past the row of startled ground crews pointing and staring goggle-eyed at the Yak's amputated tail surface.

As he taxied toward his pit, Richardson wondered again what had happened. He knew he'd just had a midair collision. With whom? He gazed out there on the course, looking for a telltale column of black smoke. He didn't see any.

It was close. So close, in fact, that no one could figure out why Sam Richardson hadn't lost *all* of the Yak's rudder as well as the vertical stabilizer and at least one elevator. One single blade of the big four-bladed propeller on Howard Pardue's Sea Fury had sliced like a machete through the Yak's rudder. Four inches in either direction would have cost Richardson *all* control of his fighter. He would have augered into the desert like a descending meteorite.

Most amazingly, neither pilot involved in the collision had seen the other—before or after. Pardue had felt a faint *thump* and, experiencing no other problems, assumed he had struck a bird. He continued his qualifying lap. Not until he landed did he find that one blade of his propeller had been slightly damaged.

It was one of those weird aviation anomalies that defied logic. It shouldn't have happened, but it did. Pardue and Richardson shouldn't be alive, but there they were, still sucking in the same dry desert air, trying to figure out what had happened.

Later, in a closed-door session of the racers' standards committee and the contest committee, it was agreed that Pardue was largely to blame. According to the rules, he should *not* have passed inside of Richardson. Pardue said that he misidentified the Yak, thinking it was a Sea Fury, a much larger—and faster—airplane; because of the disparity in scale, he believed that it was farther ahead than it turned out to be. He expected to roll out of his turn and *still* see the airplane ahead of him. Instead, while each of the airplanes was still in a hard left bank, turning for pylon 6, they merged.

Sam Richardson, for his part, was chastised for flying "unpredictably," meaning that after having gone wide on his turn, he should not have come abruptly back to the course line.

No one walked away from the debriefing feeling as though the incident had been explained. Or resolved.

Good old Howard was becoming testy. For one thing, he was *very* tired of hearing all this crap about the *incident*. He was tired of the insinuations, the innuendos that *he*—of all pilots!—had somehow screwed up. Howard Pardue, cool-handed fighter jock and experienced race pilot, had gotten himself involved in a near-fatal midair collision.

Now Pardue just wanted the subject to go away. He wanted the whole unpleasant discussion closed, and, especially, he wanted people to stop running their mouths about it. Gone, at least for the moment, was good old Howard, the amiable ostrich. In his place was an unsmiling, flint-eyed marine.

Then some fool came sauntering across the ramp. "Hey, Howard, you wanna tell me how you ran into that guy's tail?" A thundercloud would pass over Pardue's face. The pale blue eyes would drill into the guy like lasers. The foolish questioner would stagger away feeling as if he'd been zapped with a ray gun.

Pardue wasn't saying much about the incident, but what *really* pissed him off was that Sam Richardson *was*. Sam wouldn't shut up. Pardue could look down the ramp and see Richardson standing out there by his chewed-up airplane, posing for pictures, running his mouth about the incident to reporters, cameramen, passersby, race fans—anyone who came across the ramp. Pardue figured that Richardson's adrenal gland must be hot-wired to his mouth.

Both airplanes were out of action. Richardson's Yak looked as if its tail had been gnawed by a barracuda. Pardue's four-bladed propeller was hidden from the curious crowds by a tarpaulin.

A courier plane was dispatched over the mountain range to Chino, California, where the Sanders brothers, who were racing not one but *two* Sea Furies at Reno, just happened to have a spare propeller in their hangar. By the end of the afternoon, the courier was back, and Pardue had a fresh propeller blade for his Sea Fury.

Richardson's problems were more complicated. Spare parts for fifty-year-old Soviet fighters in Nevada were as rare as cowboy cosmonauts. But then, in a continuing saga of debacles and miracles, someone came up with a whole new tail from a Yak-11. A deal was made, and in two days Richardson's airplane had sprouted new tail feathers.

But the war of insults was not over. The next morning, as ground crews wandered through the pits, they saw that *Czech Ride*, Richardson's Yak, had a new racing logo painted on its vertical stabilizer: a circled P (for Pardue) with a diagonal line through it.

But even that wasn't symbolic enough. By afternoon someone added beneath the logo an even more graphic image: an outlined hand with a raised middle finger.

⌐ 7 ⌐

Hired Gun

Who was the best pilot in air racing?

It was a subject of endless speculation. You heard it asked by reporters and fans and race groupies at every watering hole in Reno. Everyone had his favorite and could cite reasons and statistics and proof positive why his guy could fly the socks off any of those other yahoos.

But it was a question you *never* heard in the hard-benched briefing room or out in the pits or in any of the places where race pilots congregated. That was part of the unspoken code: The Brethren were supposed to refrain from making judgmental observations about each other. It was a matter that went beyond professional courtesy. One of the most unpardonable sins among fighter jocks and high-risk aviators had always been running your mouth about your rivals: Who was good, who wasn't, and who might be, you know, a little suspect. You were supposed to shut up and go settle the matter in the air. Let the results do the talking.

And so it was in the racing pilots' fraternity. The race standings said it all. Or did they?

The raw statistics masked some of the more revealing details, such as who had remained coolest in the face of the worst calamity. Or who had made his slow airplane fly faster. Or who had botched what should have been a shoo-in victory.

In his secret heart, each pilot still had his own private and firmly held opinion about who was the best pilot in the business. *Himself,* of course. That much was a given. Egocentricity came as naturally to air-race pilots as breathing and swaggering.

But who—after themselves—would they name as the "best in the business?"

Well, it would be hard *not* to suggest Tiger Destefani. Destefani had made himself the dominant figure in the sport during the past decade. He had become a remarkably efficient technician, running a clean line around the pylons and managing to avoid most of the usual penalties for things like pylon cuts and deadline faults.

What the fans loved about Destefani, of course, was that the guy was fiercely aggressive. Destefani made a point of telling everyone about his single-minded mission there at Reno: *Kick ass.* It was very simple. And it didn't matter *whose* ass—his best friend's, his mother's, or the pope's. If they were foolish enough to be out there on the course with him, Tiger was going to blow their doors off.

A lot of this, of course—the swaggering, the tough talk, the pre-race blustering—was all showmanship. Destefani was a guy who *loved* playing to an audience. But those who had raced with him knew that beneath the tough talk and the gunfighter swagger was the real thing: Destefani was one hardball little son of a bitch.

Not everyone would agree that Tiger Destefani was the best race pilot at Reno. Among the "Blue Bloods"—guys who came from a more academic or technical background than Farmer Bill—was the feeling that Destefani won races for one simple reason: He had the fastest airplane. He was backed by the best crew and equipment.

When you were out in front of the pack—no prop wash, no one to pass, no jockeying for position—it was easy. Just push the throttle up and don't cut pylons.

Such sentiments reeked of the old invisible class distinction that divided the pilots in the briefing room. Some of the blue-blooded ex–military pilots were *still* finding it hard to figure how a tractor jockey from the Bakersfield alfalfa fields could blow them away.

For their money, the best all-round pilot in the game wasn't Destefani. Instead, they would point to a blond-mustached, boyish-looking character in sneakers and cutoffs.

Skip Holm was a hired gun. He didn't own an airplane, and he never paid the bills. He was one of a small cadre of pilots whom wealthy warbird owners trusted enough to turn over the controls of their precious metal.

Holm was perhaps the most blue-blooded of the Blue Bloods. He had been an air force fighter jock in Vietnam. He was a Lockheed test pilot who, while flying at Reno back in the seventies and eighties, was also performing top-secret test flights of the U-2 and the F-117 Stealth fighter.

On first meeting, without knowing his pedigree, you would take Skip Holm for just another laid-back Californian. Some flake who probably couldn't remember where he parked his bike.

There was something else that bothered people about Holm. It seemed as though he just didn't take this racing stuff *seriously* enough. He liked to joke about the whole thing, about how he was just, you know, fooling around with these people's million-dollar Sea Furies and Mustangs: "Hell, I don't even know how to start the thing. They just stick me in the cockpit, you know, get the engine going, and then I push the throttle up. Nothing to it."

That was Skip Holm's style. It was the old Chuck Yeager role, right out of *The Right Stuff*, acting cool and flippant about that which you knew could snuff you out in one dreadful heartbeat.

Still, it rubbed a few people the wrong way. To their taste, there was such a thing as being *too* cool. *It's okay to chill out, but hell, man, you have to show a little respect. After all, people do get killed out there.*

One pilot who didn't think highly of Skip Holm was a woman racer. Rather, a woman who was *almost* a racer.

She was an air-show performer. She had been recruited to fly a newly built up, alcohol-powered Sea Fury belonging to Eric Loren-zen, who owned a window-blind company and named his Sea Fury, appropriately, *Blind Man's Bluff*. Until then, there had been *no* women in the cockpits of Unlimited air racers. No one could say exactly why, but for decades the entire domain of warbirds and racing had been a male province. (A groundbreaker in the early nineties was Erin Rheinschild, a talented pilot and wife of racer Bill Rheinschild.)

The idea was, the lady would add a touch of glamour to the team. The press and the fans had already seized on this unique situation. Not even the record-setting Jacqueline Cochran had been permitted to fly back in the Thompson Trophy days.

Now all that was about to change. A lady race pilot! This was still the 1980s, before Tailhook and before the ban was removed on women pilots in military combat units. This new lady entrant was poised to break through one of the most unyielding gender-biased glass ceilings in aviation.

Of course, she had commercial value, too. Not only was she foxy enough to turn heads; it seemed that she might have what it took to attract precious sponsorship. There was only one small glitch: She had never flown anything of the size and power of the Sea Fury. Nor had she ever flown so fast so close to the ground.

Which was why, on the first day of qualifying at Reno, the Sea Fury's owner was getting *very* worried. He was standing atop his command trailer, listening to the crackling radio, watching his racer—and his handpicked pilot—thrash around the course.

She seemed to be lost.

But that wasn't the worst part. His lady pilot was flying *Blind Man's Bluff* as though she had never visited the cockpit of a high-performance fighter. Which, of course, she hadn't. An exasperated check pilot, flying a Mustang, had been assigned to chase her around the course, giving advice and trying to keep her within the confines of the racecourse.

This went on for three days of qualifying. The lady race pilot hadn't gotten better. Now it was Wednesday, the last day of qualifications, and the owner faced a dilemma: If he dismissed her, he'd look like an irresponsible schmuck for having hired her in the first place. Worse than that, he'd have the whole goddamned female flying community howling that he was a sexist slimeball who deprived women of their right to fly.

But the consequences of *not* replacing her were worse. If she failed to qualify, his expensive racer would be a static display here at Reno during the races. And, of course, there was the awful prospect that she *would* qualify—and then have an accident. It would get him and his business smeared all over the front pages. And they would say it was all *his* fault.

It was then that he turned to Skip Holm. Holm, the hired gun, happened to be without a mount at this year's race. Could he, perhaps, work something out with the lady? It would look better if Holm handled the thing. Maybe suggest that she consider *relinquishing* her seat in the Sea Fury? Could he help resolve the problem?

Holm worked something out. He simply announced that he was taking over. The lady stood there on the ramp while he climbed into the cockpit.

It was a fait accompli. Before she could protest, Holm was pulling the chute straps around him. A minute later, the big four-bladed propeller of the Sea Fury was swinging.

She was livid, of course. She was forced to watch from the ground, the fury bubbling in her like lava, while Holm flew the Sea Fury around the course. When he completed his qualifying lap,

71

roaring at more than 400 miles per hour past the finish, he hauled the nose of the fighter skyward and did a neat victory roll.

And the insults didn't end there. For months afterward, Holm went around saying he'd "saved her life." He liked to joke that it meant, at least in Oriental culture, that having saved her life, he now owned her. And since he owned her, he was putting her up for sale. And since he'd had her up for sale, he hadn't gotten any offers.

Skip Holm grew up in Dickinson, North Dakota. He went into the air force right out of college. His flying career was classic Blue Blood: He flew virtually every fighter in the air force's cold war inventory; three combat tours in Vietnam flying F-105 "Thuds" and F-4 Phantoms; selection for Air Force Test Pilot School at Edwards Air Force Base, then an assignment as an instructor at the school.

In the late seventies Holm left the air force to fly for NASA, then moved on to Lockheed as a test pilot. There he was involved in the development of some of the cold war's most secret projects: the U-2, the SR-71, the F-117 Stealth fighter. And it was during that period of his life, living in California, that he became acquainted with warbird mavens like Dave Zeuschel and Mac McClain, who invited him to do some test-flying on their old fighters. After that brief exposure, it was inevitable that Holm would be caught up in the racing fever.

It was in 1981 that someone took him to meet *Jeannie*. He didn't know what to think when he first saw her. She looked exotic, expensive—and a little bit vicious.

Jeannie was a race plane—a highly modified, hyped-up P-51 Mustang. She came from the stable of a flamboyant trucking entrepreneur named Wiley Sanders. *Jeannie* happened to be, at that moment, the most famous Mustang in the country, because she was the reigning Unlimited Air Racing champion.

Jeannie was a lady with a past. She had been around air racing longer than any of the current crop of race pilots and longer than most of the airplanes. She had competed back in the 1940s heyday of the Cleveland Thompson Trophy races under the name *Galloping Ghost*. She had changed owners several times.

Jeannie was a come-from-the-ashes airplane that had undergone a complete rebuild in 1979 after a disastrous off-airport landing that nearly totaled her. In a day-and-night, nonstop restoration project, she was barely ready in time for the 1980 Reno championships. Flown by a crafty Alabaman named Mac McClain, she captured the Gold Trophy.

Roy "Mac" McClain was an ex–air force C-130 pilot who made his living as a crop duster at his base in Eufaula, Alabama. He had come to air racing through the T-6 class, beating his competition and quickly establishing himself as a force to be reckoned with at Reno. McClain *loved* everything about race planes—flying them, working on them, and especially creating exotic new schemes to make them go faster than anything in the field.

McClain had invested all his creative energy and passion into the restoration of *Jeannie*. Now he was too ill to fly her himself. Mac was only forty-six, but he looked fifteen years older. He kept telling everyone that year that he'd been laid up with back problems. He'd be over it by next year.

Most of his friends had already guessed the truth. Thirty years of hard smoking had caught up with him, and he had lung cancer.

Jeannie needed another pilot. Not just a guy with good hands who could fly Mustangs. She needed a pilot with extraordinary skill and, most importantly, a take-no-prisoners attitude. *Jeannie* was a winner, and she needed a special pilot.

Holm walked around the Mustang, looking her over. Yeah, this airplane was different. *Very* different from your stock P-51. With that tiny little canopy and slicked-up airframe, it looked like a missile with wings.

The owner wanted to know what Holm knew about air racing. Not much, he answered. Actually, zip. What, for that matter, did he know about Mustangs? Damned little. He had been an air force fighter jock—a *jet*-fighter jock—and then a test pilot on Lockheed's aeronautical exotica. He had, in fact, a grand total of about three hours' experience in Mustangs.

So here were these guys—Mac McClain, *Jeannie*'s creator, and Wiley Sanders, her owner, peering at him, waiting for the answer to their question: Would he be interested in racing *Jeannie* at Reno?

It was a no-brainer. "Sure," he said.

At the hangar in Van Nuys where *Jeannie* lived, some aviation writers came out to get some material about the new pilot.

"How fast do you think you'll qualify?"

Skip Holm tried to think. How fast did a Mustang go? He didn't have a clue. He was about to come up with an off-the-wall guess when he glanced over at the parked Mustang. On the side of the fuselage was painted *Jeannie*'s record-setting qualification speed from 1980, the year before: *446 miles per hour.*

"Four-fifty," he said, sounding very sure of himself.

It was a typically cocky Skip Holm answer. The next month, he flew *Jeannie* out to Reno, where he set a new qualifying-speed record of 450.09 miles per hour.

The cockiness didn't stop there.

Before any rookie could race at Reno, he had to be scrutinized by a designated check pilot. The idea was, the check pilot would fly "chase," having the new guy do a few maneuvers—aileron rolls in each direction—then watch him fly a few laps around the pylons and demonstrate that he could pass another airplane in the prescribed way. And at some point the check pilot would declare a simulated emergency, whereupon the rookie was supposed to pull up, pretending his engine had just lunched itself, pick a suitable runway, and execute a simulated dead-stick landing.

It was all very cut-and-dried—the kind of stuff you did as a fighter jock when you checked into a new squadron. Skip Holm had done it a hundred times.

So he said to the check pilot, who he knew was an ex–fighter jock: "Let's make a deal. We'll go out there and get in a line-abreast formation. Then we'll dogfight, one-on-one. If I get on your tail, I'm qualified. If you win, we'll do it your way."

The check pilot glanced around just to make sure no one else was catching this exchange. He nodded. "You're on."

So that's what they did. They took off and turned left, up over the high ridge north of Stead. Then they settled into a line-abreast formation. The fight was on.

It took less than a minute. Skip Holm maneuvered into a tight trail position behind the check pilot's Mustang. He had him bore-sighted. "I guess this means I'm qualified. Right?"

No one at Reno had ever seen a rookie announce his presence so resoundingly. Holm shattered the qualifying-speed record (set two years earlier, in 1979, in the same airplane, by Mac McClain). His only real competition in the heat races turned out to be Lyle Shelton, in the R-3350-powered Bearcat he was now calling *Rare Bear*. In the first of the Gold heats, on Friday, Shelton and Holm dueled for the lead, each pampering his engine, with Shelton finally taking the flag at a speed of 416.72 and Holm in second at 414.05.

But Shelton's engine was already ailing. He would miss the Gold heats on Saturday or Sunday, leaving the field wide open to the rookie, Skip Holm. On Saturday Holm walked away with the heat race, leaving the pack well behind as he finished at a speed of 427.77. Sunday, the day of the championship trophy race, was a repeat. Skip Holm blew away the field of seven racers, winning with an average speed of 431.29 miles per hour.

⊱ 8 ⊰

Living the Dream

You could tell that he was a new guy—one of the *rookies*. It wasn't hard to figure that he was military—a fighter jock probably—by the short hair and trim figure and that barely subdued cockiness that fighter pilots tended to wear like a mantle. He could have been a model for a recruiting poster—a Tom Selleck look-alike with an engaging grin and Boy Scoutish demeanor.

And it was clear that even though he was a rookie, he had already figured out the hierarchical protocol in the Room of Hard Benches. He was sitting on a bench near the back of the room. Next to the wall. And he was keeping his mouth shut.

On the front of his black baseball cap was an embroidered logo. It looked like some sort of futuristic airplane. Over the top was the lettering STS-85.

It took a while for any of the Brethren to get around to noticing. "Hey, I know what that is," one of them said, studying the rookie's baseball cap. "That was the call sign for the space shuttle that just came down a couple of weeks ago. Did you have something to do with that?"

"Yeah, sort of." The new guy flashed the Tom Selleck grin. "I was the mission commander." Heads turned. Several of the Brethren peered over their shoulders at this new guy. Who was this rookie? One of those hot dogs that liked to come to Reno for no good reason except to get a new notch in their belt? One of the celebrity pilots who thought flying an Unlimited racer around the pylons would make a flashy little sidebar in his next press release?

The new guy's name was Curt Brown. Brown knew all about the Brethren. He knew how they felt about hotshot test pilots and astronauts and résumé builders. He was ready for them. "I'm just here to participate," he said. "Doesn't matter where I finish—in the middle, way back, or dead last. I'm just glad to be here."

And then he flashed the Selleck grin, letting them all know that, yeah, he was a new kid on the block, but he was no threat to any of them.

That was good enough for the Brethren, at least for now. What was important was that a rookie *act* like a new guy. Astronaut or not, he hadn't yet gained admission to their club—the inner circle of the Unlimited Brethren.

The race association had already gotten plenty of mileage out of the fact that not one but *three* real astronauts were entered in this year's championship races. One was Bill Anders, a courtly, retired air force general who had flown into space back in the Apollo program. Anders wasn't a rookie. He'd been to Reno before, racing his own P-51. Still, the air force general and astronaut knew his place here in the Room of Hard Benches. He was sitting in one of the back rows, showing a respectful deference to the Brethren.

Another astronaut-racer was a high-profile pilot named Robert "Hoot" Gibson. Gibson had earned several distinctions, having been assigned as NASA's chief astronaut, then picked to command the first rendezvous mission with the Russian spacecraft *Mir*. Recently retired from NASA, Gibson was making a name for himself in civilian aviation.

But Gibson wasn't there in the Room of Hard Benches this race week. The word had just come that he probably wouldn't make it this year. The Sea Fury he was supposed to fly was down with some major engine problems.

Curtis L. Brown Jr. was your basic all-American boy, the kind of kid mothers filled scrapbooks of clippings about and fathers never tired of bragging to all their cronies about. He grew up in a Norman Rockwellian environment in Elizabethtown, North Carolina, where he excelled at sports and academics and, to no one's surprise, won an appointment directly from high school to the U.S. Air Force Academy in Colorado Springs.

After graduation and commissioning in 1978, he went through air force pilot training and was assigned to fly the A-10 Warthog, stationed in Myrtle Beach, South Carolina. Brown loved the fast and low air-to-mud mission of the Warthog. He was good at it, and in a short while he was reassigned as an A-10 instructor pilot.

From then on, Curt Brown's career was on a fast track. He was selected to go through the air force's fighter-weapons course out at Nellis Air Force Base, near Las Vegas, and, a couple of years later, received the fighter jock's dream assignment—orders to test-pilot school at Edwards Air Force Base.

In 1987, while he was flying A-10s and F-16s as a test pilot at Eglin Air Force Base in Florida, Brown learned that he had been chosen for the most elite program of them all. He was going into space. He'd been selected by NASA to be a pilot on the space shuttle.

He made his first flight in 1992, aboard the space shuttle *Endeavor*. Two years later, he flew an eleven-day mission aboard *Atlantis*. In 1996 he took off again in *Endeavor*, and the next year, he commanded the eleven-day voyage of the space shuttle *Discovery*—STS 85.

By then Brown was a lieutenant colonel in the air force. He was also a bachelor, the divorced father of a young son. One summer he was given one of those assignments junior astronauts frequently received—take one of the NASA T-38 jet trainers to an air show and do public-relations work. Which meant grinning a lot and signing autographs and answering the thousand questions kids asked about how neat it was to be an astronaut.

This air show was in Tucson, Arizona. A friend, race pilot and air-show performer Dennis Sanders, dragged Curt over to meet a certain lady. Her name was Anne Brickert. She was tall, slender, and had long red hair. Brown thought she was a knockout.

As it turned out, she already knew a lot about aviation. Her brother, a warbird pilot and air racer named John Muszala, had been one of the "Chino Kids," like Steve Hinton and Jim Maloney and Robbie Patterson, who learned to fly exotic warbirds at the museum in Chino, California, before they were old enough to vote.

And the connection went further. Anne had been married for nine years to a well-known race pilot named Rick Brickert. Brickert had been chosen to fly a radically experimental airplane called the *Pond Racer*. During the Reno races of 1993, he was killed in the fiery crash of the new airplane.

Anne Brickert already knew more than she wanted to know about warbirds and Unlimited racers. But, at least for the time being, it didn't matter. She and the astronaut began dating. Anne and Curt became an item.

Like every other rookie, Brown had to be checked out by one of the Unlimited Division check pilots. It was all very basic, of course, especially for an experienced fighter and test pilot like Brown. But sometimes such check rides turned out to be *very* revealing. Over the years, many self-appointed knights of the sky had embarrassed themselves in the eyes of the Brethren by screwing up his—or *her*—check ride. Sometimes it was a simple but critical skill, like formation flying, that was missing from the candidate's repertoire.

Sometimes the rookie was unable to handle the simulated engine-out emergency landing—an often-required skill at Reno. Or sometimes the candidate demonstrated a frightening lack of what aviation psychologists called *situational awareness*, which, in shrink talk, meant that the guy had his head up his butt.

It was Monday morning, early in the week before the qualifications had gotten started. Brown took off in his Sea Fury, accompanied by Dennis Sanders in his own Sea Fury, *Argonaut*. Sanders was the Unlimited Division's check pilot this year.

Overhead the field, at a couple of thousand feet, Sanders called, "Give me an aileron roll to the right, Curt."

Brown neatly rolled the big fighter.

"Now one to the left." Brown gave him a neat aileron roll to the left.

Then they dropped down onto the course and went around the pylons. At first, Sanders led, with Brown flying close behind. Sanders called for Brown to pass. Brown passed, no problem, overtaking *Argonaut* on the outside of the line.

And while all this was going on, the Brethren watched from the pits. Over the years they had had some seriously good laughs observing one of these high-and-mighties from some rarefied test-flying facility come to Reno and *step on himself*. When such a thing happened, it was wonderful, confirming the already-exalted view the Brethren had of themselves.

But today they were disappointed. Curt Brown didn't step on himself. He jumped through all the little hoops, one after the other, that Sanders put in front of him. He rolled and passed and dead-sticked the Sea Fury. And after he'd passed the test and rejoined the Brethren the next morning in the Room of Hard Benches, he still knew what was expected of him. He kept his mouth shut.

Brown's race mount, a Hawker TMK-20 Sea Fury, was owned by a businessman named Wally Fisk. It was stock in almost every respect, still fitted with the original 18-cylinder Bristol Centaurus 2,550 horsepower radial engine. Most other Sea Furies at Reno had been reengined with the more powerful and durable Wright R-3350, cranking out about 3,500 horsepower.

After passing his check ride and being admitted to the fold of race pilots, he still had to post a qualifying time that would put him and the Sea Fury among the twenty-four fastest qualifiers. His speed of 359 miles per hour ranked him in the twenty-first position among the qualifiers.

And then, in the first heat race on Thursday, Brown improved his position by overtaking three of the faster qualifiers. The rookie came in second in his first official Unlimited race.

By Sunday, the day of the championship races, most of the Brethren had forgotten that Brown was a blue-blooded rookie. Unlike most rookies, he had gotten through the week without calamity. He hadn't cut any pylons (which several racers, not just rookies, had done). He hadn't violated the dead line (the invisible thousand-foot separation between the racecourse and the pits and audience).

But what earned the most acceptance for Curt Brown was his style. As word of his status got around—*Hey, we got a real astronaut over here . . .*—an inevitable cult of worshipers, mostly kids, flocked around his race pit. Instead of hiding in the trailer, Brown gave them his time. He signed autographs and posed for photographs. With infinite patience, he handed out advice and counsel to the multitude of kids—some of them children of the Brethren—about how they might live out their own space-flying dreams. By the end of the week everyone had reached a conclusion: This guy Brown was okay. In fact, he was a class act.

Between the two astronauts, Curt Brown and Hoot Gibson, simmered a friendly mano a mano, and unofficial competition. Brown had risen through the ranks of NASA astronauts in Gibson's shadow. Gibson, the senior of the two, had already put in a full career at NASA. He had earned a place in the record books with his homebuilt

Cassutt sport plane, flying it to a world-record altitude. Then he'd done the same thing with a hot little racer called *Pushy Galore*. Gibson was the kind of guy to whom people came with their airplanes, saying, *Please. Take my million-dollar airplane. Fly the thing.*

Brown's style was less flamboyant than Gibson's, more serious and understated. But beneath Brown's serious exterior was an ambition and drive every bit as focused as that of Hoot Gibson. Astronauts like Brown and Gibson and Bill Anders had made it to the pinnacle of the flying profession by being competitive. Throughout their careers they had gone head-to-head with their rivals—and won. And made it into space.

Now they were at Reno. And nothing had changed.

More than any of the others in the Room of Hard Benches, Bill Rheinschild could claim to be living the American Dream. He was sitting in the company of the hottest Unlimited air-racing pilots in the world, with his own Mustang, *Risky Business*, parked out there on the ramp, being tended by his own crew in his pit area.

He was a grinning, round-faced guy with an infectious kind of exuberance. He was usually the chattiest guy in those morning pre-race briefings, running his mouth and cracking jokes, then laughing at them. Though he was not yet forty, Rheinschild was already a veteran air racer: This was his tenth season in the Unlimited races at Reno.

Rheinschild was a guy who had it all: a beautiful, talented wife, model kids, lavish homes, a fleet of airplanes and boats and automobiles, the lifestyle of the idle rich. Except that Rheinschild was not idle. Nor had he always been rich.

Back when he was a kid growing up in Van Nuys, Rheinschild's hero was an entrepreneurial pilot named Clay Lacy. Among other things, Lacy was an Unlimited air racing pilot. With his Mustang named *Miss Van Nuys*, he had won the Unlimited Championship in 1970.

Rheinschild wanted to be just like his hero, Clay Lacy. As a teenager, he hung out at the airport, did odd jobs, and each time he'd saved twenty-five dollars, he'd go take another lesson at the flying school. He soloed at sixteen, the earliest possible age. By the time he was eighteen, he was working for Lacy, ferrying his airplanes and flying his Lear jets.

With his experience in Lacy's jets, Rheinschild got a job flying corporate jets for a real-estate developer while he was still finishing college at Southern Cal. In the process, he learned something about the construction business. When he graduated from college in 1980, he became an entrepreneur himself. He struck out on his own and began building houses.

It was the beginning of the roaring eighties in California. In a short while, Rheinschild was building a *lot* of houses. When he was four years out of college, he was doing $40 million a year. In four more years, he was doing $90 million.

This was the American Dream, all right, in glorious, glitzy California style. Bill Rheinschild was living out all the dreams he used to have when he was still a kid hanging out at Van Nuys Airport, cleaning bug stains off Clay Lacy's Mustang.

In 1985 he decided to fill in another part of the dream: *With the first $400,000 I make this year,* he promised himself, *I'm gonna buy a Mustang.*

He made the money, and he followed through on the promise. Not long after, Rheinschild was making the last great leap from being just another outrageously successful California yuppie to a young incarnation of his hero, Clay Lacy.

He flew his mustang to Reno. He entered the National Championship Air Races.

Rheinschild gave his Mustang an appropriate name: *Risky Business*. By the early nineties it was an apt description of his sprawling construction empire. Suddenly he was seeing the dark side of the great

California land boom. The bottom dropped out of the real-estate market. Property values—and construction costs—which, during the roaring eighties, had shot skyward like a Titan rocket, were suddenly plummeting to earth. High-rolling developers like Bill Rheinschild were going broke by the thousands. Chapter 11s became as common as California divorces.

One day Rheinschild calculated his net worth at $18 million. The next day, as he watched property values tanking in Southern California, he was informed that he was $18 million in the hole.

It was the flip side of the American Dream. For Rheinschild, it was survival time. It meant trimming back the empire. Liquidating assets like his fleet of eight airplanes. He gave up his Sabreliner executive jet. He gave up *Miss Fit,* the Rheinschilds' second Mustang.

The only thing he would *not* relinquish, not until the last shoe dropped and the bill collectors came to repossess the furniture, was the Mustang he'd bought back when his fortunes were first on the rise. *Risky Business,* the hot, clipped-wing P-51, would be the last item on the block.

It was 1994, and Rheinschild told himself to hunker down, work harder, and wait for things to get better. In due time, they did.

A lot of it was luck, Rheinschild didn't mind telling everyone. It was luck and timing—and a hell of a lot of hard work. He *knew* what a lucky guy he had been. In more ways than one.

Another lucky thing happened one night, back when he was still going to Southern Cal. He ran into this especially cute UCLA coed at the Chart House bar. He learned that her name was Erin Ellis, and as it turned out, she was interested in flying. In fact, she had just begun taking lessons, learning to fly her father's Cessna 152.

So Bill and Erin began dating. And flying together. They became each other's best friend. While Bill Rheinschild was becoming a successful home builder in Southern California, Erin earned all her flying licenses. She became a professional pilot and went to work for United Airlines.

In 1988, Rheinschild showed up for his first outing at Reno with his Mustang. It was wild and exhilarating. Racing was every bit as challenging and intimidating as he had dreamed back when he was doing gofer jobs for Lacy. That year, he made himself another one of those promises: *If I live through this, I'm gonna ask Erin to marry me.*

He did. And she accepted. And from then on air racing was a Rheinschild family affair. They never missed a year of racing at Reno. At the end of the eighties he bought a second Mustang called *Miss Fit,* and Erin Rheinschild, too, became an Unlimited air-racing pilot.

It turned out to be controversial—more controversial than either of them dreamed. Never before had a *woman* pilot actually competed in the Unlimited Division of air racing. The closest any had come was the woman air-show pilot back in the eighties who was replaced at the last minute by Skip Holm in the cockpit of the experimental Sea Fury racer. Even in the Thompson Trophy days, women were excluded from the fast company of the race pilots. Jackie Cochran, who held more speeds records than almost any of the men who had ever raced, was barred from the sport.

But times were changing. Women were launching into space and flying fighters off aircraft carriers and commanding commercial airliners, just as Erin Rheinschild herself was doing. But such changes, even in the early nineties, hadn't made a deep imprint on the True Brethren, cloistered out in the desert in their little Room of Hard Benches. Still embedded in their culture, like a fossil in a Nevada rock, was the gut feeling that air racing, damn it, was *a man's game.*

It was the same gut feeling that permeated the atmospheres of military ready rooms and aircraft carriers and the cockpits of airliners. And in the wake of events like the navy's Tailhook scandal, the whole field of gender integration had become a minefield.

Now women were invading what had always been an elite men's club—the sacred sport of Unlimited air racing. And the men—some of the men—could give you a hundred reasons why it was a bad idea:

"Sure, women can be trained to do the job, but trust me, when the sticky stuff hits the blades, they're gonna fall apart."

"It's the left-brain, right-brain thing. Women see things more abstractly than men. But there's nothing abstract about flying four hundred miles per hour over the sagebrush. The ground ain't abstract."

"It's like sticking a woman in with the Detroit Lions. You can dress her up in a uniform and pads, and if she's lucky she might not even get killed. But it doesn't mean she ought to be playing football. And it's the same thing with air racing."

Not every man in the Room of Hard Benches, of course, shared such prejudices. Certainly not Bill Rheinschild and not some of the pilots who had already flown with women in the military or in the airlines. But most air-race pilots and owners and crew members, by disposition and choice, were conservative. And in their conservative souls still burned a little torch of resistance to radical change. *Air racing, damn it, was a man's game.*

Erin Rheinschild was getting a chilly reception.

Her first race was supposed to be at Sherman, Texas—one of the several onetime efforts at a "new venue" for Unlimited racing. In the crowd were some fifteen thousand women who had turned out in the hope of seeing one of their own—Ms. Rheinschild—break one of the last gender barriers by racing in the world's fastest motorsport.

But before Erin could race, she had to pass the race committee's rigid qualification tests. And this being her first time on *any* race-course, she had problems. In the judgment of the appointed check pilot, Art Vance, her proficiency out there on the pylons was not up to their standards. He gave Erin a down.

Which, in itself, was not remarkable. Many of the current Brethren had flunked their first attempts at qualifying. All it meant, in most instances, was that they simply needed more experience in the low and fast world of closed-course air racing. They came back the next year, or the next, and most made the grade.

And that would have been the case with Erin Rheinschild except for the firestorm that was ignited among the outraged women in the grandstands. Out came the banners and public comments and urgent messages to the race promoters.

"We want Erin!"

"Air racing is a sexist sport!"

"Discrimination again!"

Even though it was a no-win situation, the race committee held to the rules. Erin would *not* be allowed to fly in the race at Sherman. But it was decided to do something even more controversial: They would give Erin Rheinschild a *second* qualification attempt.

And that was all she needed. This time she did just fine. Vance gave her his blessing, and she was qualified. She could race at the next official event.

Which satisfied everyone, of course, except the most hard-nosed of the Brethren:

"Goddamn it, *I* didn't get a second chance. It just proves that women get special treatment."

"Forget standards! Why don't we just let *anyone* come and try as many times as they want."

"Why the hell did she get *two* chances to qualify?"

And so on.

Gradually, the furor died down. In her unflamboyant way, Erin proved that she was safe and competent on the racecourse. Of course, she hadn't yet been put to the *real* test—a real race and the gut-wrenching moment of truth when the sticky stuff really did hit the blades. The moment that came, sooner or later, to everyone who flew an Unlimited racer around the pylons.

She didn't have long to wait.

. . .

It was her first race after the qualification hassle in Texas. This was another of those "new venues," an Unlimited air race in the high, thin atmosphere of Denver, Colorado.

She couldn't believe it! Here she was, rounding a pylon, flying *Miss Fit* in a low, tight line around the course, when—*Bloom!*—the Merlin engine let go.

For an instant she was stunned. It was just what the high-and-mighty Brethren were so fond of saying: *You fly one of these things long enough, it's gonna blow.*

Barely into the second race of her short career and it happened. It blew. The analogy of the racing engine and the hand grenade had been reaffirmed.

And that wasn't all. As if to *really* put the rookie race pilot to the test, the next part of the scenario was playing out like a bad movie. A black curtain of oil was splattering the windshield, obscuring her view of the world outside. The Merlin was disgorging its entire thirteen-gallon supply of oil over the nose of the Mustang.

She couldn't see.

Erin shoved aside all her dark thoughts about Merlin engines and moments of truth and the goddamned holier-than-everybody Brethren. She called a Mayday. Then she hauled the nose of the Mustang up, using the energy of its 300-plus knots to soar high over the pylons. With the safety of three or four thousand feet, she still had a chance to bail out. Through the oil-streaked sides of the Plexiglas canopy, she struggled to see the ground, the racecourse, the intersecting runways of the airport.

And then help arrived. It came in the form of the T-33 pace plane, being flown by Steven Hinton. Within seconds Hinton was tucked into position off Erin's right wing.

It would have to be a "talk down" arrival, since she could scarcely see out the windscreen. Hinton became her eyes. He talked, delivering instructions like an air-traffic controller: "Come right ten degrees ... keep it coming down ... a little steeper ..." And she responded. Down they went, locked in formation, the sputtering, oil-smeared P-51 and the lifeguard jet. "Gear down . . . one notch of flaps now . . . the runway's coming up straight ahead . . . bring the nose up a little . . . that's it . . ."

The wheels of *Miss Fit* squawked onto the hard concrete runway. It was a textbook handling of an in-flight emergency. Erin was cool. Hinton was professional. The incident put to rest any further grumbling among the Brethren about the competency of Erin Rheinschild.

In 1990 *both* Rheinschilds entered the championship races at Reno. Erin qualified *Miss Fit* at a speed of 380 miles per hour. Bill posted a qualification speed of 407 miles per hour in *Risky Business*.

In a Bronze race final on Sunday, Erin grabbed an early lead and then hung on. With each lap she widened the space between her and her closest rival, Lloyd Hamilton, who was flying his Sea Fury, *Furias*. She crossed the finish line all alone at an average speed of 387 miles per hour, half a lap ahead of Hamilton.

Bill repeated the act in the Silver race. He took charge at the start and dominated the entire contest. He roared past the checkered flag at a speed of 415 miles per hour, well ahead of Gary Levitz in his Mustang, *Miss Ashley*.

Two first-place finishes and a new page in the record books: They were the first and only husband-and-wife team to win separate first-place trophies in Unlimited air racing.

⊁ 9 ⊁

An Ill Wind

The sun is shining on some stuff in there
that should be in the dark.
—*Tom Dwelle, owner of* Critical Mass

14 September 1997

By three o'clock the wind had gotten worse. Up in the Race Control
tower, Jack Thomas and his crew were having a hell of a time just
keeping the equipment from blowing away. Twice now the canvas
awning had ripped loose and flapped around the control tower like
a runaway spinnaker. The desert grit was blasting them from behind, stinging their eyes and snatching their baseball caps from
their heads. Out there on the racecourse Thomas could see mini tor-
nadoes (dust devils, the Nevadans called them) kicking up in the
sagebrush and the dwarf trees. It was a lousy day for racing.

But it didn't matter. This was Sunday, the day of the Gold Trophy
race—and was the biggest crowd draw. Some of the events had already been canceled. The biplanes were supposed to run their own
Gold race that morning. But when the pilots of the little wood-and-

fabric racers took a look at the dust devils and the clouds of blowing sand out there on the course, they said to hell with it and pushed their biplanes back in the hangar.

The Formula Ones, which were only marginally more suited for the high winds than the biplanes, elected to go ahead and run their race. And as it turned out, they wished they hadn't.

The little 100-horsepower racers lined up for their usual shotgun start, arranged in pairs on the runway like racers at Le Mans. The flag went down. Each pilot jammed up his throttle, kicking the rudder pedals to resist the howling crosswind that was trying to blow their tails sideways to the runway. Almost instantly, one of the racers veered left, chewing into the tail of another racer. Then he made his next mistake: He stomped on the brakes and abruptly went up on his nose. The other racer, with his tail feathers gobbled into shreds by the plane behind, skittered sideways like a shotgunned quail into the sagebrush and soft dirt off the edge of the runway.

And that was just the beginning. In the heavy gusts, the little fiberglass-and-composite airplanes hammered around the course at over 200 miles an hour like bobsledders on a glacier. When the race was done, each pilot climbed out of his cockpit dripping with sweat, looking as if he'd just gone ten rounds with Tyson. "Jesus!" said one ashen-faced pilot, slamming down a Bud right there on the ramp. "I've gotta be crazy to do this shit."

The winds became worse. By four o'clock, the starting time for the Gold Unlimited, the racecourse looked like a war zone. Clouds of dirt and ripped-up dwarf trees were swirling across the plateau. Not only would the race be as rough as flying in a hurricane; the pilots would have a hell of a time just maintaining a line around the pylons. The powerful southerly wind would have the effect of constantly nudging them away from the intended track over the ground.

Low-level air turbulence was a bitch. Every air racer hated it. It was brutal on your airplane, making fragile, overstressed components even more susceptible to failure, and it was hard on *you,* each bump—*Wham! Wham!*—sending a jolt up your spine, jangling your eyeballs around in your skull, making a fuzzy blur of the instruments on your panel.

It was tough enough rolling into the turns, pulling four or five Gs, grunting to keep your vision from tunneling and losing the picture altogether. But the bumping and throbbing of the low-level turbulence, added to the Gs, was like high-speed cornering through a field of speed bumps. Your head felt as if it were being swatted with a mallet.

But, oddly, the high-G turns were the kindest to the airplane, at least in conditions of turbulence. This was because the Gs *multiplied* the airplane's effective weight. It was a matter of applied physics: A nine-thousand-pound race plane pulling four Gs had an effective weight of *thirty-six* thousand pounds. The stubby little clipped wings of a Mustang like *Strega,* instead of vibrating and flexing in the up-down *Wham! Wham!* of severe turbulence, were being weighed down and held rigid by the unyielding thirty-six-thousand-pound load imposed by the four-G turn. Under this kind of load, the bumps had little effect.

Thus the nastiest—and most destructive—turbulence was with the wings unloaded—only *one* G—at high speed on the straightaway. In this condition, the wings flexed and fluttered, taking the brunt of each invisible air bump. It was like schussing a ski slope, headed hell-for-leather over the moguls, skis pointed straight downhill. Every bump felt as if you'd hit a boulder.

The Silver race had gone off on schedule, with Bill Rheinschild jumping into the lead in his clipped-wing Mustang, *Risky Business.* For the next eight laps Rheinschild opened up his lead, with Dennis Sanders, in the family's "spare" Sea Fury, *Argonaut,* holding on to a solid second. In third place was Skip Holm, flying *Critical Mass.*

Critical Mass was the much-modified Sea Fury, owned and rebuilt by an ex-Skyraider pilot named Tom Dwelle. Dwelle was a short, outgoing man of about sixty, with whitened hair and a ready handshake. He enjoyed the surprised look on people's faces when they shook his hand, as if they thought something was missing.

It was. One of the things Tom Dwelle had been through while upgrading *Critical Mass* to an Unlimited racer was the installation of nitrous oxide. Nitrous oxide was used in other race machines— automobiles, boats, motorcycles. In air racers, the use of nitrous oxide had always been controversial. The addition of it to the fuel-air mixture of an R-3350 engine had approximately the same effect as lighting the afterburner on a jet engine. It did for racing machines what steroids did for athletes. Using it made the difference between running in the Bronze or Silver categories, which was to say *stock*— or going toe-to-toe with the big guns in the Gold.

Nitrous oxide had disadvantages. While it greatly augmented the horsepower of an already-overstretched racing engine, it shortened its life expectancy to a matter of hours. Or minutes. You never knew. Injecting the stuff into your engine was the tantamount to lighting the fuse on a keg of dynamite.

Just *handling* it could produce spectacular results. One day in 1995, while Tom Dwelle was outfitting *Critical Mass* with its on-board tank of nitrous, something went wrong. A spark, an overpressure— he doesn't know exactly what—*Blam!*—the tank exploded, removing part of his right hand, along with several fingers.

Which accounted now for that odd look when people shook tom Dwelle's outstretched hand.

Standing there in the pits that Sunday, watching Skip Holm fly *Critical Mass* around the pylons, Dwelle couldn't help having mixed feelings. This was *his* race plane, which he had lovingly restored. By all rights, *he* was the one who ought to be there in the cockpit.

He had been around the racing business for several years. Back in

1989 and 1990, he had won the Gold Trophy in the AT-6 two years running. Then, in the early nineties, at Reno, he had written a check for a wrecked Sea Fury, the troubled *Blind Man's Bluff*, which he hauled on a flatbed back to his hangar in the foothills in Auburn, California. After he and his crew rebuilt the fighter, he gave it a new name: *Critical Mass*. Dwelle appointed *himself* the primary race pilot.

Dwelle raced *Critical Mass* during its first season at Reno in 1993. In the Friday Silver race, a propeller vibration became so bad it began destroying the R-3350 engine; Dwelle called a Mayday and put the Sea Fury down safely.

Dwelle was an aggressive race pilot. *Too* aggressive, at least in the opinion of some of his peers. In 1994, after an incident of passing *between* the two Sea Furies being raced by the Sanders brothers, Brian and Dennis, followed by an acerbic exchange back in the debriefing room, the standards committee decreed that Dwelle was a danger to himself and the other racers. He was disqualified.

Not everyone agreed. A few, including Dwelle's choice as a replacement pilot for *Critical Mass*, Skip Holm, thought that Dwelle was being railroaded. "Those guys are acting like little old ladies," said Holm. "Dwelle gave them a scare, and now they're kicking him out." To others, it was simply an example of how the old boys' racing network worked. Dwelle wasn't one of them. He was one of those guys who'd come up from the other side of the pits—from the crop-dusting barnstorming AT-6 community. He needed to learn a little humility.

Humility, of course, was a scarce commodity there in primadonna country. But if Dwelle had any hard feelings about his grounding, it didn't show. Even with his mangled paw, he made the rounds of everyone's pits, shaking hands and grinning and enjoying himself immensely. Dwelle wasn't a guy to hold a grudge.

Holm was riding the bumps—*Wham! Wham! Wham!*—feeling each thump and bang resonate through the airframe. He knew this was damned hard on the airplane. At this speed, right at 400 miles per hour, every little gust and thermal felt as if one were hitting a pothole on the freeway.

Critical Mass was tricked out more like a hot racer than any plane at Reno. With its stunning poppy-red-and-black paint scheme and aft-mounted cockpit, in the style of the rakish 1930s racers like Weddell Williams, the fighter looked as if it ought to be a world-beating air racer.

But something had been lost in the transformation of the old fighter into a racer. *Critical Mass* was a dog—at least as Unlimited Gold racers went. The racer was like a gorgeous actress who couldn't remember her lines.

Now in the hands of Skip Holm, *Critical Mass* was plowing around the pylons as fast as the big fighter was able to go. And, so far, it was fast enough to keep him in a solid third place, not so far behind *Argonaut,* which he could see a couple of hundred yards ahead.

If ever something was going to break—

Thwock! Something broke. Or at least it *felt* as if something broke.

Thwock! Thwock! Christ! No doubt about it. Something *did* sure as hell break. Holm had the vague sensation of pieces—pieces of *what?*—flying past his cockpit. What the hell? Was something coming off the airplane, or was he hitting something? Birds? Rocks? Flak?

And then he had this instant flashback, like a subliminal image from his long-ago past. Was someone *shooting* at him? That's what it felt like—the thirty-millimeter rounds the North Vietnamese used to lob at him back in the bad old days. But no, he knew it couldn't be. No thirty-millimeter out here on the high desert. Something was breaking from the stress of all these goddamn bumps.

Holm, an engineer and test pilot, understood that racing applied incredible stresses to airplanes. The rate of mechanical failure went up by quantum amounts as you increased throttle and Gs on these

vulnerable old airframes. But a less understood cause of failure—
and the most insidious—was *turbulence.* Instead of the smooth and
steady application of four or five Gs as you hauled the fighter in
a hard turn around the pylon, turbulence—the *wham wham wham*
of rough air—wreaked a flexing, pulsating havoc on metal components. It was like bending a tin-can lid until it broke. Rough air
made things break.

Which was what Holm suspected was happening to him this very
minute. *Something*—he still didn't know what—had broken. Things
had gone to hell.

Holm did what he always did when things went to hell. He hauled
back on the stick and keyed his microphone: "Race Ten, Mayday!"

Critical Mass was vibrating like a hot rod with a flat tire. Holm
scanned the instrument panel. The panel was shaking so hard from
the vibration, he could barely read the gauges. But everything—
temperatures, pressures, amps—all looked within their normal parameters. He eased the throttle back in case it was something in the
engine that let go.

No change. The big, round Wright R-3350 seemed to be running
okay. The shaking was coming from something else.

Holm set the Sea Fury up for a landing on runway 27. The wind,
howling out of the southwest, would be almost directly across the
runway. The problem with crosswind landings was directional control. Landing in a crosswind, an airplane's large vertical stabilizer—
the upright fin on the tail—acted like a sail, blown sideways by the
wind. As the tail swung downwind, the nose was forced into
the wind, and the airplane tried to swerve like a jackrabbit off the
upwind edge of the runway. Such a landing demanded precise and
delicate rudder control by the pilot.

All this Holm knew from long experience. Swooping down over
the approach end of runway 27, Holm kept the left wing down,
sideslipping to prevent the fighter from drifting off the runway's
centerline.

Squawk, Squawk. The wheels of the main gear chirped down on the runway. Holm was doing his little ballet dance on the rudder pedals to keep the racer rolling straight.

Critical Mass was down and safe. It didn't take long to find out what had caused the problem. When Holm climbed out of the cockpit, mechanics were already swarming around the nose of the Sea Fury. The cowling—the cylindrical housing around the engine—was ripped open in several places. Pieces of jagged metal had torn away from the cowling and ripped large gashes in the tail surfaces. Holm stared at the damage, thinking his first impression might have been correct: It *did* look as if he'd taken hits from a thirty-millimeter.

The culprit turned out to be something less dramatic. The cowling failed because of metal fatigue—the classic tin-can effect— exacerbated by the god-awful, whamming turbulence out there on the course.

Inevitably, the phantom painter showed up when no one was watching. It took a while for anyone to notice the subtle change he'd made to the name of the crimson-colored fighter: *Critical Mess.*

Holm was out of the race, and Bill Rheinschild, in *Risky Business*, was running away with the Silver Trophy. Or so he thought. The howling devil wind was wreaking a different sort of havoc on him.

The checkered flag went down. Bill Rheinschild flashed across the finish line several hundred yards ahead of the second-place racer, Dennis Sanders in *Argonaut*. Back on the ramp, his engine still cranking to a stop, Rheinschild climbed out of his cockpit wearing his big winner's grin. And then he saw the judges coming toward him. He could tell by their faces that the news was not good. Rheinschild's big, happy grin faded.

In winning the race, Rheinschild had flown a tight line around the pylons. *Too* tight, as it turned out. On his first lap, in a hard four-G turn around the southernmost pylons, with the wind nudging him sideways, he let the Mustang slip *inside* the line between the pylons.

Not just once but twice.

That meant *two* penalties of two seconds for each of the eight laps flown. Sixteen seconds for each cut, for a total penalty of thirty-two seconds. Dennis Sanders, not Bill Rheinschild, was the official winner of the Silver Trophy.

But the haggling wasn't over.

Meanwhile, another racer was in trouble, though he didn't yet know it.

Stu Eberhardt, flying his Mustang, *Merlin's Magic*, had finished the Silver race back in sixth place. Eberhardt was a recently retired airline pilot who was indulging his lifelong whim to own exotic warbirds. Besides the souped-up Mustang, he now possessed a T-6 trainer and a newly acquired jet fighter, a pristine F-86 Sabre.

Eberhardt had been racing at Reno for six years now. Gradually, he had worked his way up the pecking order, gaining both respect and prize money as he gently pushed *Merlin's Magic* to faster lap times. Last year was the payoff: first place in the Silver.

So here he was now, way back in the pack, finishing in sixth place. What happened? Well, he knew that several of these guys—Rheinschild, Sanders, Holm—were flying Gold-contender airplanes. For reasons of their own, they were racing here in the Silver Division, flying lap speeds that put Eberhardt's nearly-stock Mustang out of contention.

Eberhardt had the nose of Mustang pointed upward, toward the high orbit where the racers went immediately after their final lap to gently throttle back and give their engineer a cooling-down session before they came back to land. That was standard procedure: Head for the cool-down pattern high over the airport after a race. It was an especially vulnerable time for the overboosted, highly tuned racing engines. The shock of powering back, cooling down rapidly—*after* the heavy running was finished—was a frequent cause of calamitous engine failures. So Eberhardt was glad that this race was over. At least his engine had held together.

Brrraapp! That was it—one heart-stopping burp—then silence. Stu Eberhardt's Merlin engine had gone dead as a stone.

"Race Twenty-two, Mayday!"

"Wind is one-nine-zero at twenty-eight, Stu. Gusting to thirty-five. Which runway do you want?"

The wind was out of the south. Runway 18, even though it was an off-duty runway and not normally used, would be a lot less problematic.

"Runway one-eight."

"Roger, you're cleared to land on one-eight."

The Mustang was coming down like a falling manhole cover. As he passed abeam the end of the runway, still flying northward, he realized that the high wind would push him rapidly *away* from the runway. Letting himself get pushed too far away, having to glide back *into* that killer wind, was a sure formula for landing in the dirt. It was a sure way to become one with the earth.

He turned toward the runway. As he was holding off lowering the landing gear, he was aware of the voices in his headset: "Gear down, Stu!" "Check your gear, Twenty-two!" "Stu, your gear isn't—"

Clunk. The fighter's big main gear clunked down. Three seconds later, the Mustang's tires screeched onto the runway. The crews in the race pits and the spectators in the grandstands sucked in a collective lungful of air.

Back in the pits Eberhardt ripped the top off a Coke can and slammed it down in one swallow. It would take a while to figure out what had gone wrong with the engine. When the crew looked inside the cowling, they saw nothing obvious—no oil leaks, no pieces missing, no broken ignition wires. Not until they opened up the induction system did they discover the gremlin—a gasket sucked up in the air intake that had been blocking the flow of air to the engine and trashing the supercharger.

That made two Unlimiteds out of action. And the main event was still to come.

. . .

The Sanders team had been coming to Reno since 1983, when their newly developed Sea Fury, *Dreadnought,* took the championship in its first Gold Trophy race. The family patriarch, Frank Sanders, had been one of the early Sea Fury mavens. Fitted with the mighty Pratt & Whitney R-4360, *Dreadnought* had been a consistent competitor in the Gold division.

Now Dennis Sanders and his younger brother, Brian, alternated flying *Dreadnought* each year. This was Brian's year to fly *Dreadnought,* so Dennis was flying their R-3350-powered Sea Fury, *Argonaut,* in the Silver race. And Dennis won.

Now, according to the official racing-association rules, Dennis had the option of forgoing his Silver prize money and "bumping" into the top class, the Gold race. It was a matter of waiving glory for Gold, since the last-place finisher in the Gold actually earned a bit more prize money than the first-place Silver winner.

But in this instance, Dennis *liked* being the Silver Class champion. He chose to keep the Silver Trophy and not bump into the Gold. He would leave that division to his brother, Brian, flying *Dreadnought.* Which meant that the Sanders brothers had a shot at a Reno record: a single family capturing both the Silver and the Gold.

And that should have been the end of it. But for reasons not clear to anyone, a member of the Reno Air Racing Association decided to modify the rules. Over the objections of the contest committee, he declared that Bill Rheinschild, now the second-place Silver winner, could exercise the option to bump into the Gold race. The decision angered not only the contest's committee members, who thought *they* were the official arbiters of the rules; it incensed the Gold Division pilots because it meant that the total prize money, instead of being divided eight ways, would now be shared by nine racers.

Rheinschild, for his part, was happy. After blowing his win in the Silver race, he was getting that rarest of opportunities in aviation— a second chance. He'd be flying again today—in the Gold.

↣ 10 ↢

Sunday Shoot-Out

14 September 1997

Destefani slipped into *Strega*'s cockpit. The wind was blowing so hard that his baseball cap was snatched from his head. Scrunching down in the hard seat, he fiddled with the parachute harness and the safety belts. He pulled the hard-shelled, military-style helmet on and stuck the two radio plugs in their jacks. Then he plugged the hose from his flight suit into the socket of the airplane's built-in ventilation system.

That was one of *Strega*'s peculiarities: no ventilation. Unlike almost all unpressurized airplanes, this particular Mustang had *no* vents or scoops for ducting outside air into the cockpit. It was a matter of aerodynamics. Air scoops installed in an airplane's skin caused drag—the perennial enemy of the aeronautical engineer. "Drag" was the aerodynamic term for the parasitic slowing effect caused by each tiny protuberance on the airframe, like minuscule speed brakes. Every exposed rivet head, antenna, and air scoop caused drag and cut into the airplane's ultimate top speed.

Air-race teams were at constant war with the arch enemy drag. In the battle to eliminate it, nothing was off limits. Everything on the airplane that could be streamlined or slickened or somehow reduced in angularity helped the airplane to go faster. Plexiglas canopies were cut down in shape and size, affording the pilots only peephole views from the cockpit. Wingspans were drastically short- ened, reducing the wings' lifting capability and giving the once-agile fighters the aerodynamic properties of a thrown rock.

With no cockpit air scoops and without ventilation in the low- altitude desert heat of an air race, the cockpit temperature of the Mustang would soar to over 120 degrees Fahrenheit.

And that was why Tiger Destefani wore a special flight suit, an outfit akin to the space suits used by astronauts, with chilled air piped into the suit from the airplane's own coolant system. The cock- pit still got hot, of course, but it was bearable, at least for the half hour of an Unlimited Race.

Lined up on the runway, waiting to take off behind Hinton in the T-33 pace plane, Destefani could *feel* the damned wind! Just sitting there on the runway, he felt the wind hammering against *Strega's* vertical stabilizer, trying to swing it around like a sail. Little whirl- winds of dirt and hunks of sagebrush were skittering past his nose.

"Pace plane ready," Hinton radioed on the race frequency.

"Race Seven ready," said Tiger Destefani. As the fastest qualifier and winner of yesterday's heat race, he had the pole position, right behind the pace plane. Each of the succeeding racers would be lined up and take off in order of their respective performances. In theory, the race field would be sorted from left to right, fastest racer to the slowest, thus eliminating dangerous conflicts at the critical start of a race. But only in theory. Unlimited racing, by definition, meant that anything could happen.

"Race Seventy-seven ready." That was Shelton, in *Rare Bear,* in the number-two position in the lineup.

"Race Eight ready." Brian Sanders, in *Dreadnought*, was checking in. The younger of the two Sanders brothers, Brian was a pleasant, heavyset young man with a mustache and a quick smile.

Behind *Dreadnought* in the lineup was Dan Martin, flying his Mustang, *Ridge Runner*. Then came Gary Levitz in the hybrid racer *Miss Ashley II*, Matt Jackson in the Sea Fury *Southern Cross*, Howard Pardue in his own Sea Fury, Lloyd Hamilton in another Sea Fury, *Furias*. In last position was Bill Rheinschild, who had just finished second in the Silver race in *Risky Business* and was now "bumping" into the Gold Division.

When all nine racers had checked in, the T-33 started to roll. Destefani sat there with his brakes locked, watching the T-33 lumber down the runway. Even though the jet was faster than most props *in the air*, it was painfully slow to gather speed on takeoff. Older jets, like the T-33, didn't have the raw, neck-straining acceleration of the overpowered, prop-swinging Mustangs and Sea Furies.

Steve Hinton had been flying the T-33 jet pace plane for the past several years, since Reno's original pace-plane pilot, Bob Hoover, and his stock Mustang, *Ol' Yeller*, had become too slow for the 400-plus-mile-per-hour Unlimited Race starts. Hinton was a former racer, a two-time Unlimited champion who had captured his first Gold Trophy at the age of twenty-six in the famous *Red Baron*. He was one of the famous Chino Kids—the pack of fortunate teenagers who had grown up flying Ed Maloney's collection of warbirds at his Planes of Fame Museum in Chino, California. Hinton, now a young man in his forties, was the president of the museum.

Hinton was leading the pack of racers around the last turn. Destefani was hugging the right wing of the T-33, with the others— Shelton, Sanders, the rest of the Unlimiteds—strung out behind him like a gaggle of geese. Trying to get into some semblance of a line-abreast formation was the tough part of a gusty day like this. They *had* to be assorted in a reasonably straight line, all headed toward the starting line, before Hinton could declare that the race was on.

The pack of racers was aimed northward now. Destefani could see Hinton nudging the T-33's nose down, which meant they were accelerating toward the starting point. Destefani could *feel* the speed building up. Through the control stick he sensed that old, familiar vibration, increasing in frequency as the Mustang sliced through the air at ever-increasing velocity. He had to nudge the throttle up on *Strega* to stay with the pace plane. He was aware of the speed increasing: 320 miles per hour; 350; 380.

Still accelerating; 400 now. The vibration in the stick was increasing in pitch. From his right he could hear the discordant roaring and bellowing from the engines of the other eight race planes coming into the line-abreast formation.

And the bumps—*damn!* It was getting rougher. Every few seconds he hit one of those severe jolts, lifting him up against the straps so hard he worried that his helmet would go through the canopy. The faster they went, the harder the bumps. Destefani had been doing this for how many years now? More than a decade. This was the roughest he could remember it ever being.

The thrumming in the stick was intensifying to a fine buzz. The wind stream over the canopy was a high-pitched howl that Destefani knew approached something around 450 miles per hour. Over the howl of his own engine, he was faintly aware of the dull, unsynchronous bellow of the other racers' engines. One engine he *couldn't* hear was that of the pace plane. The low-pitched *whoosh* of the T-33's jet engine was lost in the collective thunder of the big piston engines.

They were on a direct line for pylon 3, the easternmost corner of the 9.3-mile course. This was where the race officially began. Still clustered together, the racers would come barreling down to the pylon, each of them diving for the earth in the hope of gaining advantage over the planes on either side. From the ground it looked as if the echelon of fighters were making a strafing run. They would roar past the pylon in a hard left bank, making the 30-degree turn into a long straightaway toward the fourth pylon on the narrow northern edge of the course.

In theory, the fastest racer occupied the inside track—the coveted *pole* position—and enjoyed an enormous advantage over his competitors on the outside of his track. But coming down the chute, when Hinton declared that the race was on, the start of the race sometimes turned into a free-for-all. Each pilot jammed his throttle to the stop and tried to get the jump on everyone else, including the racer in the pole position.

From the wing-mounted smoke generators on the T-33, a trail of white air-show smoke billowed out. It meant that the race was almost on. The announcer would be calling the spectators' attention to the trail of smoke. They could spot the smoke-trailing jet and the covey of racers heading down the chute. In a few more seconds the noise of the big racing engines would be rolling down over the hills and gullies and reverberating in the grandstands.

In the front seat of the T-33, Hinton was cranking his head around, watching the formation. "You're looking good," he said on the radio, his transmissions being relayed to the loudspeakers in the grandstands.

Then the words that never failed to send an electric current through the crowd: "Gentlemen . . . you . . . have . . . a . . . race!"

Down in the grandstands, the crowd could see the smoke contrail from Hinton's pace plane arcing upward now, leaving the pack of racers to fight it out. And in the next moment they could hear and feel it—the combined thunder of nine full-throated racing engines cascading across the desert floor.

The Gold race was the last event of the race week. All the other races had now been settled, and the Silver and Bronze race pilots were now esconced atop trailers and in the pits watching the culmination of the race year. Dennis Sanders, watching from the Sanders team pit, had captured the Silver Trophy with the family's Sea Fury,

Argonaut. With him was Curt Brown, the astronaut and rookie race pilot, who had managed to fly his stock Amjet Sea Fury to a fourth-place finish in the Bronze race. Skip Holm, in Tom Dwelle's pit, was still assessing the damage incurred by *Critical Mass* when the engine cowling shed its parts at 400 miles per hour.

Pylon 3, the easternmost corner of the course, was the first turn point at the beginning of the race. It was where the most frantic jockeying for initial position took place. If someone was going to do something reckless or maniacal or egregiously stupid, it was here. Sometimes a racer, wingtip to wingtip with a rival, would dive for the ground, using the speed gained in the dive for an initial speed advantage. And for a few seconds, as they aimed like hell-bent ban-shees for the same tiny little pylon sticking up out there in the desert, the lower airplane would be *out of sight* from the other. And there they would arrive—simultaneously—rolling into a steep turn to make that first pylon turn, trying to occupy the same precious few feet of airspace.

With the racers all breaking loose from the formation and diving for position—*anything* could happen. In the lead race plane, Deste-fani felt his pulse accelerating. After a year of working and tweaking and scheming, here it was again: *the start!* A thousand times in the past year he had closed his eyes and imagined this moment. It was the kickoff. In terms of excitement, it was the equivalent of a cata-pult shot from an aircraft carrier. Or the liftoff of a space shuttle from its pad. It was the most exciting—and dangerous—moment of the race. It was also the most likely place for disaster.

It was a scenario that had played out—*for real*—in enough past races to give every pilot cold sweats. Each of them, in his most pri-vate thoughts, had replayed the scene: the sudden, blood-chilling appearance of *another airplane*, right there in your face, filling up your canopy, his propeller carving like a scythe through your wing—*Krrrunnnch!*—the brown earth and the clear blue sky whirling and tumbling, exchanging places, the desert rising to meet you until . . .

It was ghastly. No one liked to think about such an awful possibility. But it was impossible *not* to think about it, at least while you—and all eight of your colleagues—were charging down the chute, each trying to pass you, each trying to occupy the same tiny piece of airspace just to the outside and above pylon 3.

Destefani had the throttle up on *Strega*. The Mustang was going balls out, "down the chute," approaching 500 miles an hour. He could feel the entire airframe humming like a tuning fork. Up ahead he saw pylon 3 sticking up from the brown earth and sagebrush like a tiny clothesline pole.

Destefani had an advantage, of course. He was in the pole position by virtue of having qualified in the fastest time. In the second starting position, just off Destefani's right wing, was Lyle Shelton in *Rare Bear*. And though everyone, including Shelton, had the same distance to fly to the first pylon, Destefani knew that anyone who wanted to get there ahead of him was going to have to pass him on the outside.

Which Destefani knew was exactly what that damned Shelton was trying to do. When it came to jockeying for starting position, Lyle Shelton could be as diabolical as Wile E. Coyote. In races past, Shelton had been reprimanded for diving at the start pylon, going out of sight of his nearest rival. He had scared the hell out of them.

Destefani had full power on the Mustang now. If anyone—Shelton or any of the others—intended to take away his advantage, they would have to make their play now. They would have to get around him. Or under him.

Destefani took a quick glance over his right shoulder. They were out there, up, down, wide, and close, scattered like quail. He tried to pick out the distinctive white-and-gold, barrel-shaped profile of *Rare Bear*. He didn't see it.

Where was Shelton?

That damned engine problem. *It was back.* The old roughness or unbalance or whatever the hell it was. Shelton felt it as soon as he advanced the throttle on *Rare Bear,* going for full power down the chute.

Actually, it had never gone away. The problem seemed to reside somewhere inside the big R-3350 radial engine, lurking there like a hidden parasite. After last year's fiasco, when the engine self-destructed and John Penney called a Mayday after only two laps, they had rebuilt the engine. And though the rebuilt version had run well enough, it never seemed to deliver full power. The thing ought to be delivering something over 4,000 horsepower, but it was clearly coming up shy of that.

They didn't know why. Between qualification runs and the early race heats, Shelton's ground crew had labored over the engine, tweaking and polishing, looking for obvious flaws. They found nothing. The engine was fine. It just wasn't running well, that was all.

Now, with the power up, it was running with a new roughness that worried Shelton. He wasn't so concerned about a simple loss of power. He'd been through plenty of those. But when a power plant with the mass and torque of this big R-3350 started shaking and throwing its weight around up there on the nose, that was *very* serious. You had to back off on the power *quickly* or something vital was going to break.

He didn't need these problems. He was having enough trouble just getting *himself* back in the groove after four years out of the cockpit. But this had been a week of ongoing grief. First the mysterious center-of-gravity problem that made the Bearcat want to pitch its nose upward. Now a rough-running engine.

He was below and behind *Strega.* At the instant Hinton declared, "Gentlemen, you have a race," *Strega* had shot ahead like a jackrabbit. And that's where he was now, coming up on the first pylon—still ahead. Shelton was a couple of seconds back and below, in second place. Already he was feeling the turbulence of Destefani's prop wash.

Rare Bear and *Strega* had been rivals since back in the eighties, when Destefani first showed up at Reno with his new Mustang.

Each year, *Strega* had gotten a little faster, and Destefani had learned a little more. Now he was running away from everybody. He'd won the Gold race at Reno five times now—one short of Shelton and two wins short of Darryl Greenamyer's seven victories.

And now the little hardball son of a bitch was doing it again. And it was pissing off Lyle Shelton, back after his four-year layoff. This was not where he wanted to be, back here in second place, looking at Tiger Destefani's tail feathers.

Screw it, thought Shelton. The engine might be a little rough, but at least it was running. Temperatures and pressures were okay—nothing in the red. He wasn't going to back off. Keep pressing Destefani and—who knows?—maybe something would go wrong with *his* airplane. Hell, this was Reno! Anything could happen.

Brian Sanders, flying *Dreadnought,* was also playing a waiting game. Going around the first pylon, he was in the number-three position—exactly where his qualification time placed him in the lineup. And that was just fine with him. Sanders's strategy was simple: Hang on to your nice, safe number-three position. Don't let the challengers from behind get past you. Don't try to overtake the hotshots *Strega* and *Rare Bear.* Let them slug it out for the front position. Maybe one of them would push too hard. Maybe one of them would make a mistake. Maybe something would break.

For several years now *Dreadnought* had not been a front-running contender for the Gold Trophy. Though the Mustangs and Shelton's clipped-wing Bearcat had gotten slicker and faster every year, *Dreadnought* seemed to have reached its ultimate performance. You could push a blunt mass of metal through the air only so fast. But the big fighter was still the fastest Sea Fury in the racing business. On a good day—which meant a very *bad* day for *Strega* and *Rare Bear*—*Dreadnought* could still saunter across the finish line with the top prize money.

The waiting-game strategy had worked before. It worked the

first year they ran *Dreadnought* at Reno, back in 1983. Flown by test pilot Neil Anderson, the Sea Fury was fighting it out with a trio of hot Mustangs—*Dago Red, Strega,* and *Precious Metal.* One by one, each of the Mustangs faltered, like overstressed Thoroughbreds. Both *Dago Red* and *Strega* called Maydays and made emergency landings. As the last Mustang, *Precious Metal,* was challenging *Dreadnought* on the final lap, his engine burped, and pilot Don Whittington made one of those instant economic decisions: *Don't blow this hundred-thousand-dollar engine!* He backed off on the throttle. *Dreadnought* roared across the finish line in first place.

It worked again in 1986. *Dreadnought* outlasted its rivals to win the Gold. And in four other Gold races, *Dreadnought* had persevered to capture the second-place money. That's the way it played out sometimes at Reno—a war of attrition. For such wars, *Dreadnought,* with its Pratt & Whitney R-4360 "corncob" radial, was particularly well suited. The big Sea Fury was the flying equivalent of a Peterbilt eighteen-wheeler. After the prima-donna Mustangs and the hypersensitive *Rare Bear* had trashed their fickle engines, there would be *Dreadnought,* cruising serenely around the course like a man-of-war.

And then during the 1996 race, with Dennis Sanders at the throttle, the big Pratt & Whitney finally let them down. He called a Mayday and made a classic dead-stick landing back at Stead. It took the brothers the entire year—until a week before the 1997 races—to rebuild the R-4360. They made it, and here was *Dreadnought,* again roaring its big throaty roar.

Brian nudged the throttle forward. He could feel the torque increase on the big Pratt corncob. Fifty yards ahead and to his left, he saw *Strega,* closely trailed by *Rare Bear.* They were rolling into the turn around pylon 3.

And then Brian noticed something—a puff of . . . what? Oil? Smoke? It was spewing in little puffs off *Strega's* right wingtip.

And that wasn't all: A grayish, intermittent wisp of smoke was streaming from *Rare Bear's* exhaust stacks.

These were clues to what lay ahead. To Sanders it meant that things were going to get interesting during the next eight laps. All he had to do was hang in there. And wait.

Where the hell was the oil coming from?

Tiger Destefani saw the first filmy traces smearing his windscreen. It had appeared right after he pushed the throttle up at the start of the race.

Oil, when it found its way outside the crankcase of the engine, was bad news. Leaking oil inevitably made its way to your windscreen. It blurred your view and made it damned difficult to see pylons, other racers, the ground. Enough oil on the windscreen and you had to call it quits. If it got bad enough, you couldn't see to land. Then you had to fly in a skid, peering out the side, or jettison your canopy and try to land the fighter by sticking your head around the windshield. It was not a graceful way to land a nine-thousand-pound fighter at 120 miles per hour.

Or the oil might be a warning that *something* was going to hell up front. If it was an oil line that split or disconnected, you could count the seconds until the great, final, heart-squeezing *Gulp!* from your engine. Then dreadful silence.

In the absolutely *worst* case scenario, the engine would lose all its oil before you shut it down. The engine would seize. The prop would stop and become an inert, four-bladed speed brake. The sleek Mustang would descend with the glide characteristics of a bowling ball.

Strega was leading the pack. They were rounding pylon 6, heading southward down the long stretch called "the valley of speed." Despite the bothersome oil film, *Strega's* engine was howling like a hungry beast. So far, so good, thought Destefani. He had a couple of seconds' lead on *Rare Bear*. He could hold on to this advantage, probably even widen it, as long as his overstrained Merlin stayed intact. Or as long as he could see out of his windscreen.

. . .

111

This was very strange, thought Shelton. The gremlin was gone! Or at least one of the gremlins—the one that was bedeviling his R-3350 engine. Just as abruptly as it had come, it was gone. The roughness in *Rare Bear's* four-row corncob engine was smoothing out.

Of course, *smooth* was a meaningless adjective on a day like this. Shelton was getting hammered so hard by the turbulence—*Whump! Whump!*—it was difficult to feel or hear subtle changes in the airframe and engine of the Bearcat racer.

Yes, he was sure of it: The engine *was* smoothing out. He had no idea why, just as he had no idea why the damned thing had roughened up to begin with. Because of the power problem, he had already lost precious ground to *Strega,* which was ripping along up there like a runaway horse with the bit in its teeth. Just behind and to the outside, *Dreadnought* was nipping at Shelton's heels. He knew that Brian Sanders was waiting for him to make one little mistake—get sloppy on a turn or lose just a little more power—and he'd pass.

Shelton tried nudging the throttle up a tiny increment. The engine responded. Still smooth. He nudged it up some more. Still okay. Great! Maybe the thing was going to behave. With the added power, *Rare Bear* was moving ahead of *Dreadnought* again.

Up ahead Shelton could see *Strega,* still holding his commanding lead. And a few hundred yards ahead of *Strega* was the pack of slower racers, about to be lapped by the leaders. In dead-last position was *Southern Cross,* a mostly stock Sea Fury being flown by Matt Jackson. Ahead of Jackson was a cluster of racers who were providing the only real action for the spectators. Gary Levitz, in the hybrid Mustang *Miss Ashley II,* was swapping positions with Daniel Martin in his Mustang, *Ridge Runner.* Bill Rheinschild, flying *Risky Business,* was working his way through the lineup and was trying to overtake Martin. The two Sea Furies, Howard Pardue's *Fury* and Lloyd Hamilton's *Furias,* were waging their own private duel coming down the western straightaway.

Shelton had almost full power on *Rare Bear* now. The big, round engine was giving that distinctive basso-profundo howl that made it such a favorite among the air-race groupies in the grandstands. Shelton thought, Hell, it was almost like old times. Except that he could hardly see because of the goddamned turbulence that was banging him around the cockpit.

Still, he couldn't help sensing that something was missing. The power wasn't there. It just wasn't the same ass-kicking, balls-out brute thrust that *Rare Bear* had demonstrated in years past. The Bearcat ought to be ripping through the air at over 500 miles an hour—if everything was right. Something still wasn't right.

He nudged the throttle up some more.

Lap six.

Except for the place swapping back in the fifth, sixth, and seventh positions, the lineup hadn't changed. *Strega* had a firm lock on first place. If anything, Destefani's lead was opening over *Rare Bear.* Brian Sanders was still hanging on to third place, playing his waiting game, fighting off the occasional challenge from Gary Levitz in the exotic-looking *Miss Ashley II.*

Levitz's racer was the only one at Reno this year that could truly be called *experimental.* All the others—the Mustangs, Bearcats, Sea Furies, Yaks—still possessed their basic airframes. Except for clipped wings and beefed-up engines and slickened airframes, they were the same classic fifty-year-old fighters.

Miss Ashley II was something else. Though the fuselage resembled that of a Mustang, the similarity ended there. Instead of a Merlin engine, the racer mounted a 2,300-horsepower Rolls-Royce V-12 Griffon 57 engine removed from a Shackleton patrol bomber. In place of the Mustang's four-bladed propeller, it had *two* three-bladed props, rotating in opposite directions, which prompted Skip Holm, who conducted a test flight on the new racer, to dub it the "Scissors Plane."

The racer's swept wings looked as if they belonged on a jet. In fact, they did. The Scissors Plane had the wings, landing gear, and cut-down horizontal tail of a Learjet. In plan view, banking hard around a pylon, *Miss Ashley II* looked more like a modern jet fighter than a World War II warbird. Of all the Unlimited competitors, it *looked* fast.

But the Scissors Plane wasn't seriously fast. Not yet. Its qualifying speed of 392 miles per hour had earned only ninth place in the starting positions. At this point, Levitz and Bill Rogers, his engineer-partner, didn't care. They were ecstatic that their new toy was just hanging together. For a first-time Unlimited racing airplane, *Miss Ashley II* had already astonished everyone by reaching this level of competition—the Sunday Gold race.

Behind Levitz was Dan Martin. Martin was a guy who had "retired" from racing several years back, declaring that he had had enough. Now he was back with a vengeance, racing his Mustang *Ridge Runner* and flying in the Gold. On the second lap, Martin managed to slide past Levitz, briefly claiming fourth place. It didn't last. By the next lap, Levitz had again pushed his Scissors Plane ahead of Martin.

Meanwhile, Bill Rheinschild, who, by strict interpretation of the rules, shouldn't have been in the Gold race, was gobbling up the back pack. Already he had left the plodding *Southern Cross* in the dust. Then he skimmed around the two Sea Furies—Howard Pardue in *Fury* and Lloyd Hamilton in his *Furias*. Coming down the western leg in the valley of speed, Rheinschild zoomed ahead of Dan Martin in *Ridge Runner.*

Matt Jackson, flying *Southern Cross,* wasn't zooming past anyone. He was running dead last. He'd been here before, and he knew what to expect: Before the race ended, he would be passed *again*. The front-runner, *Strega,* had almost a 100-mile-an-hour advantage over him. That meant that somewhere around the seventh lap Tiger Destefani—having gained a nine-mile lead—would be chewing up his tail. And if *Rare Bear* and *Dreadnought* were holding together, they wouldn't be far behind.

That was fine with Jackson. Hell, it was part of the game. If they wanted to pass, they had to go around the outside of his line. All he had to do was keep boring along.

He took a quick peek over his right shoulder. Sure enough, there it was, right on schedule: the long, tapered snout of the world's fastest P-51. From this angle, *Strega* looked like a low-flying cruise missile hell-bent toward a target. Jackson heard, for an instant, the mean, hard growl of the Merlin engine as the Mustang went sailing past him.

Four seconds later, also on schedule, appeared the next player. It was just what Jackson expected to see: the stubby, barrel-shaped profile of *Rare Bear*. As the Bearcat swept past his right wing, Jackson could sense the resonant drone—a different, deeper sound than the higher-pitched growl of *Strega*. The Bearcat was so close, Jackson could see the big lettering on the gold-painted nose—*Rare Bear*—and even the little lettering beneath the cockpit with the pilots' names.

Then he noticed something else. The gold-painted cowling. Shit, he couldn't believe it! Pieces were coming out of the thing! It looked like *Rare Bear*'s engine compartment was shedding its parts.

It was. Inside Lyle Shelton's tightly cowled engine compartment, the peekaboo gremlin was back. And this time he was *really* raising hell.

A welded portion of a header—an engine exhaust stack—had ruptured. A jet of raw blue exhaust flame was blasting the inside of the engine cowling. The intense heat was singeing wires, melting hoses, cutting like a blowtorch through the aluminum skin of the cowling. What Matt Jackson had seen as *Rare Bear* zipped by him was debris spewing from the inferno inside Shelton's cowling.

But Lyle Shelton didn't yet know any of this. All he knew was that something *sounded* different. That big basso-profundo noise of the R-3350 had changed to something metallic. Something ominous.

And that damned roughness was back. But worse than before. It felt as if several cylinders in the big twin-row radial had stopped firing. The thing was hammering and shaking like an old Ford trac-tor. What was it? Ignition? Induction problems? *Something* was defi-nitely going to hell up front.

Shelton decided to do the prudent thing: He throttled back. He was just coming up on pylon 6. He nudged the stick back, pulling *Rare Bear* up to about five hundred feet. He wanted an altitude cush-ion in case he wound up making a dead-stick landing on one of the runways here at Stead.

There was a fine line between being prudent and being *too* pru-dent. If you throttled back every time you didn't like some little irregularity in your engine, you'd never win an air race. You'd never even be in the running. Lyle Shelton hadn't won six Unlimited Championships at Reno by being prudent.

And then he noticed something else. As he rounded pylon 6, dis-tracted by the hammering of the engine, he realized he was looking *straight down at the pylon!*—and at the upturned faces of the pylon judges. Damn! With that motherless desert wind howling from his right, he had drifted too close to the line and cut the pylon.

He immediately dismissed the matter. So be it. Shit happened, and getting penalized for a pylon cut was minuscule shit compared to lunching your engine out here on the back stretch.

The engine was getting too rough to ignore. He had two laps to go. Winning the race was obviously no longer in the cards. With the engine now throttled back, he had zero chance of overtaking *Strega*. In fact, taking second place was no longer an option. Looking down over the right edge of his canopy, he saw the distinct shape of the Sanders *Dreadnought*—passing him.

Shelton's mission was just to finish. Hang in there, keep this corn-popper motor running, take the checkered flag. And get a paycheck.

With his engine sputtering and shaking, shedding more pieces, the old fighter pilot hung in there. *Two more laps.*

And then one more.

Despite the shaking, he kept enough power on the engine to stay ahead of Levitz and Rheinschild and the rest of the pack. It was as though Shelton *willed* the dying R-3350 engine to keep running. *Don't quit, baby . . . Keep running . . . Just one more lap . . .*

Rare Bear sputtered down the home stretch and took the checkered flag. Even with the sixteen-second pylon-cutting penalty, he had still hung on to third place.

And that was it. As if sensing that the job was done, the engine emitted a final, urgent death rattle.

Shelton pulled up steeply. He turned leftward into the center of the runway complex, making a quick assessment of his options. The wind was southwesterly, blowing like hell across runway 27, which was the active runway. Looking down, he saw that he was in a good position for runway 18, which was a closed runway.

At this point, Shelton didn't care whether runway 18 was open, closed, or being used for a flea market. It suited his needs perfectly.

"Race Seventy-seven is gonna land on runway one-eight." Shelton's voice was cool, laconic—the old Gary Cooper act. It was *High Noon* time.

"Roger, Lyle," said Jack Thomas in the tower. "Are you calling a Mayday?"

Silence. Seconds passed. It was a simple-enough question. Was he in so much trouble he couldn't talk?

Shelton finally answered. "Yeah," he drawled on the radio, *really* putting on the Cooper voice. "Guess you better make that a Mayday."

Everyone listening to the frequency cracked up. It was vintage Shelton. *Better make that a Mayday?* It could have been a line right out of *The Right Stuff.* Ol' Lyle made declaring an emergency sound like calling for a pizza.

Landing the Bear in *normal* circumstances was a handful. For one thing, it had no flaps to give it a slower landing speed. And the stubby fighter had a tendency to ground-loop—the tail swinging around and swapping ends with the nose—as soon as you put the wheels down on the runway. To make matters worse, the pilot had *no* forward visibility. He had to keep it on the runway by feel and by peripheral vision.

But today was something else: Putting the stubby-winged Bearcat down in a gusting 50-mile-an-hour wind—*without power*—would be as demanding a feat as anything in aviation.

From the stands they watched the Bearcat descending over the gullies and sagebrush toward the end of the closed runway. The gear came down. The wings were wobbling in the turbulent air.

They saw *Rare Bear* sweep over the end of the runway, right wing down into the quartering wind, main wheels—*Squawk Squawk*—planting themselves on the concrete, the blind rudder dance as Shelton fought to keep the Bearcat tracking down the centerline, the tail wheel lowering gently to the runway.

The Bearcat rolled to a stop, the propeller motionless. The emergency was over. Ol' Lyle had pulled it off again.

From his high perch above the airport, the new Unlimited champion, Tiger Destefani, observed Shelton's landing. *Good idea,* he thought. *Runway one-eight.* With this kind of wind it didn't make sense risking your airplane in a stiff crosswind just because runway 26 happened to be the "active" runway. Screw 'em. He would do the same.

"Race Seven will take runway one-eight also."

"Roger, Tiger," said Jack Thomas. He knew better than to argue with anyone about which runway to take. Not with a wind like this. "Wind is two-one-zero, thirty-five. Gusts up to fifty. You're cleared to land on one-eight."

Destefani set up a left-hand approach to runway 18. Jesus, it was rough! Now that he'd slowed down to approach speed—something under 200 miles per hour—the turbulence was kicking him around like a kite.

Concentrate on the landing, he told himself. Tack on a few extra knots. Don't let it float. Paste it on; then keep it there. Don't let the tail swing around in the wind or you'll be off in the boondocks for sure.

Destefani was coming up on the end of the runway. The airspeed was back to 120. He was "crabbing" the Mustang—flying sideways over the ground, keeping the plane's nose angled into the wind. The nearer he flew to the ground, the worse the turbulence became. It felt as if the Mustang were being snatched this way and that in the jaws of a beast. He fought the turbulence with the control stick— jabbing left, right, fore, and aft, resisting each violent lurch.

As he swept over the end of the runway, a thought flashed through his brain: *Where was Shelton?* Destefani knew that *Rare Bear* had already landed on runway 18—but where was he now?

Up there. For an instant Destefani tore his eyes away from the approach end of the runway and looked down toward the far end. There was the Bearcat—*still on the runway.* Which was no surprise. Shelton's engine was probably dead as a stone.

But how far down the runway? Four thousand feet? Five thousand? Or less? Then Destefani had another thought. Actually, it was more like a subliminal image: This would be *really* ugly if *Strega* ran into *Rare Bear*—on the runway!

It was the wrong thing to be thinking at the moment. He had a more immediate problem: Getting this airplane down in one piece.

The end of the runway swept under him. He was over concrete now. Throttle back . . . break the descent . . . not too much . . . keep the thing coming down . . . *don't let it float* . . . don't eat up precious runway. . . . Shelton was down there somewhere, still on the runway, and once you land this sucker, you can't see over the frigging nose. Paste it on the runway!

Destefani pasted it on the runway.

Thwump! The main wheels hit the concrete. *Strega* bounced back into the air, into the gusting wind. *Don't let it float. Get it on the runway.*

He pasted it back on the runway.

Thwang! The main wheels hit again. This time the nose was lower, and the Mustang didn't bounce back into the air.

But that sound—that *Thwang* when the wheels went back on—was a different noise. It had an ominously *metallic* feel to it. Destefani had a good idea what it meant.

He was doing his own blind-rudder dance now, fighting the wind, keeping *Strega* going straight down the runway. He got on the brakes, wanting to get slowed before he caught up with Lyle Shelton, who was somewhere up ahead.

He had the Mustang under control. The tail wheel lowered to the runway, making it easier to keep the airplane tracking straight ahead.

Destefani let *Strega* roll up to where Shelton was stopped in the Bearcat. He shut down his engine and rolled to a stop behind *Rare Bear.*

When the big four-bladed propeller had stopped rotating, it was obvious what had happened back there on the bounced landing. And there was no doubt about the meaning of that metallic-sounding *Thwang!* The last four inches of each propeller blade was curled inward at a sickening angle. Each blade looked like a Q-Tip.

Destefani climbed out of his Mustang. He waved at Shelton, who was standing there, leaning against the wing of his disabled racer, still playing the Cooper role. Over on the other runway, 26, the rest of the pack was landing. Destefani saw the big silver Sea Fury, *Dreadnought,* rolling out. Everyone was coming home safely.

Destefani walked around to the nose of his airplane. He looked at the Q-Tipped propeller. He quickly did a rough calculation: A new propeller cost about fifty thousand. That was for starters. When a propeller hit the runway, it almost always caused damage inside the engine. That might be, oh, another hundred thousand. And, of course, there might be airframe damage. They wouldn't know until they'd torn the thing down.

Destefani turned his back on the damaged airplane. To hell with it. He'd think about all that later. He'd just won the National Unlimited Air Racing championship!

The ground crews were already on their way with the tugs to haul the broken racers back to the pits. They could see Destefani strolling over to have a chat with Shelton, his perennial rival.

It was classic Destefani. He was stuffing a fresh wad of Skoal under his lip. And he was giving them the Walk—the old cool-handed, loose-hipped swagger. *I'll tell you what you're gonna see out there: twenty-three losers—and me.*

The Gunfighter was back.

⊱ 11 ⊰

Hors de Combat

Splooot!

Destefani fired a glob of tobacco in a perfect six-foot arc, smacking the concrete just beneath the right wing of *Strega*. He glanced over at Kerchenfaut. For once, the yakky crew chief was keeping his mouth shut. He was standing there, gazing off toward the brown desertscape, pretending not to notice the activities of the insurance adjuster.

It was early afternoon, and the devil wind of Sunday had retreated back into the Sierra. Stead Field looked like the aftermath of a rock concert. The port-a-john crews were busy loading the long rows of blue stalls onto flatbeds. Cleanup crews were picking up the trash and emptying the litter barrels. The concessionaires were folding their tents and loading up vans with their display stuff.

The Unlimited racers' pits were mostly empty. Gone were the eighteen-wheel-trailer rigs and the RVs and the support vehicles. They had loaded up and headed out the front gate. Gone, too, were most of the race planes. Those that were left were being fueled and preflighted for their flights back to home base.

Four racers—*Strega, Merlin's Magic, Rare Bear, Critical Mass*—had been wounded in action. They wouldn't be going anywhere, at least not soon.

Watching the insurance adjuster go over the damaged *Strega*, Tiger wondered how much the guy knew about P-51s. It didn't take a hell of a lot of expertise to notice that the outer four inches of each propeller blade looked as if it had been used to chew up concrete—which, in fact, it had. But did he understand what kind of damage such chewing was likely to do to the engine? Did he observe that in the process of devouring concrete, the blades had gouged up several large chunks and hurled them into the radiator that was mounted back in the belly scoop?

This whole idea of insuring your race machine was foreign to Destefani. Insuring a race plane? Until this year he'd never carried one damn penny's worth of insurance on *Strega*. It just ran against his penurious farmer's nature to throw away assets for *nothing*. He had always regarded the Mustang as just another piece of machinery, like a tractor back on the farm: If he broke it, he'd fix it. It was his problem, and he'd figure something out. If he broke something so spectacularly as to total the airplane, *c'est la guerre*. He'd probably be totaled with it.

At least that's the way it always had been. But now circumstances had changed. During the past year Destefani had been receiving an unwanted education on the subject of California community-property law. He and Mary, his wife of twenty years, were on the outs. After a couple of years of warring and counseling and reconciling and warring again, they had made a final split. He had stormed out of the house and moved into a place in Bakersfield. A classic California-style, scorched-earth divorce was in full gallop.

Now Mary and her lawyers had taken an intense interest in the well-being of *Strega*. The race plane was community property, and if

Tiger were to make a smoking hole in the desert with *Strega*—or himself—by God, she would want her rightful share.

The adjuster finished his work. He and Destefani came to an amicable agreement about the extent of damage. The propeller, of course, was the most obvious casualty. The price for four new blades on a Mustang propeller could swell to over a hundred thousand. The damage to the radiator had been noted and would be included in the settlement. What about the engine? With the cowling off, they could see a nasty crack in the nose section of the crankcase—the round piece that formed a housing for the engine-to-propeller reduction gears. Would they find greater damage inside? Replacing a crankshaft or propeller shaft or reduction gear—now *that* could get very expensive.

Privately, Destefani doubted that the engine was damaged. The cracked nose section, by itself, was no big deal. It was a single-cast piece, and he had spares on the shelf back in his hangar. The radiator, too, could be replaced. Even the Q-Tipped propeller blades, he suspected, could be trimmed by four inches or so and made to turn at a different speed. At least it would be an interesting experiment.

Still, *Strega* was a mess, and some inner damage had been done to Destefani's pride, too. He was trying to be philosophical about the incident, but it was hard not to feel bummed out after damaging your airplane—in a landing accident, for God's sake! Landing accidents were things that happened to student pilots and ham-handed amateurs, not hot-rock race pilots.

But, of course, ultraperformance race planes like *Strega* and *Rare Bear* were not your docile flying-school Spam cans. These warbirds sat perched on their main mounts and tail wheel, the nose so high in the air, the pilot had *zero* forward visibility. Landing one of these squirrelly, overpowered, clipped-wing machines, not seeing beyond the racer's massive snout, trying to peer out of a cut-down Plexiglas canopy the size of a washbowl—was a challenging feat even in smooth air. On a day like yesterday, with that devil wind rolling like an invisible tsunami over the desert—bad things were bound to happen.

The truth was, such things happened often enough at Reno that pilots just laughed it off. Some of the incidents became the stuff of racing lore.

Bob Hoover, for instance. One day at Reno, back in the eighties, the great Hoover, pilot's pilot and icon of aviation, was taxiing past the pits, on his way to takeoff. The fans were waving madly. So Hoover did what he always did. He smiled and waved back to the folks—*his fans*—who were waving even more frantically, pointing at something. What the hell were they pointing at?

And then he found out. *Klang! Krunch! Whang!*—the propeller of his Mustang gobbled up the front of a tow truck. ("Who the hell put that truck there?" Hoover demanded.)

In 1982, Lloyd Hamilton was taxiing his Sea Fury on a city street in Reno, returning to the Reno airport from a publicity parade, when he proceeded to swing the tail of the fighter over a parked police motorcycle. (The police affixed a "kill" symbol—a silhouette of a motorcycle—on the side of his fighter.)

In 1992, after dropping out of the race with engine problems, Shelton executed a masterful landing in *Rare Bear*. Then, while rolling out, he "ground-looped"—did an out-of-control, end-swapping maneuver—twirling off the runway in a geyser of dirt and mesquite and lizard crap. (And fifty thousand adoring fans roared in applause.)

C'est la guerre. Shit happened. Even so, pride was involved. Destefani knew that during the next twelve months he would replay again and again in his head those last seconds of the Sunday Gold race: the gusty wind . . . trying to paste it on the runway . . . *Whump!*—the first bounce . . . the nose coming down again . . . *Whang!*—that sickening sound of metal against concrete . . .

He was just glad that he had *won* the damned race. The fallout on his pride would have been immeasurably worse if he had lost *and* trashed his airplane.

The immediate question was what to do with *Strega*. Was it more practical to fix the damage here at Stead, make her flyable, and ferry her back to Bakersfield? Or disassemble her, remove the wings, stuff the airplane onto a flatbed, and haul her back to California?

Neither, as it turned out. Team *Strega* had run out of time and assets. Like the crew of every other race team, his guys were volunteers. They took vacations from their real jobs every year in order to go racing with him at Reno. Now it was return-to-reality time. Even Kerchenfaut, who was the team leader and the only paid member of the crew, had to get back to his corporate job in Silicon Valley.

After a caucus with his crew, Destefani towed *Strega* into a hangar. It was still mid-September, but out there on the empty ramp at Stead you could feel the season changing. Winter was lurking somewhere just beyond the high ridge of the Sierra. *Strega* would spend the rest of the year in Reno.

PART TWO

Y Y Y Y

The Road to Reno

You're shaking again. You can hardly control the ship after she's on the ground. Your heart beats louder than the engine. Uniform soaked, sopping wet. Hands tremble. Knees buckle as you climb out to meet the reporters and photographers with a big, forced smile. . . . Headache. Muscle ache. Exhaustion. Oh, for a great big soft bed.

Air racing is like that. . . . It's the most dangerous profession in the world.

—Col. Roscoe Turner,
"Air Racing Was Like This,"
Pegasus, August 1956

⊁ 12 ⊁

Thompson

This is the last race I'm gonna run in.
I've suddenly realized that I've bitten off more than I can handle.
—Bill Odom, *before the 1949 Thompson Trophy races*

Before Reno, it was Cleveland. In the 1930s, Cleveland was the Mecca, the sacred site of the National Air Races, where you could come every year to see the likes of Jimmy Doolittle and Roscoe Turner fly specially built racers that flew *faster* than military fighters of the day.

Since 1929 the Thompson Trophy race had been the highlight of the National Air Races. It took its name from the Thompson Products Company, a Cleveland automotive-and-aircraft-parts maker, which sponsored the trophy. The idea was, Thompson Trophy racing would be the spawning ground for subsequent high-performance military aircraft.

Race planes of those days were exotic, one-of-a-kind creatures. Every airplane-crazy kid in the country could draw you a sketch of Doolittle's famous GeeBee, a barrel-shaped, low-winged monster with the cockpit set so far back it was almost in the vertical stabilizer.

The GeeBee (from the initials for the Granville Brothers, the Gee-Bee's builders) was one of those blood-stirring airplanes that had charisma. It also possessed the nasty trait of killing its pilots. Of the four pilots who raced the GeeBee, all except Doolittle had died in spectacular crashes.

The golden era of racing ended with World War II. When the sport returned to Cleveland in the late forties, the world—and aviation—had changed forever. Jimmy Doolittle and Roscoe Turner were no longer on the scene. Hot racers like Doolittle's GeeBee and Turner's Weddell Williams racer were museum pieces. For the price of a new DeSoto you could buy a surplus Mustang or Corsair—fighters with twice the speed and horsepower of the old Cleveland racers.

The first postwar Thompson Trophy race at Cleveland was a war-surplus event. None of the 1930s racers were competitive against the field of ex–military fighters there at Cleveland. The first winner was a Bell P-39 Airacobra, flown by Bell test pilot Tex Johnston. Johnston's Airacobra was fitted with a highly modified Allison V-1710 engine, delivering something over 2,200 horsepower and giving the fighter an unbeatable average speed at Cleveland of 373.9 miles per hour. It broke Roscoe Turner's 1938 record by 90 miles per hour.

The 1947 race was won by an ex–navy pilot named Cook Cleland. Cleland had managed to acquire three of only a few F2G-model Corsairs ever produced and equipped them for racing. The F2G was the lightened and reengined version of the famous Chance-Vought F4U Corsair.

In the opinion of those who flew each of the world War II fighters, the Chance-Vought F4U Corsair was the best all-round fighter of the war. It was the first fighter in the world to exceed 400 miles per hour in level flight and could carry a load that was equal to the weight of a Japanese Zero. Corsairs went to war in February 1943, flown by Marine Corps units at Guadalcanal. Powerful and rugged, the big Corsair was still agile enough to turn and maneuver with the nimble

Japanese Zero, shooting them down with a kill-to-loss ratio of eleven to one.

Pilots called it by various names—"Hose Nose," because of the fifteen-foot length of fuselage between the aft-mounted cockpit and the propeller. Or "Old Bent Wing," referring to its unique inverted-gull wing. To marines fighting on the beach, it was "the Sweetheart of Okinawa."

The Japanese had another name for it. In a high-speed dive, the Corsair's air-inlet ducts emitted a unique high-pitched shriek—a banshee scream that struck terror in the hearts of the enemy. They called it "Whistling Death."

The Corsair was undeniably sexy, with that rakish long nose, the cockpit planted so far back, it looked like part of the tail. It was a fighter that the navy and Marine Corps would keep in production until 1952, receiving over twelve thousand of them. The French navy, too, favored the Corsair, operating them off their tiny aircraft carriers into the mid-1960s.

During the last year of the war, when Japanese kamikaze fighters began sinking American ships, the navy placed an urgent order for a new, fast-climbing interceptor to combat the suicide bombers. The result was a souped-up Corsair, the F2G (in navy designation, "G" indicated Goodyear, which would produce the new Corsair under license). The F2G was a lightened Corsair airframe mated to the huge new Pratt & Whitney R-4360 engine. The fast, new fighter was supposed to reach 450 miles per hour.

By war's end, only ten F2Gs had been delivered. When they became surplus, several were acquired by air racers, including Cleland.

Cook Cleland was a worthy successor to the legendary Roscoe Turner. He was a gusty guy, thirty-one years old, who always wore his trademark polka-dot tie when racing. As a highly decorated, carrier-based fighter pilot during the war, Cleland was credited with sinking a Japanese carrier and shooting down four Japanese airplanes. He was the 1947 Thompson winner, and except for engine problems, he would have taken the trophy again in 1948.

Now Cleland wanted to rack up a win in 1949. And he was making no secret of his plan to come back and do it again in 1950, which would put him in a tie with Roscoe Turner, the only other three-time winner at Cleveland.

Nineteen forty-nine was the year of the Super Corsair. Of the field of entrants for the Thompson Trophy race, four were F2G Super Corsairs. Cleland's team alone was entering *three* Super Corsairs, but Cleland's own F2G was so modified that it little resembled the stock model. A total of forty-seven inches had been clipped from the span of each wing, with end plates capping off the tips of the stubby wings. To the already-overpowered R-4360 engine, he added a hydrogen-peroxide injection system that boosted the total power to something well over 4,000 horsepower. By 1949 standards, Cook Cleland was flying a *very* fast race plane.

Cleland's Corsair had one major adversary at Cleveland this year: a beautiful and radically modified P-51C Mustang named *Beguine*. The C-model Mustang still had the original "birdcage" canopy instead of the later-model bubble canopy. (Surplus "D" models, with the bubble canopy, were not yet available because they were still on active air force duty.) Instead of the standard P-51 belly scoop and radiator, *Beguine* had clipped wings and a slick belly, with wingtip-mounted air scoops and radiators. She was painted a dark green, with the opening notes of Cole Porter's "Begin the Beguine" flowing down the side of the fuselage.

Beguine was a flashy racing machine. Appropriately, she was owned by one of the world's flashiest pilots, Jacqueline Cochran. Cochran, who had led the famous WASPs (women ferry pilots) during World War II, already held several speed and distance records. All things being equal, she would have been the pilot to race her own airplane at Cleveland. But this was 1949, and all things were not equal. The rules of the Cleveland Air Races prohibited women from racing in the Unlimited event. Cochran was forced to hire a pilot to race her new Mustang.

She considered a test pilot she had heard about, a lanky young man named Bob Hoover. But Hoover was still an unknown in those days, and Cochran wanted someone with plenty of name recognition. She had to have a pilot whose own press clippings were an appropriate match for her dazzling new race plane. She wanted *Beguine*—and its pilot—to make headlines.

She got her wish. *Beguine* and its pilot would make headlines around the world.

Bill Odom had press clippings, all right. He had gathered them like souvenirs during a two-year spurt of round-the-world record flights in a Douglas twin-engined A-26 Invader, followed by a lightplane solo distance record flight in a Beechcraft Bonanza from Hawaii to Teterboro Airport in New Jersey. During the postwar years, Bill Odom had made himself one of the best-known aviators in the United States.

He was a thick-waisted, balding man of thirty who looked closer to fifty. Odom looked less like a fighter pilot than he did a transport driver, which he had been during the war years. He had served as a ferry pilot and later flew lumbering transports over the "Hump" in China. He had logged little time in fighters and none at all in sophisticated racers like *Beguine*.

Which was raising eyebrows that year at Cleveland. *Odom?* Of all the hot fighter jocks Jackie Cochran could have chosen, why pick a guy who was obviously miles behind his airplane? Odom was flying *Beguine* around the course, in the qualification laps and in the preliminary Sohio race, like a guy getting his first practice in a new airplane, which was exactly what he was doing.

He was even scaring himself.

Half an hour before race time, Odom was talking to Bob Hoover. Odom was trying to get himself in a frame of mind to race, but he was having trouble. They had stashed *Beguine* in a closed hangar because the racy-looking Mustang attracted so much crowd attention, they couldn't keep people away.

"This is the last race I'm gonna run in," he said to Hoover. "I'm gonna leave this to you fighter pilots in the future."

They rolled the hangar door open and wheeled *Beguine* out to the flight line.

The thunder reverberated across the grandstand as they leaped into the air—three mighty Super Corsairs (Dick Becker's F2G was out with mechanical problems), six Mustangs, and one pointy-nosed P-63 King Cobra. It was the last time the big Unlimiteds would make a racehorse start, with all the overpowered race planes taking off in a line-abreast formation, like ponies at Belmont.

Odom was in seventh place. But as they turned onto the course, rounding the first pylon, he was already overtaking the slower traffic.

He had a plan that had been worked out for him by Benny Howard, a famous racer and airplane builder: *Move into third place as soon as you can. Stay there and bide your time until the tenth lap. Then push it up and take over first place. Stay there for the remainder of the race. Win!*

And that's what Odom was doing. *Beguine* was moving ahead, passing the stock Mustangs and the King Cobra. By the time they finished the first lap, flashing past the grandstand, he had moved *Beguine* all the way up to third. Just where he was supposed to be.

The trouble was, the course was still unfamiliar to him. Pulling hard around pylon 1, beginning the second lap, he had to search, scanning the distance ahead. *Where was the next pylon? There it was.*

Rounding pylon 2, turning left, his vision tunneling under the unaccustomed burden of four Gs, Odom tried to pick up the next pylon. *Somewhere up there . . . it ought to be. . . . Damn! Over there . . . to the right.*

He had overshot the turn. He was already too far to the left! Now he was *inside* the course; he had to get this thing back to the right! He snatched the stick hard to the right, rolling the Mustang out of its left turn, back to the right.

He pulled hard on the stick, yanking the racer's nose around, feeling the G's come back on.

Odom felt *Beguine* shudder. *Whoa! What's happening?* The damn thing was *still* rolling to the right. Too far to the right.

He hauled the stick back to the left, trying to stop the roll. It was too late. *Beguine*'s nose was pitching downward, rolling inverted.

It happened in less than two seconds. Bill Odom stared at the scenery filling his windscreen like the image in a zoom lens. He saw streets, backyards, a house, rising to meet him.

It took several seconds for the sound to reach the grandstands—*Kaboom!*—and even then, because it was so far away, it sounded more like a distant thunderclap. The spectators—fifty-two thousand of them on that September Sunday afternoon—were still riveted on the front-running racers, the three Super Corsairs.

"Where's *Beguine?*"

"What's that black smoke over there?"

"Jesus, did he go down in those houses?"

Beguine had exploded into the side of a house at 400 miles per hour. A ball of flame belched upward, engulfing the house, rolling across the earth like a napalm charge.

The house, on West Street in the suburb of Berea, Ohio, was the home of a young couple, Bradley Laird and his wife, Jeanne. Mrs. Laird and her thirteen-month old son, who had been playing in a playpen in the backyard, were killed. So was Odom.

And so were the Cleveland Air Races as well as the Thompson Trophy.

Even before the smoke had subsided, recriminations were flying like missiles.

"Odom never should have been in the race," declared Cook Cleland, who won the Thompson Trophy race. "It's no worse than a good combat mission, but a man should have plenty of time in fast single-engine planes before he is allowed to fly the Thompson."

Bob Hoover, standing atop a hangar at the airfield, saw it happen: "Any fighter pilot who ever flew P-51s knew that you had a neutrally stable, if not unstable, airplane, and when you started to pull G with it and pulled back on the stick, you would immediately have to start pushing to compensate because the airplane would want to dig in on you. *Beguine* just dug in so fast when he overcontrolled and pulled, and he didn't back off quick enough and push. The aircraft snap-rolled."

An airplane was likely to "snap-roll" when its nose was abruptly yanked back while changing direction of flight. One wing—the one *inside* the turn—stalled, causing the airplane to roll violently in that direction.

Which was what happened to Odom. When he realized he had overshot the course line to his left, he overreacted, yanking the nose too hard while turning back to his right, and stalled the right wing. The Mustang snap-rolled into the ground—a classic instance of overcontrolling a fighter.

Not until after the crash did Jackie Cochran learn about Odom's real experience. Though he claimed to have logged 350 hours in fighters, it turned out that he had almost none. Bill Odom was more of a self-promoter than anyone realized.

Newspapers, congressmen, and even the influential *Aviation Week* magazine ranted about the tragic deaths of a young housewife and her child. For months the debate raged on about banning not only air racing but air shows of all kinds.

One immediate result was obvious: Air racing at Cleveland was finished. What was even more obvious, in the clarity of hindsight, was that racing *should* have been banned at Cleveland and at every other site where high-performance planes flew dangerously low over populated areas. The crash of a race plane into an underlying neighborhood had been a calamity waiting to happen.

The sensible solution, of course, was to move the National Air Races to another venue, away from Cleveland, away from any populated area. But in the pall of smoke that still hung over the Cleveland suburb where Odom crashed, the zeal for racing had been extinguished. Big-time air racing was a pariah among motorsports. No one had the stomach for promoting such an event. In the public view, air racing was a dangerous anachronism, like throwing Christians to lions.

There would be no 1950 Thompson Trophy race. Or any other Thompson race for propeller-driven racers. Cook Cleland, who now had two Thompson victories to his credit, retired from racing without matching Roscoe Turner's record of three wins. His beautiful F2G Super Corsair retired with him. When the Korean War ignited a year later, Cleland returned to active navy duty and again distinguished himself in combat, commanding a squadron of Corsairs.

Thompson Trophy racing was a closed chapter in history. It would never be revived, at least in its old high-profile racehorse-starting, anything-goes Cleveland version. For fifteen years the sport of racing big, grossly overpowered airplanes around pylons languished, waiting for someone to bring it back to life.

✈ 13 ✈

A Benevolent Dictator

No problem.

That's what everyone remembered about Bill Stead. "No problem," he always said, usually meaning that it was no problem *to him.*

Bill Stead was a guy in a hell of a hurry. He didn't have the time or the inclination to deal with the petty crap—the nitty-gritty little *problems*. He had bigger things to attend to. Like the resurrection of the National Air Races.

Everything Bill Stead did was *fast*. He liked fast cars, boats, airplanes. As a kid he'd gotten into hydroplane racing and soon made himself one of the top dogs in that arcane motorsport. He won the national championship in 1958 and again in 1959, then became the team captain and manager of Harrah's big hydroplane racing operation.

And he'd always been crazy about airplanes. As a kid he'd been fascinated by the pomp and color of the old National Air Races at

Cleveland. Stead learned to fly at an early age and had owned a string of airplanes—a Navion, T-6, Howard DGA, Grumman Sea Bee, and then moved up to what he considered the ultimate warbird, an F8F Bearcat.

Stead was the stepson of a well-to-do Reno rancher. His family owned a large parcel of land north of Reno, out in the flats between the town of Sparks and Pyramid Lake. On their spread was a windswept, dusty little airfield called Sky Ranch, that had been used off and on by the air force as a touch-and-go training field.

Stead was a compactly built, muscular guy with the rugged good looks of a cowboy actor. But the quality that made him successful was his ability to motivate. He was a natural salesman. He was also a visionary, one of those people who dreamed grand dreams, then got other people hooked.

In the 1950s, while Stead was still winning and promoting hydroplane races, he was already talking about one of his grandest dreams. He wanted to somehow revive championship air racing, which, after the stigma of Bill Odom's crash in 1949, had vanished from the American landscape. Stead even had the perfect place in mind for such races: his own airfield, out there across the big sprawling valley from Pyramid Lake, beneath the High Sierra.

It was all so clear to him—a new version of the old Thompson Trophy races out there in the wide-open spaces of Nevada. And having envisioned his dream with such clarity, Stead had no doubt about *who* was going to make it happen: He was. *No problem.*

In early 1963, Stead began making it happen. The state of Nevada in those days was still a small community. It was the kind of place where everything—politics, social life, business—was conducted on a first-name basis. A handful of well-connected families—ranchers, businessmen, hotel and casino owners—presided over most of the state's affairs.

Bill Stead, coming from such a family, was acquainted with each of the major players. He began making his rounds, promoting his scheme for a national-championship air race at Reno. It made such perfect sense. Hell, they had *everything!* The weather, the airport, the wide-open spaces, and best of all, they had Reno, the ideal tourist facility for a high-octane event like air racing.

And *that* got their attention. The gaming industry of Reno thrived on crowds like the one Stead was talking about.

Stead was tireless in promoting his idea. He was a man in constant motion. He hustled everyone—the state legislature, the Reno Chamber of Commerce, the military (which still maintained an air force base at Reno), his old contacts from hydroplane racing. He even enlisted Bob Hoover, who by now was working as a test pilot for North American. Hoover flew out to Reno and offered advice and guidance from his experience at the Cleveland races.

Even history was on Stead's side; 1964 happened to be the year of Nevada's centennial. The governor, Grant Sawyer, appointed Stead to the state's Centennial Commission, and he wasted no time selling his fellow commissioners on the notion of a National Championship Air Race.

Like a complicated mosaic, the pieces were slipping into place. When knotty problems arose, Stead did what he always did: He charmed someone into working it out for him. Through all the difficult organizational stages, he managed to stay above the fray, focused on his dream of high-powered racers flying around pylons. Bill Stead's dream was going to come true. He was going to get his race. Right there in Reno!

All he needed now were racers. The problem was, almost none of the pilots who had flown at Cleveland or knew anything about pylon racing were still active. Stead worked the telephone, calling up everyone he knew with a hot warbird, persuading them to come to his reborn championship air race. Instead of the Thompson Trophy race, the fastest division would now be called the Unlimited Class. The format, he promised everyone, would be just like Cleveland's.

Some believed him. They came to Reno. And they couldn't believe it.

I can't believe this shit!

That was the most commonly heard expression. You kept hearing it all day. The pilots couldn't believe what they were being asked to do.

This wasn't at all like Cleveland. It wasn't like anything they had imagined. They were appalled. What Stead wanted them to do was take off and land—for each race—at his little strip out there at Sky Ranch, *not* from the Reno municipal airport, some fifteen miles away, as they wanted to do.

The problem was, Stead's "strip" was a barely discernible, sand-covered, metal-mat runway of only about two thousand feet. The strip would hardly accommodate a Piper Cub, let alone a nine-thousand-pound, hyped-up Mustang fighter. Worse, sand and dirt were blowing across the place in dense clouds that clogged your nostrils and filled every exposed fissure on your airplane.

Stead was being obstinate about it. They damn well *would* use the Sky Ranch facility, such as it was, because that was where the race was. It was also where the spectator bleachers were erected, and most importantly, it was where the vitally important *television* cameras were placed. ABC was there to cover the "new" National Championship Air Races. Everyone had come to Sky Ranch to see the pilots and the airplanes. And, by God, that's where they would be—on the ground—in the center of the show.

This was when the race pilots, being the prima donnas they truly were, showed their true form. They told Bill Stead to go screw himself. The racecourse itself was dangerous enough, with pylons that they couldn't find and high-tension lines strung across the middle of the course. But this damned runway! It looked like something from the Afrika Korps.

The year 1964 marked a whole new era of racing and a new

generation of pilots. Each of them that first year was a rookie. None of the old Cleveland competitors—Cleland, Becker, Johnston—had signed up for Stead's reincarnated version of the Thompson Trophy race. Among the gaggle of new pilots were some unknowns whose names would become very well known in the years to come: Greenamyer, Lacy, Slovak, and a hung-over navy lieutenant named Lyle Shelton who showed up to help on Lacy's crew.

Bill Stead's own Bearcat, dubbed *Miss Smirnoff,* was sponsored by the vodka maker and was being raced this year by the world hydroplane racing champ, Czechoslovakian pilot Mira Slovak. For publicity purposes, Smirnoff had come up with a special mixed drink they were calling the Smirnoff Bearcat, which consisted mostly of vodka, mixed with more vodka, with an optional dash of bitters.

Stead, the entrepreneur showman, had lined up a weeklong aeronautical carnival. Besides the Unlimited racers, there was also biplane championship racing, a class for Formula One (100-horsepower homebuilts) racers, and, unique to the 1964 races, a women's Cherokee 180 (a Piper fixed-gear monoplane) race. Stead even organized a race for World War II Stearman biplanes, featuring four of the ungainly machines, all local crop dusters, motoring around the pylons at a stately 100 miles an hour.

Stead offered the fans more than air racing. The weeklong event at Reno included the National Balloon Championships, antique and experimental aircraft judging, parachuting championships, and the U.S. National Aerobatic Championships. A daily air show featured performers like Bob Hoover doing his now-famous act in the Mustang and a host of aerobatic performers that included the U.S. Air Force aerobatic demonstration team, the Thunderbirds, flying F-100 fighters.

And this being Reno, the wind blew every day. And with the blowing wind came the whirling clouds of dirt and sand and sagebrush. By Friday, the first day of the three-day championship Unlimited heats, the wind was howling almost directly *across* Bill Stead's little metal-matted runway out there at Sky Ranch. Which just made the matter of landing out there even more problematic.

The pilots were balking. Stead was holding firm: The pilots *had* to land on the goddamned Sky Ranch runway after their race or they would be disqualified. And the pilots were telling Stead the same thing they'd been telling him all week: Go screw yourself.

At the briefing that morning, when it looked like the standoff between Stead and his prima-donna pilots would terminate the short-lived revival of racing, an active-duty navy pilot named Walt Ohlrich, who was flying a borrowed Bearcat, stood up and proposed a compromise. Suppose the pilots took off from the Reno airport and flew their race, then landed there at Sky Ranch—once—then departed again for Reno. That way the television crews could get their interviews and footage of the pilots with their airplanes. Everyone, including Stead, could save a little face. After a requisite amount of grumbling, the pilots, one by one, agreed to the compromise.

All except one. Darryl Greenamyer, whose F8F-2 Bearcat was probably the most modified of all the racers that year, flatly refused. His Bearcat had a tiny, hard-to-see-out-of bubble canopy not much bigger than a bowler hat. Worse, it had sealed, inoperative landing flaps, which gave the fighter a landing speed of something around 120. Greenamyer had already made one tentative touchdown on Stead's runway, and then, not liking what he saw—or *didn't* see—he poured the power to the Bearcat and flew back to the Reno municipal airport.

Now the other pilots were taking a fresh look at Greenamyer. All they knew about him was that he was a feisty little guy with blue blood credentials, working as a test pilot under the famous Tony LeVier out at Lockheed, in Palmdale. What they didn't yet know, of course, was that they were looking at the pilot who would become the winningest racer—and the champion prima donna—of Reno Unlimited Air Racing.

As it turned out, Greenamyer *did* race but still refused to humor Stead by landing his Bearcat out there in the blowing dirt and pot-holed cow paths of Sky Ranch. So instead of coming in fourth, which was where he finished in the standings, Greenamyer was de-moted to last place.

The winner of the 1964 Unlimited Air Racing Championship turned out to be the Czech Mira Slovak, flying Bill Stead's own *Miss Smirnoff.* Though Slovak finished the final "championship" race well behind the front-running Mustang, *Bardahl Special,* flown by Bob Love, he was named the overall winner because of the arcane scoring system the organizers had imported from the sport of hydroplane racing. By these rules, the winner was determined not by the results of the final race but by a cumulative total of points earned during *all* the heat races that week.

To the fans, of course, it was an unsatisfying result. They had just witnessed a race in which Love's Mustang had clearly beaten all tak-ers during the championship heat—*and didn't win the trophy.* From that year on, the rules would change: Forget accumulated points. The racers in the championship contest would be those with the best finishing positions in the heat races of Friday and Saturday. The championship event on Sunday would be a flat-out, winner-take-all air race.

But at least for that year, 1964, both Mira Slovak and Bill Stead had reason to celebrate. Stead's Bearcat, *Miss Smirnoff,* had won the Unlimited Championship. And best of all for Stead, his long-held dream—a resurrected national-championship air race—had come to pass. *He* had made it happen, and it had been a success.

Well, almost. Actually, the extravaganza lost money, but not so much that Stead's investors weren't willing to give it another shot. The year 1964 was a learning experience for both the racers and the organizers. Even though the air races had gone into the red, new sponsors and investors were suddenly taking notice. The cham-pionship air races had given the little gambling resort of Reno a healthy splash of national attention. Best of all, it brought a swarm of fresh tourists to the hotels and casinos.

The 1965 races were scheduled again out at Stead's Sky Ranch, which made none of the would-be racers happy. But the same unpredictable Sierra weather that had scoured the 1964 races with dirt and tumbleweed this year produced a different phenomenon: rain. From the skies poured a steady torrent that washed out the first three days of qualifying for all the race classes.

For the pilots, the rain was a blessing. It held down the dust. Moreover, at least temporarily, it gave the soft, treacherous runway at Sky Ranch a firmness that suited the big, stiff-legged Mustang and Bearcat fighters.

Even Darryl Greenamyer seemed to be satisfied, although his rivals were learning that Greenamyer was a guy who was *never* happy unless he was pissed about something. And Greenamyer had been pissed for most of the past year because of his disqualification from the prize money in the 1964 race.

This year, Greenamyer was rolling back into Reno like an outlaw riding through Dodge City. He had put together a team of the best airframe and power-plant talent to transform his Bearcat into the hottest racer in the world, including two savvy engineers from Lockheed, Pete Law and Bruce Boland. He had a brilliant metal fabricator named Phil Greenberg and a top-notch crew chief, Ron Waagmeester.

Greenamyer's team had done a complete rebuild of his Bearcat. The wings were clipped, with new, more efficient wingtips installed. A tank for water injection was added, and a huge four-bladed Skyraider propeller was mounted. The weight of the airframe was drastically reduced by removing the entire hydraulic system. A one-shot nitrogen bottle was used to raise the landing gear. It was then lowered and locked back into place purely by gravity. The already-minuscule canopy had been replaced with an even tinier, more aerodynamic model.

That first day on the ramp at Reno, when the other racers got their first close-up look at the Greenamyer Bearcat, a sudden realization dawned on them: *This is not just another warbird pumped up for a race.* Greenamyer's machine was unlike anything they had ever seen before. This thing was like a specially bred racing animal.

Unlimited Air Racing had just moved into a new era.

Stead put on the same kind of show for the 1965 races that he had booked the year before. The National Aerobatic Championships were again held at Sky Ranch. And the hot-air balloons were back, skating across the desert in a hare-and-hound competition. The air show once again featured the crowd-pleasing air force Thunderbirds and the ubiquitous Bob Hoover in his yellow Mustang.

Stead, the speed addict, could no longer keep himself out of the races. He had bought a homebuilt racer he named *Little Miss Reno* and was flying it himself this year in the Formula One class. He had already raced it in a competition at Lancaster and planned to follow the Formula circuit with it after Reno.

The 1965 Unlimited Championship race was being touted as a navy versus air force contest: a field of three ex–navy Bearcats running against three former air force Mustangs. Though World War II was over—the *real* war with the Germans and Japanese—this was what they had left: interservice competition matching obsolete, pointy-nacelled air force machines against obsolete, barrel-shaped, tailhook-equipped navy fighters.

The results were inconclusive. Since the heyday of the hot propeller-driven fighters, the argument had gone on about which fighter was the fastest, the most maneuverable, the deadliest.

Or the sexiest. World War II fighter planes were now *objets d'art,* each possessing its own cult of admirers every bit as devoted as the fans of a film star.

Just as air force pilots had a land-based culture that was distinctly different from that of the navy and marine corps, so were their fighting machines. It started back in the thirties, when the navy eschewed the long, in-line, liquid-cooled engines like the Allison and Merlin and hung big, round Wright or Pratt & Whitney radial engines on their fighters. What came was a lineage of stubby, blunt-nosed Grumman fighters, all looking like winged beer barrels. A single exception was the Chance-Vought F4U Corsair, a long-nosed fighter with graceful inverted gull wings but powered by a Pratt & Whitney R-2800 radial.

Meanwhile, the Army Air Corps (forerunner of the U.S. Air Force) was proudly flying their narrow-snouted fighters like the Mustang, the P-40 Tomahawk, and the twin-boomed P-38 Lightning—all mounting streamlined, liquid-cooled engines. The only round-motored fighter of the Army Air Corps was the Republic P-47 Thunderbolt, a radial-engined fighter that looked—and flew—like a Sherman tank.

In the charisma department, the beautiful P-38 was an undeniable superstar. Already in full production when World War II began, the Lockheed Lightning was fast, sexy, and unique. With its two long tail booms, each mounting an Allison V-1710 and pod-mounted cockpit, the P-38 resembled no other fighter, friend or foe.

Though the P-38 lacked the top end speed and maneuverability of the P-51, it possessed two exceptional traits: an awesome rate of climb and devastating firepower. As fighters went, the P-38 was *big*—nearly twice the weight of the Mustang and with a third greater wingspan—with an immense capacity for guns and ammunition. In its nose was mounted a 20-millimeter cannon and four 50-caliber guns, making the Lightning eminently suited for the job of long-range bomber escort. It was so feared by the Luftwaffe that they called it the *Gabelschwanz Teufel*—fork-tailed devil. In the Pacific the P-38 wreaked havoc upon the Japanese, producing the two leading American aces of the war, Maj. Richard Bong, with forty kills, and Maj. Tom McGuire, with thirty-eight.

In April 1943, Lightnings from the 339th Fighter Squadron, based in Guadalcanal, flew 550 miles to intercept and shoot down the

Mitsubishi transport carrying Admiral Yamamoto, architect of the Pearl Harbor attack.

In later years, even though almost ten thousand P-38s were constructed, the beautiful Lightning became more and more an endangered species. By the 1990s, only a few were still flying. The best known was Lefty Gardner's *White Lightnin'*, still enchanting the crowds at Reno.

The year 1946 also marked the last moment of glory for the much-maligned P-39 Airacobra. Even before World War II began, the Airacobra had been relegated to training duty and for export to America's allies.

Cook Cleland's dominance of the 1947 Thompson race was the beginning of the reign of round-motored, ex–navy fighters. Cleland and his big 4,000-plus horsepower Super Corsair ran away with the 1949 race, setting a closed-course record that lasted into the 1970s.

"Ho-lee cow!" Those words, or some similar utterance, were the standard reaction of a pilot on his first flight in the Bearcat. He would shove up the throttle—and the little fighter clawed into the sky like a runaway rocket.

The F8F Bearcat was the last of the line of chunky little Grumman fighters. Though it had the same engine—the 2,100 horsepower Pratt & Whitney R-2800—as its beefy predecessor, the F6F Hellcat, the Bearcat was smaller, lighter, and infinitely more nimble.

Pilots loved the Bearcat. Never had they had their hands on a fighter so light on the controls or with such a breathtaking rate of climb. The Bearcat could scramble into the sky at a rate of 4,800 feet per minute, which made it the hottest propeller-driven fighter in American livery.

And the last. By the time the F8F reached its first navy squadron, it was too late to join the war in the Pacific before the Japanese surrender. The Bearcat's only taste of combat came in the service of the French Armée de l'Air, fighting in the fifties in Vietnam.

Strega

Rare Bear

Dago Red

Tsunami

Pond Racer

Critical Mass

Miss Ashley II, the "scissors" plane

Voodoo—after Bob Hannah's close call

Robert Gandt

The Gunfighter—Bill "Tiger" Destefani

Robert Gandt

Lyle Shelton

Bruce Lockwood

Bob "Hurricane" Hannah

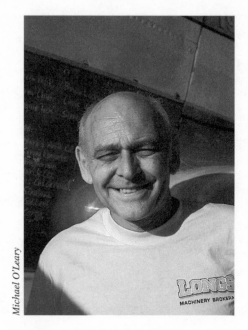

Michael O'Leary

Bill Kerchenfaut, Reno's winningest crew chief

Michael O'Leary

Bob Hoover in *Ole Yeller*

Skip Holm, hired gun

Robert "Hoot" Gibson

The Room of Hard Benches

Home pylon

Though the Bearcat reigned for a few more years as the top dog in the aerial-gunfighting department, its future was preordained. The smell of kerosene was wafting across air bases around the country. The day of the prop fighter was over.

Because the F8F was still a front-line warplane, no surplus Bearcats were available during the time of the Thompson Trophy races. Not until the resurrection of Unlimited Air Racing at Reno in 1964 did race fans get to see what a Bearcat could do.

And then, for the next six years, it was a one-plane show. Bill Stead's Bearcat, *Miss Smirnoff*, flown by Mira Slovak, was the first winner, followed by Darryl Greenamyer in his *Conquest I*, taking five of the next six Unlimited Championships. Later, Lyle Shelton burst onto the scene, beating all contenders with his record-setting *Rare Bear*.

Another latecomer to air racing was the British-built Hawker Sea Fury. Though the Sea Fury was conceived in the early forties as a long-range, air-superiority warplane for both the RAF and the Royal Navy, the big fighter never saw action in World War II. By 1945, with the end of the war imminent and jet fighters on the production line, the project was canceled.

During the postwar years, the Sea Fury went into production as a fighter-bomber to be flown from the tiny decks of the Royal Navy's aircraft carriers. Powered by an 18-cylinder Bristol Centaurus 2,550 horsepower radial engine, the Sea Fury proved itself to be a rugged warplane. It was armed with four 20-millimeter cannons and could haul an impressive combination of thousand-pound bombs and rockets.

The Sea Fury finally saw action in the Korean War, flown from British carrier decks against targets in North Korea. One day, a flight of the big propeller-driven fighter-bombers was jumped by North Korean MiG-15s. Though outclassed by the MiGs—then the hottest fighter in the world—the Royal Navy Sea Furies managed to shoot down one of the jets and escaped the skirmish without losses. It was the Sea Fury's supreme moment of glory.

So successful was the Sea Fury, it went into service with air forces around the world, including those of Egypt, Burma, Cuba, Canada, Australia, West Germany, Iraq, Pakistan, and the Netherlands. By the 1960s, when propeller-driven fighter-bombers were being phased out everywhere, Sea Furies were discovered by civilian warbird aficionados.

The Sea Fury was introduced to Reno in 1966, first flown by Lyle Shelton and later campaigned by racers like Lloyd Hamilton and Frank Sanders. Most racers chose to reengine the Fury with either the Wright R-3350 (as installed on the German Sea Fury), cranking out 3,700 horsepower, or the massive Pratt & Whitney R-4360, as installed on Sanders's *Dreadnought*, delivering over 4,000 horsepower.

In terms of top end speed, the Sea Fury punched into a wall of air at about 450 miles per hour. Beyond that speed, it seemed that no amount of extra cleaning up or additional horsepower could push the big, blunt-nosed fighter into the 500-plus range, where the hottest Mustangs and Bearcats dwelled. Still, pilots loved the Sea Fury both for its brute strength and for its straightforward handling characteristics. The Sea Fury was an honest, easy-to-fly airplane that made an average pilot look good and made a good pilot, sometimes, a winner.

Few other fighters from outside America made it to Reno. In the early days of Cleveland, pilots had raced the famous Supermarine Spitfire without spectacular success. For all its good looks and glamorous wartime record, the Spitfire was not a flat-out race plane.

Nor were any of the other World War II birds—the German Messerschmitt 109 or the Focke-Wulf 190 or the Japanese Zero or the British-built Hurricane. They were too slow, too underpowered, too rare. Only a handful of Russian-designed fighters, Yak-3s and Yak-11s, all fitted with American-built engines, had raced at Reno. None could match the speeds of *Strega* or *Rare Bear* or *Dreadnought*.

. . .

The 1965 navy–air force competition ended with mixed results. Darryl Greenamyer's Bearcat sailed away with the first-place trophy. Chuck Lyford's Mustang clung to second place, followed by another Mustang flown by Clay Lacy. Mira Slovak, the previous year's overall winner, flew his Bearcat to fourth place. Another Bearcat-and-Mustang duel was fought by Walt Ohlrich and a rookie named Lyle Shelton, bringing up the rear of the pack.

But the day belonged to Greenamyer. His winning speed exceeded the previous year's record by 10 miles an hour. He had evened the score after his disqualification at last year's race. Greenamyer's victory in 1965 was the first in the longest string of wins in Reno racing history. He would go on to stamp his indelible print on the culture of air racing.

In all the euphoric postrace celebration, everyone was in agreement: The 1965 air races had been a success. The fans loved it. The little city of Reno had garnered huge media coverage. Local hotels and casinos had raked in new profits.

There was only one bothersome irritant that no one could quite figure out: They were *still* losing money.

But Bill Stead was already working on that one. By now even he could admit that cramming thousands of fans and dozens of temperamental race planes into the swirling dust bowl of Sky Ranch had been an exercise made in hell. It was the eternal air-race promoter's problem of *venue*. Where do you conduct a wide-open, high-octane event like Unlimited Air Racing *and* provide creature comforts to your paying customers as well as your participants.

Stead had a new place in mind. The *perfect* place.

The Reno Army Air Base had been constructed prior to World War II. During the war the base had been used for glider training. In the cold-war era it was renamed Stead Air Force Base in honor of Bill Stead's own brother, Croston Stead, who had lost his life in a

P-51 accident while flying there with the Nevada Air National Guard. Stead Air Force Base later served as the headquarters of the air force's survival school, as a helicopter training center, and the headquarters of the Nevada Air National Guard.

It was ironic. Bill Stead had tried the year before, in 1965, to stage the Reno Air Races there at the military base, but the air force had turned him down. The air base would have been the perfect facility because it had *three* long, intersecting concrete runways, suitable for handling the hottest racers in the game. Its big, spacious ramps would be ideal for erecting bleachers that would accommodate tens of thousands of spectators. And it possessed all the amenities of a modern airport: hangars, access roads, taxiways, a control tower. However, in typical military wariness, the air force wanted no part of a civilian free-for-all between a bunch of wild-assed race pilots.

And then, in 1966, they made an announcement: Stead Air Force Base was on the hit list. The air force was closing the base, and the field would revert to civilian control. Which meant to Bill Stead that his old nemesis—the *venue* problem—would be solved. The National Championship Air Races would, in all likelihood, move to a new and permanent home.

It was sweet irony staging *his* air races at the perfect facility that just happened to bear the name of *Stead!* It was the break he'd been waiting for since he first conceived the idea of racing at Reno.

For Bill Stead, life was good. The grand dream he'd had of the resurrected National Championship Air Races had come true. The 1966 Reno races would be the grandest aerial speed contest ever held.

The only trouble was, Stead wouldn't be there to see it.

⊁ 14 ⊁

If You Can't Beat 'Em . . .

No one knew what happened on 28 April 1966. It was one of those unexplained mishaps in aviation, the kind the investigators attribute to "cause undetermined."

Stead was gliding back toward the runway with the little racer when something went wrong. The airplane rolled out of control and pitched downward. It impacted the ground, nose first, with a sickening *Whump!*

Speed had always been the elixir of Bill Stead's life. Having entered himself in the 1965 Formula One races, he was frustrated with the dogginess of his race plane, *Little Miss Reno*. He had barely qualified in the little midget plane and finished at the rear of the pack in the final heat races.

So Stead, being Stead, had done the natural thing: He went looking for another, faster airplane—the fastest he could find. What he found was a midget racer called *Deerfly*, and it was, officially, the fastest airplane in the Formula One class. *Deerfly* had waltzed away with the championship in 1965. Now Bill Stead was determined to savor for himself that sweet taste of victory. He wanted to roar past the checkered flag in first place.

Which was why, in the spring of 1966, he was out in St. Petersburg, Florida, practicing for a race on the Formula One circuit. The side of his hot little racer was emblazoned with "Smirnoff," the sponsor of Stead's own racing team, which now included both his sexy white Bearcat and the new midget racer, wearing the number 84.

They never figured out the cause of Stead's accident. From the twisted wreckage they could only conclude that he had experienced some sort of mechanical failure. A locked flight control? A severed control cable? No obvious answer could be extracted from the destroyed pieces.

At age forty-three, Bill Stead was gone. But what he had dreamed—and made happen—was firmly entrenched out there on the boulder-strewn moonscape of Truckee Meadow. Championship air racing had a life of its own. In the years to come, it would swell in magnitude and spectacle. To the astonishment of its promoters, it would even make money. The only missing—and critical—element would be its benevolent dictator.

Meanwhile, Darryl Greenamyer kept winning. He won in 1966. Again in 1967. And he kept winning. His streak continued unbroken until 1970, when his one-shot, nitrogen-bottle, gear-retraction system malfunctioned and he flew the championship race with his right main landing gear hanging down. It was the first time in the seven-year history of the Reno races that a Mustang—this one flown by California pilot Clay Lacy—had taken the Gold Trophy.

For Mustang devotees, it had been a frustrating period. They *knew* that their beloved Mustang—the hottest, most charismatic fighter ever constructed—was *supposed* to beat all the other lesser fighters, including the crude, round-motored machines like the Bearcat. The trouble was, the Mustang's temperamental Rolls-Royce Merlin engine, with its liquid coolant system and geared-reduction box, had this maddening propensity for going *Bloom!* at the most critical juncture of every damned race. It was like flying a hand grenade.

By contrast, the rugged Pratt & Whitney R-2800 radial engine on Greenamyer's Bearcat was as powerful and predictable as a farm ox. Greenamyer only needed to push his engine to its normal takeoff-power maximum. His Bearcat's winning speed had been achieved almost purely through airframe sophistication. Every hole had been sealed, every protuberance smoothed, every gram of superfluous weight discarded. His racer, *Conquest I*, had the nimble grace of a dancer and the punch of a heavyweight.

But this was 1971, and Greenamyer's rivals had also learned a few things. The unchallenged reign of the Greenamyer Bearcat was almost over. In the qualifying trials, Greenamyer's speed of 406 miles per hour was only fourth best. For the first time in Reno racing, the first six qualifying racers *all* posted speeds over 400 miles per hour. A hot Mustang named *Roto-Finish Special*, flown by Gunther Balz, won the pole position with a scorching 419 miles per hour. Right behind him, at 418, was Lyle Shelton, flying *Phoenix I*, the Bearcat he had rescued, restored, and reengined with a mighty Wright R-3350 radial.

In previous years, the Unlimited Championship races had been exciting but predictable. The front-runner usually stayed in front. The only real dueling for position took place among the slower racers in the back of the pack. The year 1971 was different. For months to come, the fans would be talking about what happened at this year's trophy race.

Mike Loening (son of the aviation pioneer Grover Loening) grabbed the early lead in his sleek Mustang, *Miss Salmon River*. He was chased by three other Mustangs and by Lyle Shelton, whose R-3350-powered Bearcat was now the match of anything at Reno. Back in fifth place was Greenamyer.

Greenamyer was biding his time. By now he had learned one certainty about Mustangs: They were fast—and fragile. If you just
waited a few laps, they would start blowing engines.

And the Mustangs were staying true to form. Loening's overstrained Merlin engine self-destructed on the second lap. After hol-
lering, "Mayday," he set up his pattern, then landed *downwind*, hot
and heavy, and proceeded to give the spectators a close-up-and-dirty
view of a P-51 Mustang fighter careening off the far end of the runway, through a concrete fixture, disappearing in a geyser of sand
and sagebrush. When the cloud of silt had abated, they could see
that Loening was okay. He was still sitting there in his cockpit, gazing out at the tableau of descending dirt, looking as if he had just
been rear-ended by a garbage truck.

Scratch one Mustang.

On the fourth lap, Greenamyer made his move. And as he moved,
Shelton moved with him. The two Bearcats, nose to tail, advanced
to the front of the pack.

Meanwhile, yet another Mustang—this one flown by Howie
Keefe—belched a cloud of smoke like a dyspeptic dragon. Keefe
yelped a "Mayday" and pulled the smoking fighter up in an emergency landing pattern. He, too, landed hot and heavy. And not to be
outdone by Loening, he went barreling off the *opposite* end of the
runway, treating the fans to yet another Mustang-induced geyser of
sand and sagebrush.

Scratch two Mustangs.

The Bearcats were still going. Entering the final lap, Greenamyer
was in the lead, but only by a few feet. Shelton was clinging to him,
looking for the tiniest advantage so he could pass.

Greenamyer wasn't giving any advantage. He was flying a tight
line, nearly scraping the paint from each pylon, skimming the floor
of the desert. From the stands it looked as if the two fighters were
welded together, coming down the home stretch in tight formation.

Greenamyer took the checkered flag with a speed of 413.99 miles per hour. Shelton finished in his shadow at 413.07. It was the closest Unlimited Championship race Reno had ever seen.

It also marked the beginning of a twenty-seven-year war.

Greenamyer and Shelton disliked each other even before the events of the 1971 race. Neither could say exactly why. It was just one of those inevitable clashes of chemistry. Shelton and Greenamyer were like two dogs in the same yard, each circling and snarling and protecting his own turf.

Shelton was not alone, of course, in disliking Darryl Greenamyer. The air-racing world was split into two nearly equal camps—those who admired the guy and those who considered Greenamyer an eminently suitable target for machine-gun practice. The most commonly heard description of Darryl Greenamyer was "That cocky little son of a bitch!"

Greenamyer, for his part, returned the contempt in full measure. He liked to wrap himself in that same icy, blue-eyed arrogance, grinning like a Cheshire cat, reminding everyone that he was—and had just proved it for the sixth time—the winningest pilot in the history of air racing.

This year, Shelton had a specific grudge against Greenamyer. He was protesting Greenamyer's victory in the Unlimited Trophy race. In his opinion, Greenamyer had violated the rules. When a Mayday was declared during a race, the pilots were required by the rules to pull up to a minimum safe altitude until the emergency was resolved. But during this year's two Maydays—Loening's and then Keefe's engine seizures and subsequent off-the-runway excursions—Greenamyer *had not* pulled up. He had held his same tight line, hugging the floor of the desert, while his rivals, including Shelton, pulled up and lost ground behind him. Shelton, who had lost the race by a matter of seconds, was complaining that Greenamyer used the situation to win the race.

There were other complaints. Greenamyer had flown dangerously low, according to several observers. And on the southern leg of the race he had flown outside the boundaries of the course, swooping too close to the pits, ramp, and the grandstands.

After a huddle, the contest committee decided to levy fines against Greenamyer for three different rules infractions. But they disallowed Shelton's protest. Greenamyer was still the champion. He could keep his trophy and the prize money.

The matter was closed, or so everyone thought. But between Shelton and Greenamyer now festered the kind of cold-eyed contempt that fighter pilots reserved for enemies they wanted to blow out of the sky. *That cocky little son of a bitch!*

Greenamyer couldn't have cared less. He flew home with his trophy. All that petty carping about low flying and course boundaries and such—to hell with it. That was history, he figured.

He figured wrong.

Greenamyer's war with the rest of the world was just beginning.

The FAA, which governed *every* aerial event in the country, also maintained a watchful presence at the Reno races. Muddling along at its own stately pace, the FAA had reached a conclusion: *Hey, if this guy Greenamyer was dangerous enough to merit a fine from his own race committee, then he obviously violated some federal air regulations, too.*

So they did the worst thing the FAA could do to a pilot like Darryl Greenamyer: They suspended his pilot's license. Greenamyer, who made his living as a professional test pilot, was grounded.

Which was why, in April 1972, he found himself in court trying to prove that he, in fact, did *not* fly outside the FAA's designated racecourse boundary. After a protracted case involving charts of the racecourse and witnesses and experts, he won his case. He had his license to fly. He'd beaten the bureaucracy. It meant he could race again next year.

Wrong again.

He had to contend with yet another bureaucracy. The Reno race committee now invoked its own labyrinthine logic: If Greenamyer actually flew so recklessly as to receive a fine (from us), which was an offense heinous enough to receive a suspension from the FAA (thrown out but obviously not without merit), then we have to demonstrate how serious we are about safety here at the Reno races.

So the race committee demonstrated how serious they were: They banned Darryl Greenamyer from next year's race.

The T-shirts were ubiquitous. You saw them in the grandstands, the pits, around the hotel bars, wherever race people gathered. Nobody knew for sure where the T-shirts came from, but the message printed on them was clear: *If You Can't Beat 'Em, Ban 'Em.*

The fans were letting the race officials know how they felt about the banning of their favorite racer. Air-racing aficionados loved Greenamyer precisely for the reasons that he had been banned: because he was flamboyant both in the air and on the ground. And because he was a winner.

Greenamyer could be seen out there on the ramp that year, anyway. And so could his natural-metal-surfaced Bearcat, *Conquest I.* Since he couldn't fly in the races, he had selected a NASA test pilot named Richard Laidley to fly his Bearcat.

But when the racing began and the spectators got their first look at the Greenamyer Bearcat roaring around the course, they all had the same thought: *If that's not Greenamyer, it's somebody just like him.*

It was pure déjà vu. Laidley was flying the Bearcat, if anything, even *lower and tighter* than the hard-charging Greenamyer. Laidley was coming so low around the pylons that the judges, thinking for sure his wingtip would catch the ground, ducked for cover. They could see the little vortices being kicked up in the dirt by the Bearcat's propeller.

Watching the low-flying Laidley, Stan Brown, the chief race judge, just shook his head. He tried not to notice the glacial stare of the unsmiling FAA official standing next to him. *Damn*, thought Brown. *Here we go again.*

Laidley's tight line kept him in first place until the end of the fourth lap. It was then that Gunther Balz, flying his sleek Mustang, *Roto-Finish Special*, made his move. From back in the pack he shot past second-place Lyle Shelton's Bearcat, then took the lead from Laidley.

Balz was making history. For the first time, a Mustang was beating the invincible Bearcats and staying in the race. In the bleachers, the fans were on their feet. Now this was a race!

Three more laps. Two more. Now the fans were collectively holding their breath, *willing* that howling Merlin engine to hang together just a little longer.

The final lap. Would he make it?

The Mustang's engine held together.

Balz's Mustang ripped across the finish line in a new record speed of 416.16 miles per hour. It was nearly 3 miles per hour faster than the record set the previous year by Greenamyer's Bearcat.

Now Laidley, who had finished close behind Balz, was the new object of the race committee's wrath. For his low flying around the course, he was disqualified.

For the Greenamyer crew, this was the end of the line. Not only had Greenamyer himself been banned from this year's race; now his designated pilot, Laidley, was *disqualified*. No second-place trophy. Worse, no prize money. *Nada.*

Greenamyer was disgusted. This was it, he told everyone. Screw it. He was finished with racing. *Adios* to the assholes. Reno had seen the last of Darryl Greenamyer.

No one who knew Greenamyer believed it.

✈ 15 ✈

Red Baron

Someday that thing is going to bite somebody in the ass.
—*Mac McClain, circa 1978*

Whenever he wanted, Steve Hinton could close his eyes and summon a defining moment in his life. It was an image of *brown*—the monotonous beige desertscape of Nevada—and of gullies, sagebrush, and boulders the size of trucks. All rushing up to meet him. It was an image Hinton could summon whenever he needed to remind himself of why he didn't race anymore.

It was the Gold Trophy race of 18 September 1979, and Hinton was flying the hottest air racer in the world—the *Red Baron*. The Mustang was so highly modified, they gave it a unique designation: RB-51. It's most exotic feature was the big Griffon engine, a more powerful variant of the Rolls-Royce Merlin, which had been installed in late-model Spitfire fighters. Just like Gary Levitz's experimental *Miss Ashley II* twenty years later, this Griffon-powered Mustang had *six* contrarotating blades—three whirling clockwise and three counterclockwise. The Griffon was a 2,239-cubic-inch power plant that, in its stock version, produced 2,300 horsepower.

The Dave Zeuschel–modified engine in the *Red Baron* was cranking out something closer to 4,000 horsepower.

The *Red Baron* represented a breakthrough in Unlimited Air Racing. Veteran racer—and master salesman—Mac McClain was the creator and initial promoter of the *Red Baron*. He had sold the idea of a *Red Baron* racing team to Idaho aviation entrepreneur Ed Browning. Browning then gave McClain the go-ahead for the development of the Mustang they called the RB-51, including the switch from the traditional Merlin engine to the Griffon, with its scissors-like, contrarotating propellers.

For the first couple years, McClain was the RB-51's only pilot. He raced the new machine at Reno in 1975, blowing the engine, and again in 1976, when he dropped out with a canopy that would not lock. But these were problems peculiar to any new racer, as McClain well knew. The *Red Baron* was proving itself to be the fastest Mustang in the world. McClain was looking forward to the 1977 Unlimited Race.

Meanwhile, the self-exiled crown prince of air racing, Darryl Greenamyer, was back. Watching the formation of the *Red Baron* organization, Greenamyer had glimpsed an opportunity. He was rebuilding a Lockheed F-104 Starfighter, an exotic supersonic jet fighter with the lines of a lawn dart, to make an attempt on the world speed record. He managed to persuade Browning to include his F-104—relabeled the *RB-104*—in the *Red Baron* stable. Browning also recruited Greenamyer—a six-time Reno winner—to fly his stock Mustang, *The Flying Undertaker,* at Reno in 1976. Greenamyer showed his old prowess by taking second place in the Gold. Browning was impressed.

So impressed, in fact, that for the 1977 race, he appointed Greenamyer as the *Red Baron*'s new pilot. Gone from the roster was the racer's developer and original pilot, Mac McClain. In the cockpit now was the legendary Greenamyer, with a new patron and a new shot at Reno glory. McClain, angry and disappointed, packed up and left the team.

The Unlimited Race in 1977 was a classic Greenamyer performance. Flying the *Red Baron,* he grabbed an early lead, then widened it. None of the other competitors came close enough to threaten him. He flashed across the finish line with an average speed of 430.70—a new race record.

Having won his seventh Unlimited Championship, Greenamyer stayed in character. He announced that he was taking a walk, Gold Trophy in hand. Again. Off to pursue new adventures. Thanks and *adios.*

Again, no one believed him.

Meanwhile, the record-setting *Red Baron* needed another pilot. Mac McClain, soured by being bumped in favor of Greenamyer, wasn't coming back. He had found himself a new Mustang project and a new sponsor, truck baron Wiley Sanders.

For the next several months, during the long season between Reno races, the number-one subject of speculation was: Who would race the RB-51? Who could fill the shoes of the great Greenamyer?

And then Ed Browning, owner of the *Red Baron* team, surprised the hell out of everyone. Instead of casting about for another veteran test pilot and racer like Greenamyer, he chose someone from inside the team. He named a guy who had been *working* on the airplane and who, on only a few occasions, had been drafted to ferry the thing to where it would be raced.

Steve Hinton was a tall, skinny guy with a hawklike beak and an obsession for hot fighters. Though he was twenty-six, he looked more like eighteen. Standing in the company of grizzled veterans like McClain, Lefty Gardner, and John Crocker, Hinton looked like one of their sons. Though no one wanted to come out and say it, it probably hadn't hurt Hinton's chances of being chosen to race the RB-51 that he happened to be engaged to Karen Maloney, daughter of the museum's founder and boss, Ed Maloney.

Despite Hinton's lack of experience, savvy gamblers were still placing their bets on the *Red Baron.* Even without Greenamyer in the cockpit, it was clear to everyone who knew racing that the RB-51 had no real competitors this year.

Which was exactly the way it seemed, watching the qualifications early in the week. Hinton qualified the RB-51 with a respectable 425 miles per hour; his closest rival, Cliff Cummins, in *Miss Candace*, clocked at only 400 miles per hour. And then, on Saturday, the day before the championship race, some things happened to take everyone's mind off the coming Unlimited contest.

Anyone who knew anything about racing had a feeling about this one: Something wasn't right.

It was the first lap of the T-6 consolation race. The big droning T-6 Texans were bunched up in a tight cluster—*too* tight—going around pylons on the pace lap. They were so close, you could tell that something was going to happen.

And it did—the most dreaded occurrence in racing. Two of the T-6s came together. One, flown by rookie pilot and flight surgeon Dimitry Prian, chopped up the propeller of the other T-6, then disintegrated in a shower of chaff and metal debris. The other T-6, with veteran Don DeWalt in the cockpit, fell like a dropped safe and impacted the desert in a mushroom of dirt and smoke. Both pilots were killed.

After fifteen years of racing at Reno, the unthinkable had finally happened—a midair collision. Sure, there had been other fatalities, but they involved air-show performers and, in one instance, an incapacitated pilot. A midair was a pilot's worst nightmare. And it had finally happened.

A grimness settled over the crowd like a pall. Still numbed by the tragedy of the T-6s, the fans watched the start of the Unlimited heat. Bill Whittington, flying a rare P-51H, declared a Mayday and aimed his Mustang for runway 26, right in front of the stands. He had a propeller-control problem and was eager to land.

Too eager, as it turned out. Whittington's problem was so urgent that he opted to land *downwind,* which added to his already-excessive speed over the runway. Then he compounded the problem by plunking the fighter nearly halfway down the eight-thousand-foot strip of concrete.

Again, everyone who had watched these big racers more than a few times knew without doubt what would happen next. Off he went—*Ploooof!*—into the sagebrush and sand, just as several of his predecessors over the years had done. Except that Whittington's Mustang wasn't just dribbling off the end of the concrete. He was hauling ass, hopping and careening across the desert like a derailed locomotive.

Ahead lay a fence. And standing along the fence was the usual crowd of nonpaying spectators, gathered outside the field's perimeter to watch a free show. Now the freeloaders were getting a *real* show—an up-close-and-personal view of a P-51 Mustang fighter bearing down on them like a buzz saw.

"Ground-loop it!" Bob Hoover was yelling on the radio. Hoover was in the chase plane directly overhead. He could see the carnage at the fence about to unfold. "Ground-loop it!"

A ground loop was usually an accidental maneuver, but it was also an effective way to stop an out-of-control fighter on the ground. It amounted to a reversal of direction, swinging the airplane's tail around in a violent arc, swapping ends.

And that's what Hoover was yelling at Whittington to do, *Stop the damned airplane!* Slew the Mustang's tail around and stop before he caromed into the fence and sliced up the freeloading spectators like salami.

Whittington finally got the idea. Still lurching across the desert at nearly 50 miles per hour, he stomped the rudder pedal. The Mustang veered around. The landing gear broke away. The fighter skidded sideways along on its belly, shedding pieces as it went. In an eruption of sand and sagebrush, the Mustang kept bumping and sliding toward the fence, closer, and ground to a clattering stop.

A shower of Mustang pieces and dirt and sagebrush and coyote crap rained down on the goggle-eyed freeloaders along the fence. Several were reported to have soiled their underwear. Others made instant vows *never* to go near another air show. Free or otherwise.

The Sunday Gold Trophy race went as the gamblers had predicted. Almost.

As usual, it began with Hoover leading his flock of racers down the chute, heading for the starting pylon, giving them his standard peel-off blessing: *Gentlemen, you have a race . . .*

Just as expected, the RB-51, flown by Steve Hinton, surged into the lead. But then something not at all expected happened: Somebody else surged right up there with him.

It was Don Whittington, older brother of the luckless Bill Whittington, who had terrified the freeloaders at the fence the day before. Whittington, flying his hot Mustang, *Precious Metal,* was staying right on Hinton's tail.

Then, rounding pylon 1 on the first official lap, Whittington *passed* Hinton. And then Hinton nudged the throttle up in *Red Baron* and retook the lead.

On the next lap, Whittington again passed.

And Hinton again retook the lead.

The fans in the grandstands, chilled into numbness both by the frigid Sierra wind and by the tragedies of the day before, were on their feet. Now they had something worth watching. This was a real race!

So it went for six laps: Whittington passed. Hinton retook the lead. Back and forth, the two Mustangs only a few feet apart. When they roared past the finish line, Hinton was in front, but only by a few feet.

The fans loved it. This was what they had come to see. The *Red Baron* had again won the Unlimited Championship, but by only seven-tenths of a second. Hinton averaged 415.46 miles per hour, while Whittington came in at 414.77. It was one of the most closely contested Unlimited Races in history.

Too damned close, grumbled some of the old-timers that night at the bar. They *knew* the RB-51 should have walked away with the race; 415 miles per hour! That was a snail's pace for the *Red Baron*. Hell, it was 15 miles per hour slower than Greenamyer's record-setting speed last year.

Of course, the only record that history would remember was that Steve Hinton was the 1978 Unlimited champion. At twenty-six, he was the youngest pilot ever to win a Thompson or Unlimited Trophy. But to the guys at the bar, one thing was for sure: The kid wasn't another Greenamyer. Not yet.

Next year, in the summer of 1979, Hinton took the *Red Baron* up to Tonopah, in the north Nevada flats, to go after the world's 3-kilometer speed record. And though he managed to set a new record—499.018 miles per hour—it was a frustrating accomplishment.

On the first attempt at the record, Hinton blew the RB-51's Griffon engine. He was able to land it without any problem, and the *Red Baron* crew quickly installed the spare Griffon engine. But it was their *only* spare, and the Reno races were less than a month away. And that meant that after this next record attempt, they'd be going to Reno with that same overstrained Griffon engine still churning in the *Red Baron*. The 12-cylinder, water-cooled Griffon, the team was learning, could be just as bitchy and temperamental as its sister engine, the Merlin.

And though the RB-51 had managed to shatter the world's record, it still came up tantalizingly short—less than 1 mile per hour—of the magic 500-mile-per-hour barrier. It would have had immense symbolic value to break through the 500 wall.

So that meant Hinton and his team still had unfinished business. Sometime after Reno, they promised themselves, they'd take the *Red Baron* back for another shot at the 500 mark.

No one, including Hinton, was happy about racing the *Red Baron* again in the Reno Unlimited contest without a fresh engine. But everyone was keeping his reservations to himself.

Everyone but Mac McClain, the RB-51's original pilot. McClain was now involved with a new Mustang racer called *Jeannie,* but he stayed abreast of developments over at the *Red Baron* team. One morning, before the qualifying heats, McClain was standing on the ramp gazing at the long-snouted *Red Baron's* contrarotating propellers and its trim, bulletlike lines. The Mustang looked like a killer angel. "Someday," he said to no one in particular, "that thing is going to bite somebody in the ass."

Things were looking good, though, for Steve Hinton and the *Red Baron* team as the 1979 race week commenced. They had a new, deep-pockets sponsorship in the form of Michelob. The *Red Baron* wore a glitzy red-and-white paint scheme, the name of the new sponsor adorning the fuselage.

By the end of Tuesday, things were *really* looking good. That was the day Hinton ran the RB-51 around the course to rack up a new-record qualifying speed of 441.90 miles per hour. A wave of cheers ran through the *Red Baron* team. The Griffon engine they were so concerned about was holding together! The RB-51 was still the fastest mount at Reno, right?

Well, not really. On Thursday, Mac McClain took his new mount, *Jeannie,* around the course at a qualifying speed of 446.93 miles per hour. Which trashed, by a considerable margin, the record just set by Hinton and sent a seismic tremor through the *Red Baron* camp.

McClain again. The guy was turning into the *Red Baron* team's worst dream. McClain was behaving like a rejected baseball player who had come back to hit bases-loaded homers against his old team. It had already begun to dawn on a few people that McClain was perhaps more than just a good ol' Alabama boy—a guy who liked to mess with machinery. Now they remembered that it was

McClain who had conceived the original RB-51 concept and then went on to make it a winner. Now he was doing it with another Mustang. McClain was turning out to be one of those rare characters who not only *built* hellaciously fast airplanes; he could fly them, too. And in these Reno qualifications, the good ol' Alabama boy was blowing their doors off.

Jeannie, McClain's hot new Mustang, was still in the teething stage. She was fast as hell, but still troubled by problems that attended every new and exotic race plane. McClain's crew had slaved over the racer right up to the minute of its departure for Reno. Just before the deadline, the Mustang arrived at Reno, still unpainted, looking like a refugee from a boneyard.

Even as McClain was pulling up after his record-setting qualification lap, his pit crew could hear a perceptible *Pop! Pop! Pop!*—an ominous backfiring from the finicky Merlin engine. It was a portent of the problems they would face later in the week.

Friday was the first day of the heat races. Usually, these early races didn't mean much. Their main purpose was to provide some preliminary racing for the fans and to determine the eventual pole starting positions for the next heat race on Saturday, which in turn sorted out the racers for the Sunday trophy race. The only real competition during the heat races was between the back-of-the-pack airplanes, jockeying for their slots in the Silver and Bronze events Sunday. The faster, Gold contenders tended to dog it during the early heats. With their more temperamental, fine-tuned engines, the idea was to play it cool on Friday. Take a leisurely stroll around the course. Save the motor for the big push Sunday.

Not today. Mac McClain was changing the script. At the start of the first Unlimited Gold heat, McClain startled the hell out of everyone in the field by cramming the throttle to *Jeannie*, roaring hellbent for the first pylon as if this were the last race of his life. A surprised Steve Hinton shoved his own throttle up and clung to

McClain's tail. Just behind him, John Crocker, flying *Sumthin' Else,* did the same.

The tepid first Unlimited heat race had just turned into a grudge match.

McClain was giving no quarter to the red-and-white scissors-bladed Mustang fastened to his tail. You could almost see the grin spreading over the Alabaman's face. How sweet it was! He was competing against the very airplane that he had built into the most formidable racing machine in the world and from which he had been so rudely deposed as its pilot.

And he was kicking ass.

The fans came alive. What was supposed to be a ho-hum promenade around the desert was turning into a bitterly fought contest. For what stakes? No one knew. Nor did anyone care, at least for the moment. All the careful engine-saving gamesmanship and the clever strategies of big-time air racing—all that was being thrown to the desert wind. The pilots were in the grip of a primordial instinct: *Beat that son of a bitch!*

Which was what Mac McClain was doing, but not by a wide margin. A few plane lengths behind, Steve Hinton was battling John Crocker for second place. As the three racers howled down the straightaway in front of the grandstands, it was clear that nobody was sparing his precious engine. For whatever quirky reason, each was shoving his throttle to the limit. To hell with babying the motor.

Mac McClain got his sweet retribution. *Jeannie* flashed across the finish line a few feet ahead of *Red Baron,* which was a foot ahead of *Sumthin' Else.* McClain's speed was 413.80, while Hinton's was 413.07. John Crocker finished at a laggardly 412.67.

What did it mean? Nothing, at least officially. But rarely had anyone at Reno seen such a closely contested *heat race.* The fans had gotten more excitement than they expected on a ho-hum Friday afternoon. For very personal reasons the pilots had flogged their engines like jockeys whipping their mounts. Now they could only hope they hadn't flogged them *too* much.

. . .

As it turned out, Friday's heat race was the first—and last—time that Mac McClain would taste the sweet contentment of blowing away the *Red Baron*.

The Saturday Unlimited heat race started out looking exactly like the day before. Just as he had done on that day, McClain seized a quick lead. He seemed bent on continuing his humiliation of the *Red Baron* organization. McClain held his lead as the cluster of Unlimiteds roared around the pace lap.

Then things went to hell. Entering the second—and first official—lap, McClain pulled up, calling, "Mayday." *Jeannie's* engine was sputtering, running rough. McClain managed to put the Mustang down without incident on runway 08. *Jeannie* was out of that day's race.

Which left Hinton and Crocker to slug it out for the lead. But with McClain gone from the fray, most of yesterday's feral, gut-shooting competitiveness was gone, too. Crocker slid into a comfortable lead, and Hinton seemed content to cruise around the course in the number-two position. The front-runners, being conservative, saved their motors for the big one tomorrow.

Without having to battle for position, Crocker was able to sail across the finish line at a zippy 420 miles per hour. Hinton came home four seconds behind him. The race's only significance was that Crocker would get the pole position for the start of the Gold race Sunday.

For the fans, it had none of Friday's excitement. Just another predictable heat race. And just as boring.

Sunday was one of those perfect autumn afternoons in Reno, the sky so clear you could see all the way west to the High Sierra range. For once, the capricious Reno wind was not howling down across the high desert. In the stands, an overflow crowd smeared themselves with sun lotion and basked in the warm Nevada sun. A hum of excitement crackled across the grandstands and through the pits.

The championship Gold Trophy race was shaping up to be one of the best contests in Unlimited history.

But down in the pits, in the *Jeannie* camp, Dave Zeuschel, the master Merlin engine builder and anointed caretaker of *Jeannie's* power plant, felt like pulling his hair out. It was the same damned inexplicable problem, the kind of thing that made racers and crew chiefs go crazy. What the hell was wrong? At first he was sure it was just bad spark plugs, something he could readily fix. But just as he thought they'd cleared the problem, it came back. Was it bad fuel? Why wasn't anyone else having the problem?

It was maddening. Only a couple of hours from the championship race and they still weren't sure they'd found the problem.

Meanwhile, the serious bettors at Reno were putting their money on *Red Baron*. They were convinced that Hinton had been holding back, even yielding the pole position to Crocker after Saturday's race, saving his Griffon engine for the main event Sunday. When Hinton headed for the pylons in the trophy race, *Red Baron* would blow them all away.

In the *Red Baron* pit area, no one was having such sanguine feelings. After the record-breaking assault up at Tonopah, then the balls-out, go-for-broke race on Friday, and yet another hard push yesterday, they were just keeping their fingers crossed. The Griffon wasn't any different from a Merlin when it came to self-destructing. Both engines, when tweaked and stretched and pumped like these race motors, were like powder kegs with the fuse lit. There was no question about *whether* the damn things would blow. Just when.

The same silent supplication was playing like a mantra in everyone's mind that Sunday afternoon: *Please, not yet. Just one more race . . .*

"Gentlemen, you're looking good. . . . Gentlemen . . . you . . . have . . . a . . . race!"

Showtime. Hoover's Mustang peeled away, and the Unlimited racers shot ahead like quarter horses out of the chute. John Crocker, who now owned the pole position after winning the Saturday heat race, seized a quick lead heading downhill toward the first pylon. Hinton slid into a loose number-two position, from where he could watch and wait for Crocker to make a mistake.

At least he wouldn't have to worry about McClain.

Jeannie—and McClain—were no longer in the race. McClain had just gotten airborne, still joining up on the pace plane with the other contestants, when things started going to hell. The engine was bucking and popping like a jackhammer. As the other racers were heading down the chute, McClain was rolling the wheels of his Mustang onto the concrete of runway 08 back at Stead Field. The gremlin that had been troubling *Jeannie*'s Merlin engine was back with a fury. *Jeannie* would not be racing today.

It was now a two-plane race. Down in the grandstands, you could hear the fans groan. They were disappointed because today's race had been hyped as a 400-plus-mile-per-hour grudge match between the *Red Baron* gang and McClain's bunch, the Wiley Sanders team, who owned *Jeannie*. And, of course, they had been surprised by the hard-charging John Crocker, whose *Sumthin' Else* was now blazing around the course at near-record speed—ahead of *Red Baron*.

The truth was, John Crocker was just as driven to score a win here at Reno as McClain or Hinton. For four years he'd been a contender for the Gold Trophy, and each time he'd seen the prize slip from his grasp. In 1976 he'd led the pack across the finish line, only to be told that he'd been disqualified for breaking the deadline (the invisible southern boundary of the course, along the east-west runway, that separates the racers from the pit area). In 1977 he'd lost his propeller control during a practice session and wound up putting it in short of the runway, causing serious damage to a wing spar on the Mustang. Staying true to form in 1978, his engine again blew, drenching the slick Mustang in oil and black gunk and ending yet another run for the Gold.

FLY LOW, *FLY FAST*

Now Crocker was out in front. And no way in hell was he going to give Hinton, back there in the RB-51, *any* chance to steal it from him.

By the fourth lap Crocker had opened up a substantial lead on *Red Baron*. And as Hinton flew down the straightaway in front of the pits, it was obvious why he was losing ground to Crocker: The RB-51's Griffon engine sounded like a chorus of chain saws. Hinton was using just enough power to stay in the race and try to hang on to second place. Without full power on the Griffon, he had no chance of catching Crocker.

Meanwhile, Crocker was pushing his Mustang, *Sumthin' Else*, to the limit. He was moving so well ahead of the pack, his crew chief told him on the eighth lap he could ease off a little on the throttle. Pamper the engine a little. You've got the trophy in the bag.

It was then that Hinton received a strange report from his crew on their discrete radio frequency: *He was gaining on Crocker.* How could that be? Did Crocker also have a sick engine? If so, the last laps of this trophy race would be a contest of cripples.

So he shoved the throttle up again—and immediately wished he hadn't. The sick Griffon engine sounded sicker. It was making noises like a dying concrete mixer. But Hinton hung in there. One more lap. Maybe Crocker's engine would fold.

Crocker's engine, of course, was doing fine. Hinton had gained on him because McClain, knowing that the *Red Baron* was no threat, was babying his own engine. And then, when *his* crew reported that Hinton was moving up, he just shoved the throttle again. No problem. And the gap again widened.

John Crocker took the checkered flag a full ten seconds ahead of Steve Hinton in the *Red Baron*. He finished with a respectable 422 miles per hour, while Hinton came in at 415 miles per hour.

As Hinton hauled the RB-51's nose up from his final lap, experiencing that rush of relief and exhilaration every racer felt after the last lap of a trophy race, he had the vague notion—a momentary uneasiness—that his rough-running engine was sounding even rougher. But hell, it was still running, still developing power. Anyway, the high power demands of the race were behind him. Even with the sick engine, he had managed to hang on to the second-place trophy. He had made the best of a bad situation. All he had to do now was land.

He didn't think it was necessary to declare a Mayday. Not with the engine still running the way it was. He would just expedite his landing. The slower-running airplanes in the race were still coming down the straightaway toward the finish line.

All he had to do now was make a right turn toward the southeast. Get rid of his excess altitude and kinetic energy. Set up for a landing on runway 26.

It was then that Hinton, still slowing the Mustang and maneuvering to land toward the west, made the worst decision of his flying career. He turned *away* from the airport.

It was one of those little mistakes, seemingly innocuous at the moment. He *knew* the engine was going bad. He *knew* he had to get the thing on the ground. After all, he'd had plenty of warning; the damned Griffon engine had started behaving like a popcorn machine by the fourth lap. He'd throttled back, turning the race over to Crocker. All Hinton wanted was to hang in there, just finish the race, collect what prize money he could, and avoid racking up one of those ignominious DNFs (did not finish) in the race results.

The fans, of course, didn't yet have an inkling of what was happening up there with Hinton's faltering airplane engine. They were still watching the late finishers battle it out for the last places in the Gold Trophy race, listening to announcer Sandy Sanders go on in his breathless style: "And here they come, folks, number eighty-five, the *Fat Cat* Mustang flown by Clay Klabo, taking the flag in fourth place."

For that matter, Steve Hinton himself didn't know what was

happening, either. He was in a left turn now, *away* from the safe haven of Stead Field's long concrete runways. His plan was to crank it around in a big, meandering leftward circle several miles out there southeast of the airport, then bring it back to land on runway 26.

He saw that he was still high, still zipping along with plenty of extra airspeed left over from his 400-plus mile-per-hour dash to the finish line. He started to lower a few degrees of landing flaps, get rid of some airspeed, get the Mustang slowed down. With the throttle retarded on the RB-51, some of the engine roughness seemed to have subsided.

It was an illusion. What Hinton didn't know was that inside the clanking Griffon engine a deadly chain of events was already in progress.

A bearing had failed, which now caused the engine's custom-built supercharger gears to drop out of their track, which caused the gears to disintegrate. The debris from it, in turn, ruined the engine oil pump, resulting in a cessation of oil flow to the internal components of the Griffon, which, without its supply of precious lubricating oil, *was about to seize!*

And so it did. The RB-51's mighty Griffon engine stopped dead. And so did all six contrarotating propeller blades. Even worse, they went flat, perpendicular to the airstream, giving the Mustang the gliding characteristics of an anvil.

Then the twenty-seven-year-old pilot depressed his microphone button and transmitted his version of what fighter pilots in distress have *always* said in times of calamity: "I'm in deep shit now!"

And he was.

Hinton had never peered out over the nose like this—airborne, at least—through *stopped* propeller blades. Normally, his only view of the propellers when he was flying was just the blurred silver disc of the whirling blades up there over the nose.

Now he could count the things. All six blades. They looked like big paddle-shaped speed brakes. Each flat-pitched blade had the effect of stopping the Mustang's slick forward progress through the air. The big, unmoving propeller was dragging the *Red Baron* to the floor of the desert like an anchor.

One truth became instantly clear to Hinton: He wasn't going to make runway 26. He wasn't going to make *any* runway. He was going to plop down somewhere there in the deep valley that lay short of runway 26. And he could see what was waiting for him down there: rocks, gullies, hills, boulders the size of Buicks. All the same ghastly hue of *brown*.

Every eyeball at Stead Field was riveted on the tiny red-and-white object descending into the valley out there off the end of the runway. The announcer, Sandy Sanders, was telling the crowd, "Steve Hinton has called a Mayday, folks, and he's going to land the *Red Baron* on runway two-six."

No one believed it. Not even the most unknowledgeable race spectator thought that the little falling object out there was going to land anywhere except in the Nevada boondocks. Each observer had the same tightening sensation in the gut, watching the *Red Baron* drop out of the sky like a felled pigeon. Overhead, they could see Bob Hoover's yellow Mustang racing toward where the RB-51 was making its rendezvous with the earth.

As Hinton's racer was settling into the valley to the east of the airport, those listening to radios were treated to a snippet of real-life melodrama. Just as the Mustang disappeared into the sagebrush, Hinton keyed his microphone for the last time: "Tell Karen I love her."

It was like a line from a 1960s teenage movie. Karen Maloney was Hinton's fiancée. It was so corny and melodramatic, so unexpected, coming as it did from the cockpit of a doomed fighter, it electrified everyone who heard it.

The RB-51 dropped out of sight.

Seconds later, the hushed crowd saw what they most feared to

see. From the floor of the valley spewed a geyser of dirt like a vol-
canic eruption. Then a pulsating orange flash . . . and the thick gush
of evil black smoke.

In the grandstands, spectators groaned. Race fans burst into
tears. Grizzled crew chiefs in the pits swore and turned their eyes
away from the towering column of black smoke.

Bob Hoover observed the carnage from above. Circling the site,
he radioed what he saw to Race Control. They, in turn, passed the
information on to the announcer's stand, where Sandy Sanders
grabbed his microphone and blurted out the news to the fans.

"Folks, it looks like we've lost Steve Hinton!"

It was a hell of a ride. First came the impact of the 170-mile-per-
hour landing—*Kablam! Blam!*—tortured aluminum ripping over the
desert, bumping and jolting, banging through the rocks and dwarf
trees like a goddamn runaway ammunition truck.

Was it going to blow?

Stupid thought. Hell, it *had* to blow. The airplane wasn't an airplane anymore, just a high-octane fuel bomb, skipping along with
its fuse burning. Of course it would blow. Hinton tried to hunker
down in the seat, instinctively seeking a fetal position.

He had the vague impression of going uphill. . . . Yes, for sure, he
was going up an incline. . . . *Oh, shit!* A boulder the size of a truck—
Whump!—the wing shearing away, flipping over the fuselage like a
piece of cardboard, gushing fuel—*Kabloom!* There it was, the explosion. . . . He could see the orange inferno, *feel* the intense heat of the
flash. . . .

Still ricocheting along, still going uphill—*Wham!*—another rock,
the other wing shearing away—*Boom! Boom!*—more explosions,
more flame . . . all behind him.

Cresting the hill, pieces flying off the airplane like confetti . . .
wings gone, canopy gone.

Going *downhill* now—*Crump!*—hitting something with the nose . . .

the engine separating from the front of the fuselage, lurching, sliding . . .

Where was the fire?

Still behind him. Everything behind the crest of the hill . . . all the big pieces, wings, tail section . . . the fire and smoke . . .

The lurching stopped. At least he thought it had stopped. He was still strapped in the seat, numb, no feeling, not sure, even, if he was alive. His ears were still roaring with the dreadful cacophony of the crash. Nothing was recognizable. Nothing seemed to be left of the *Red Baron.* Every scrap of metal around him looked as if it had been through a shredder. Behind him, the pall of black smoke was billowing into the Nevada sky.

New sensations . . . something coming . . . engines and sirens . . . the *whop-whopping* of helicopter rotor blades. And he wasn't totally numb anymore. Something hurt. Everything hurt. Jesus, it hurt like hell!

They radioed the news back to the announcer's stand. Sandy Sanders was moved to seize his microphone and issue an amendment to his death pronouncement: "Folks, they have just taken a living, breathing Steve Hinton to the hospital via helicopter."

You could feel the wave of relief that swept over the airfield. The fans in the grandstands were cheering and hugging each other. They had been through an emotional wringer. Many who had wept openly when Sanders announced that Hinton was gone were now bawling with joy. *He was alive!* It was a miracle. The whole thing had played out like the script of a Tom Cruise movie.

In the *Red Baron* pits, the crew had been in the depths of despair. The loss of the *Red Baron* was tragic enough, but Steve Hinton was one of *them.* He had been one of the original crew members of the project, turning wrenches and doing gofer jobs and paying his dues. When the orange fireball erupted from the floor of the desert, it was like losing a family member.

Now there were grins and handshakes and hugs all around. Never mind, for the moment at least, that the world's fastest Unlimited race plane had been transformed to tinsel.

John Crocker, after four frustrating years, had finally triumphed at Reno. But it was an empty victory. Before he could land and collect his prize and revel in the glory of his first Unlimited Championship, Hinton's crash had captured the crowd's attention. Crocker was a forgotten entity. No one cared *who* won the damned race. The crowd was fixated on that ominous column of black smoke rising from the desert—and the fate of Steve Hinton.

Now that the smoke had dissipated and Hinton was alive, the matter of who won the race seemed anticlimactic. The Unlimited Championship . . . Oh, yeah . . . Who was the guy who finished first? John *who?*

Crocker was a good sport. He accepted his trophy and thanked everyone. And he expressed his relief that his friend, Steve Hinton, was still with them. Then he and the team of *Sumthin' Else* got on with their own celebration.

Hinton was a mess. After being extracted from the wreckage of the *Red Baron,* he was airlifted to the Washoe County Medical Center. His injuries included a broken left ankle, a smashed right kneecap, multiple bruised and broken ribs, back injuries, lung damage, and so many lacerations and cuts that he looked like the victim of a glass-factory explosion.

Hinton was a tough kid who possessed the rude good health of youth. In two days he was sitting up and cracking jokes with friends. In a month he was back home. In a short while, he was flying. In due time he was even racing again.

But it would never be the same. Racing had nearly killed him. And in the years to come he would see it kill his friends.

✈ 16 ✈

Hoover

There are old pilots, and there are bold pilots.
But there are no old, bold pilots.
—*aviation adage*
—*exception to aviation adage:*
R. A. "Bob" Hoover

The nose. That's what you noticed on first meeting Bob Hoover. Hoover had a proboscis on him like the prow of an icebreaker. That long, bulbous nose had been exposed to so many unwanted sun rays, so many hard days and late nights, you expected it to glow in the dark.

Hoover had always been tall and skinny, but in later years, wearing his broad-brimmed, straw sun hat and the Nomax flight suit, he looked like one of those Don Quixote stick figures. At an air show back in the seventies, Tennessee Ernie Ford had called him "a two iron with an Adam's apple."

That was one of the paradoxes about Hoover that always fooled people. They'd see him out there on the ramp at the air show, that lanky stick figure with the straw hat and the flight suit, and they figured him to be someone from an assisted-living facility. A spindly old guy they wouldn't trust to park a golf cart.

And then they saw him fly.

He would crank up the twin-engined Shrike executive aircraft right there in front of the crowd. He would take off, then haul the nose way up high and *roll the thing!* Right over the runway.

That was for starters. He'd come ripping back down the runway, giving the folks four-point, then eight-point, then sixteen-point hesitation rolls. Never mind that this was a twin-engine corporate airplane. Hoover was flying the Shrike as if it were a Pitts Special.

But Hoover's trademark—the heart stopper that air-show spectators never forgot—was the "energy management" sequence. From thirty-five hundred feet over the field, he would dive the Shrike right down to the runway, with *both* engines shut off and the propellers stopped.

Then he pulled up into a loop.

And then an eight-point roll.

He would set up for an approach to the runway, touching down first on one wheel, then pulling up and touching back down on the other.

When he had finally landed the engineless Shrike, Hoover would roll off the runway, onto the taxiway, not a sound coming from the stone-dead engines, rolling, rolling, in front of the grandstands, to a stop.

On the exact spot from where he started. The crowds loved it.

Then he would get out, wave his big straw hat at the crowd, and some would gasp. *God, that old guy is . . . ancient!*

You knew, watching Hoover fly, seeing that big-nosed, grinning, hound-dog face, that you were watching a piece of history. By all rights, he shouldn't have been there. He was an anachronism, a throwback to a bygone era when flamboyant daredevils like Clyde Pangborn and Roscoe Turner and Johnnie Livingston lit up the skies. Hoover should be dead or retired or grounded for terminal craziness.

However, in the sensible, regulated 1990s, he was still comporting himself as if it were the free-for-all, wild-assed Thompson Trophy days of the 1930s. Hoover was a dinosaur who didn't belong in the modern world. He shouldn't be breathing the rarefied air of modern history. But he was still breathing, still flying.

He was one of those larger-than-life characters who seemed to be present at *every* momentous event in aviation. Hoover's career epitomized the fighter pilot's axiom: *Thou shalt go where the action is.*

In 1944, when Bob Hoover was twenty-two, the action was in the skies over Europe. In a swirling dogfight with Luftwaffe Focke-Wulfs, his Spitfire was shot from under him, and he parachuted into the Mediterranean. After being captured, he managed to escape from a German stalag, steal a Luftwaffe FW-190 fighter, and fly away to freedom.

As a test pilot after the war, he flew the P-80 chase plane during Chuck Yeager's history-making first supersonic flight in 1947. It was Hoover, in fact, who had been designated as Yeager's backup pilot for the history-making flight.

Hoover proceeded to put his stamp on every facet of flying. He was the North American Aviation test pilot on the F-86 and F-100 fighters; captain of the United States's world aerobatic team; master air-show pilot. Millions of air-show spectators thrilled to his aerobatic performances in his twin-engined Shrike Commander.

Since the first Reno races back in 1964, Hoover and his yellow Mustang had been as much a part of the scene as pylons and the howling Sierra winds. It was always Hoover who would lead the pack of Unlimiteds down the chute, accelerating to race speed. Approaching the starting pylon, Hoover would line up his covey of racers in an echelon off his right wing. When everything looked right, he banked sharply up and away. "Gentlemen," he said on the radio, "you have a race."

That's the way it had been for years: Hoover bringing the pack down the chute, giving the crowds that little electric shock over the radio: "Gentlemen, you have a race!" They loved it.

But over the years the world changed. The Unlimiteds got faster, hitting speeds in excess of 500 miles per hour. Meanwhile *Ol' Yeller*—and Bob Hoover—weren't getting any faster, just older. Some of the Unlimited racers were heard to complain that Hoover and his Mustang were just taking *too damned long* to get the racers lined up and headed down the chute. Sometimes, chasing around out there over the desert with Hoover, they would be perilously low on fuel before the race had begun. And, of course, *Ol' Yeller,* being a doggy stock Mustang, couldn't fly at the speeds the hot Unlimiteds needed to start a race.

Legend that he was, Hoover was definitely beyond his prime. He was well into his seventies now and looked every day of it. He had always been tall and skinny, but now, on a bad day, he looked like a cadaver in a flight suit.

He still did his engine-out routine in the Shrike, but a few people, including some in the FAA, thought it was time for the old guy to quit. The tough part was: How did they get rid of an icon like Hoover?

Not that they hadn't tried to get rid of him. For several decades the FAA had been pursuing Hoover as if he were a trophy fish. Wherever he showed up to do an air show, he could expect a clipboard-wielding FAA examiner to cite him for some infraction of federal air regulations.

The real reason they hated Hoover wasn't his age. It was because he was, by definition, a "celebrity pilot." He got away with his daredevil, rule-flaunting stuff and rubbed their noses in it. So they issued violations for everything from reckless flying to not possessing parachutes to overflying populated areas.

Hoover was well connected both in the military and in government. He had buddies like Barry Goldwater, Jimmy Doolittle, F. Lee Bailey. Hoover managed to beat most of the violations issued by the FAA. So they issued more.

And he continued to beat them.

And they kept trying to get him. *Get Hoover.* It became a holy war—the feds versus Robert A. Hoover. The war had begun to consume more bureaucratic energy than running the Pentagon.

And finally, one day in 1992, the feds got him.

It happened at an air show in Oklahoma City. Two zealous FAA inspectors who had witnessed Hoover's performance declared—two months after the show—that his performance was marginal. In their judgment, Hoover, at age seventy, no longer had the requisite skills to fly airplanes. Hoover's medical certificate was rescinded, which, in effect, nullified his license to fly. For the first time since he'd been captured by the Nazis half a century ago, Hoover was grounded.

Thus began a three-year range war between pilots and the FAA over the treatment of Bob Hoover. That a government agency could arbitrarily deprive a citizen of his right to fly without due cause or evidence sounded a battle cry around the country. Pilots like Chuck Yeager, Leo Loudenslager, Tom Poberezny, and a host of air-show stars testified in his defense. Attorney F. Lee Bailey volunteered to represent him. A group called the Friends of Bob Hoover raised a massive legal-defense fund.

Hoover had friends in the air-racing community, too. One was Bill Rheinschild, who introduced Hoover to Dr. Brent Hisey, a neurosurgeon and new owner of the veteran Mustang racer *Miss America*. Hisey put Hoover through an extensive set of exams. The results all showed that Hoover still possessed his cognitive and physical capabilities.

Hoover also produced a video made while he was flying a T-28 Trojan with a safety pilot. During the aerobatic routine, the T-28's engine began self-destructing, backfiring and quitting. Hoover managed to land the big trainer, without power, at the end of the runway at Torrance, California.

Armed with the video demonstrating his undiminished ability to fly and Hisey's battery of successful physical exams, Lee Bailey presented Hoover's case to the administrative-law judge. The judge ruled in Hoover's favor. And then the National Transportation Safety Board reversed the decision.

Thus began a series of unsuccessful appeals that went all the way to the U.S. Supreme Court. For Hoover it was a nightmare. To him, the government's strategy was obvious: Stonewall the case. Let time take care of the issue. In a few more years, their contention would be valid: Bob Hoover *would* be too ancient to fly.

The "Hoover affair" sent a seismic wave through the aviation community. The same government agency that regulated *everyone's* right to fly was revealing itself to be a merciless inquisitor. If the FAA could snatch the right to fly from an icon like Bob Hoover, they could do it to anyone.

In the meantime, Hoover *did* receive a license to fly—in Australia. After taking an arduous written exam and an even tougher flight check, he was issued a first-class commercial-airline pilot rating that allowed him to perform his air-show routine anywhere in the world—except the United States.

Hoover continued petitioning the FAA. He submitted to a withering battery of further neurological, physical, and psychological tests. He passed them all.

He was still grounded.

And then, in October 1995, Hoover received a phone call. His license was being reinstated. No explanation or apology was given.

What happened? Somewhere inside the dark sanctum of the FAA, something had cracked. Hoover would never learn what. But it seems clear that the unrelenting pressure from thousands of angry Hoover supporters in the aviation community had taken a toll.

In the range war between Hoover and the FAA, the FAA suffered the most battle damage. It would take years, perhaps forever, to restore the agency's credibility in the eyes of the nation's pilots.

So here it was, 1997, and Hoover was back. It was a touchy situation, because by now the T-33 jet pace plane, flown by Steve Hinton, was a fixture in the Unlimited competition. And even though Hoover's Mustang, *Ol' Yeller,* was back, too—it was sitting out there on the ramp at Reno after a long restoration period—the P-51 was not slated to start any more Unlimited Races. Those days were over, since the Unlimiteds had gotten used to coming down the chute at speeds unattainable by artifacts like *Ol' Yeller.* In fact, it was rumored that *Ol' Yeller* was for sale.

But Hoover *was* on the slate for the air show that accompanied the races. And he was even scheduled to do an air show with the P-51, even though he hadn't flown the Mustang for over five years.

Everyone remembered the old days when he would do things like land on one wheel, then pour the power to the Mustang, pull the nose up, and do a *roll* right over the runway, then land again on the other wheel. Another thing Hoover liked to do was take off and stay low, dropping out of sight into a depression beyond the end of the runway. In the grandstands, spectators would hold their breath. *Oh, my god, what happened?* After several heart-stopping seconds, Hoover would reappear, roaring back at them from another direction, scaring hell out of everyone and enjoying himself immensely.

Well, that was then, and this was now. No one on the Reno airshow committee was happy about letting Hoover make what might be his terminal appearance. His engine-out stuff with the little twin-engine Shrike was one thing, but doing aerobatics with an aging fighter like *Ol' Yeller* was quite another. The last thing the Reno air races needed was for the legendary Bob Hoover to give himself a Viking funeral right there in front of a hundred thousand fans.

On the other hand, the fans still loved the old guy. The word was already out: *Hey, you don't want to miss the air show today. Hoover's going to fly the Mustang.*

Fly it he did. One last time.

It wasn't the old Hoover razzle-dazzle show, but it was still vintage Hoover, if a bit more sedate. More chamber music than symphony. You could see that the love affair between Hoover and the Mustang fighter was an ongoing one. There was the spindly old guy with the bulbous nose, looping and rolling and even doing a little Tennessee waltzing—landing on one gear and then the other—for his fans. And they loved it.

This time, when he parked *Ol' Yeller*, it was for the last time. A buyer had appeared, and the yellow Mustang was sold.

It wasn't the end of the Hoover era. He was still flying the Shrike. But you knew that a certain page in history had been turned. Hearing the growl of *Ol' Yeller*'s Merlin engine out there at Reno, you knew it was Bob Hoover's swan song.

⊱ 17 ⊰

The Trouble with Air Racing

Reno is the kind of place
where you can get 100% credit on your word.
Unless, of course, you break your word. Then you get zero.
—Harry Parker, proprietor of Reno western-wear store

What was wrong with air racing?

It was the same rhetorical question race pilots and owners and lovers of the sport had been asking each other for the past ten years—a subject of every race crew's late-night beer session.

It was hard to figure. How could it be that the fastest motorsport in the world wasn't being embraced by all those same bubbas and speed freaks and groupies that convened by the millions to watch something as two-dimensional and mundane as stock-car racing?

The numbers were depressing. Air racing no longer attracted ever-greater audiences; instead, the spectator count leveled off and then began falling. It was as if the public had already looked into the future and read the obituary of air racing—that quaint aerial diversion that a few crazies amused themselves with back in the twentieth century. Air racing seemed to be returning to the netherwold it had occupied after the fiery crash in Cleveland in 1949.

For fourteen years the sport of air racing seemed as dead as the great air ships and the pony express. And then, in 1964, came Bill Stead, the benevolent dictator, to seize the moment and bring air racing back to life. For the next ten years the National Championship Air Races operated either in the red or barely enough in the black to pacify their biggest creditors.

In the 1970s air racing started taking off. Crowds were showing up. Every year at Stead Field in Reno, the grandstands filled up a little more. In 1981 they topped the magic benchmark of one hundred thousand spectators. It appeared that air racing was going to make a breakout. Hit the big time.

The breakout never happened. The eighties came and went, and Unlimited Air Racing remained just what it had always been: a sequestered, once-a-year event that drew approximately the same finite number of airplane-heads and warbird aficionados. Same participants, same crowd. It was an annual convocation of dinosaurs.

Not until the 1990s did anyone realize that the previous decade had been the high-water mark of Unlimited Air Racing. Audiences were the largest, the purses fattest, and the field of entrants the most exciting. The same groups were showing up every year in their chartered planes and buses and staking out their own blocks of seats in the grandstands. They formed fan clubs around their favorite pilots and planes. "Reno" was their annual pilgrimage.

And that became the biggest problem: Reno. Air racing had no other venue. Reno was all there was. For several years *venue* was the operative buzzword of the racing business. Everyone was in agreement: Air racing needed new *venues*.

Sure, they kept trying. And it always came back to Reno. Despite their efforts, there was never an extended air-racing season or tour or circuit where, as with NASCAR or tournament golf, the players could accumulate points and vie for standings. At Reno—the only venue—they shot it out, eyeball-to-eyeball, once a year. Then they went home to tend their wounded egos and broken airplanes and begin the dismal process of scraping together the assets to come back next year.

Part of the venue problem was the peculiar nature of Unlimited Air Racing. It required vast amounts of unencumbered real estate—so far removed from humanity that the only imperiled creatures were a few rabbits and rattlesnakes.

It came down to a matter of topography: Where did you stage a race for about a hundred thousand spectators—over a totally uninhabited space? There were only a handful of such places, mostly in the open spaces of the West, all possessing the same snake-and-coyote charm as Reno's Stead Field.

Not that they hadn't tried. In years past promoters had staged Unlimited Races at Phoenix; Denver; Hamilton Field, north of San Francisco; out in the Yucca Flats of Mojave, California; and on the beach at Cape May, New Jersey. None were moneymakers. In most cases the promoters lost their shirts. And not just the promoters. In some well-remembered instances, the winning racers climbed out of their airplanes to learn that their prize money had already vaporized.

Meanwhile, NASCAR, which had gone through its own dirt-grubbing, low-rent years, managed to burst out of the doldrums. It happened so quickly, no one could quite believe it.

Until the late 1970s, NASCAR was still considered a good old beer-guzzling Bubba activity, confined to oval tracks that had been cleared in pastures all over the South. Then two fortuitous events coincided to change everything for NASCAR. The first was an accord struck between big tobacco firms and the government that would end cigarette advertising on television. R. J. Reynolds, biggest of the tobacco firms, was looking for another medium in which they could display their logo. And then it struck them like a thunderclap: NASCAR! They could sponsor the entire series of NASCAR events. For the company from Winston-Salem, it seemed a natural audience—the Winnebago-driving, Confederate flag–waving, car-crazy yokels from down-home America.

During the next decade, R. J. Reynolds threw huge sums into the race purses. Going even further, the company remolded the entire NASCAR sport into its corporate image. The Grand National Series was renamed the Winston Cup. Race schedules were streamlined to attract the maximum number of fans.

The next fortuitous happening, given R. J. Reynolds's looming presence, was inevitable: *television*. Until 1979, the only TV coverage of NASCAR racing was on segments like ABC's *Wide World of Sports*, taped and sliced up for delayed programming. But then, for the first time, the Daytona 500 was covered *live*. Nothing was left out, including spinouts, crashes, and one spectacular fistfight. Two years later, ESPN began its own live coverage of NASCAR. By the 1996 Daytona 500, 70 million households were watching. Stock-car racing had suddenly burst upon the national consciousness.

Other sponsors—Budweiser, Quaker Oats, DuPont, Ford and GM, auto parts and oil companies—clamored to get on board the juggernaut. Race teams were picking up sponsorships worth millions. It was incredible! Race cars were festooned with big name brands. Champion race drivers became cult figures whose endorsement deals sometimes swelled to ten times their race winnings. There seemed to be no end to the flow of money into the sport.

Meanwhile, out in the mesquite-and-roadrunner country of Reno, air-race promoters watched and scratched their heads. *Stock cars?* What the hell was going on? It had been all too easy for them, just as it was for the prima-donna pilots, to look down their noses at a sport as . . . déclassé . . . as stock-car racing. Wasn't stock-car racing a redneck thing that originated with moonshiners and booze runners? Weren't NASCAR fans mostly guys with toothpicks in their mouths and yellow-eyed rottweilers in the backs of rusty pickups?

By comparison, air racing was a sport that appealed to a rarefied class of mostly college educated, affluent aviation enthusiasts. To the air-race elite, the difference between their sport and stock-car racing was as great as the gulf between polo and mud-wrestling.

. . .

Thus did Reno become to air racing what Daytona Beach was to stock-car racing. And in some people's opinion, *that* was air racing's biggest problem.

For half a century Reno had been trying to shed its image of a low-rent Las Vegas. Despite everything they tried—museums and symphonies and grand conventions in their hotels—the image didn't change. Reno was, above all else, a gambling town.

But it wasn't your Côte d'Azur, *Casino Royale*–style gambling, or even glitzy Las Vegas gambling. Reno looked and felt like a place where dirt-grubbing prospectors, cattle herders, and card sharks still came to play. Despite the blinking lights and glittery signboards, you couldn't get over the feeling that the dirt streets had just been paved last week.

In every lounge, lobby, and waiting space in town, you heard the same electronic chirping of the slots: *Pleep-pleep-pleep-pleep.* You saw the same vacant-eyed gaze of the eternally hopeful losers from Wombleyville and Wasatch and Burley Flats as they shoved coins into the machines. Every so often—often enough to light up their eyes like neon bulbs—they'd hear the *Chinga-chinga-chinga-chinga* as half a pound of quarters came shucking down the chute. Jackpot!

Daytona and Reno were polar opposites in geography and climate. But in terms of spirit and quintessence, the two towns were soul sisters. The life stream of each came from the flocks of tourists, low-budget conventions, and boozy seasonal events like spring break and bike week. Each city was a motorsport Mecca. Each offered to its pilgrims similar amusements: You could get drunk, laid, and tattooed and, in the case of Reno, married, divorced, and bankrupted in the casinos. All this while watching your favorite race.

But Daytona had something that Reno had always lacked: a benevolent dictator. NASCAR was the single-minded creation of a legendary promoter named Bill France. Big Bill France was a tough, six-foot-five ex-mechanic with a vision: Stock-car racing was going to be the hot new sport in America. And, by God, he was going to build the biggest, glitziest, most expensive damned stock-car speedway in the world, right there in his hometown of Daytona. France happened to possess the critical mix of charm and brains and balls to make it happen. For twenty years he ruled NASCAR like a personal fiefdom, then turned it over to his sons, who continued to keep it under their control.

And *that*, went the argument, was exactly what air racing had always lacked. The closest thing it had ever had to a dictator, benevolent or otherwise, was Bill Stead. And he had been replaced by a committee.

Air racing and stock cars—all motorsports, for that matter—had one thing in common. You didn't read about it in the promotional material or in the newspapers or hear it talked about by race officials, but everyone knew it was there. It was the dark side of the racing business and an inherent ingredient in the promotion of any motorsport.

It was the prospect of *mayhem.*

The problem with air-race fans, just like NASCAR and motorcross fans, was that they got bored. They didn't come out there just to watch expensive vehicles go around and around the course in a relentless left-hand orbit. That stuff got tiresome in a hurry.

What the fans came to see—a certain block of them, anyway—was something more basic. More visceral. What they wanted to see was *action! Destruction!* And though it couldn't be openly admitted, *blood!* The more of it the better. They wanted some good old high-velocity violence—pieces flying like shrapnel and the air reverberating with that gut-warming *Kaaa Whang!* And, best of all, they were waiting for the mesmerising specter of an orange fireball erupting like magma from Vesuvius.

It was then that you would see the other face of motorsports viewing. The spectator would slip into an atavistic state. He'd become transfixed, staring openmouthed, nostrils flared, spellbound by the spectacle of a human being, not much different from himself, getting his carcass splattered like an armadillo on the turnpike. The spectator would feel shocked and sickened—and utterly intoxicated.

No one had ever put a name to this fever or even acknowledged its existence. But everyone who promoted motorsports knew what it was. And they understood that without it they might as well be selling tickets to a taffy pull.

It wasn't just the lack of a venue or a benevolent dictator that troubled air racing. There was something else wrong with it—a problem more intractable: The supply of hardware was running out. Warbirds in the 400-mile-per-hour category were becoming too old, too rare, too valuable to lose.

Which was why, on any given night at the air racers' watering holes in Reno, you could hear them talking about it. It would be late, the groupies gone home and all the day's events dissected. Someone would clunk his glass down on the bar and ask the same old rhetorical question: *Why didn't someone have the balls to build a new race plane?*

Such a question, on the surface, sounded like heresy. These were, after all, grizzled old Merlin mechanics or fabricators of Mustang and Bearcat and Sea Fury airframes. They were guys with a vested interest in the preservation of heavy metal. For them, nothing would ever match the awesomeness of a 3,000-horsepower Merlin or a big, round, twin-rowed radial driving a fifty-year-old killing machine.

But each of them, in his innermost thoughts, knew the truth: Time was running out on the warbirds. It was making less and less sense with each passing year to put these precious artifacts at risk for something so trivial as a trophy. Or worse, a paltry prize check that barely paid your bar bill when you checked out of Reno.

Several famous racing machines had already been "rescued" from the pylons by collectors. *Stiletto,* a highly modified Mustang that had been raced by Skip Holm, was recently bought and returned to its original military condition. So was Lloyd Hamilton's Sea Fury, *Baby Gorilla*. As the price of warbirds soared past a million dollars per copy, more valuable race planes would be rescued and restored. Risking such an object in something as frivolous as an air race was like renting out the *Mona Lisa* for a stag party.

And even if the price of the object was not an obstacle, a natural law of physics was still at work. Scientists had a word for it: *entropy*. In everyday language, it meant that everything eventually wore out. In the final count, time and travail would defeat you. The old warbirds, constructed of frangible metal and powered by increasingly delicate power plants, were wearing out. Despite the brilliant efforts of builders and fabricators like Dwight Thorn and Pete Law and Nelson Ezell, the warbirds were becoming as obsolete as pterodactyls. And so, in a sense, were the men who flew them.

Which meant that air racing, unless it replaced its hardware, was doomed. Unlike NASCAR or Grand Prix racing, for which auto manufacturers pumped out exotic racing versions of their own street products, there were no street versions of air racers. No one had manufactured a propeller-driven fighter for nearly half a century. No one since the advent of the kerosene-sucking turbine engines had produced a piston-powered reciprocating engine that even approached the mighty Merlin or the corncob radials from Wright or Pratt & Whitney.

Why didn't someone have the balls to build a real race plane?

Well, actually, someone did.

One description, above all others, you heard applied to John Sandberg was: "Damn good mechanic." He wasn't one of the theoretical, advanced-design guys, like Bruce Boland or Pete Law from Lockheed, who were working on the record-setting Unlimiteds. Or a master engine tweaker like Dwight Thorn or Mike Nixon. Sandberg was a tinkerer. He was a burly, round-faced guy, a Minnesota Scandinavian, who was as much at home in a blacksmith shop as in a sheet-metal shop. If something didn't work, well, damn it, he'd just take it apart and try it another way. And if that didn't work, then, hell, try something else. He'd find *something* that worked.

Such tinkering drove other, more fastidious mechanics crazy. Bill Kerchenfaut worked for Sandberg for a while up in Minneapolis. "John didn't care a damn about the scientific process," Kerchenfaut complained. "He just couldn't help fiddling with things."

He approached flying the same way. Sandberg never possessed anything more advanced than a private pilot's license, but he taught himself to fly the hottest warbirds. And he did it the old-fashioned way: He got in the cockpit and flew them. His first fighter was a barrel-shaped Grumman F4F Wildcat. Sandberg's first, but not his last, major accident was in the Wildcat, which he flipped upside down in an off-runway landing.

Later, he owned a Bell P-63 King Cobra, with a mid-mounted engine, named *Tipsy Miss*. Sandberg took the P-63 to Reno in the seventies, where he turned the racing over to old warbird maven Lefty Gardner.

The King Cobra had problems that even Sandberg's constant fiddling could never fix. The airplane-engine combination experienced vibrations that caused one engine shutdown after the other. It was in *Tipsy Miss* that Sandberg experienced his *second* major accident, bellying the fighter into the boondocks and again walking away.

All this while moldering inside his tinkerer's brain was a flea speck of an idea: *I'm gonna build my own racer.* Not just another ancient Mustang or Bearcat tortured into going faster than the thing was ever designed to go. Sandberg's racer would be an all-new, built-from-scratch airplane designed for no other purpose than to go blisteringly fast around the pylons of Reno.

He approached Lockheed engineer Bruce Boland, who had been involved in the development of several record-setting racers, including Daryl Greenamyer's winning Bearcat, *Conquest I.* Boland, in fact, already had a design: an abortive project commissioned a few years earlier by Greenamyer. The airplane had a sleek, Mustang-like fuselage, with the familiar belly scoop for coolant air. But the racer was smaller, more streamlined, with the cockpit placed in the aft of the fuselage, just in front of the angular, jutting vertical stabilizer.

One night in a California bar, after several rounds of margaritas, Boland and Sandberg hit on the perfect name for their hypothetical racer. The name came from an ocean phenomenon being talked about along the Pacific Coast—a thing called *tsunami.*

It took nearly seven years. Boland put together a team that included fellow engineer Pete Law and master mechanic Ray Poe. In a Santa Monica metal shop the strange-looking craft slowly took shape. With a wingspan of twenty-seven feet and a twenty-eight-foot fuselage (a stock Mustang had a *thirty-seven-foot* span and a thirty-two-foot fuselage), *Tsunami* was the most compact airplane ever to mount a Merlin engine.

Not since the Thompson Trophy days back in the thirties had anyone constructed an Unlimited racer from ground zero. If *Tsunami* turned out to be successful—and there were plenty of naysayers predicting that the strange-looking craft would never get off the ground—it would mean that Unlimited Air Racing had a future. Let them venerate the dinosaur warbirds in the air museums. Let entropy run its course.

In 1986 they took the partially completed *Tsunami* out to the wide-open spaces at the Fighter Rebuilders facility in Chino for final assembly and flight testing. Frank Sanders, the old warbird maven who was still glowing with the success of his big R-4360-powered Sea Fury, *Dreadnought,* took one look at *Tsunami* and rendered a typical judgment: "They've reinvented the wheel," Sanders said. "Just another homebuilt Mustang—without the guns."

Sandberg's guys just narrowed their eyes and ignored Sanders. In any case, they'd gotten used to such remarks. "It just made us work harder," remembered Steve Hinton, fully recovered from his 1979 crash and now *Tsunami*'s test pilot. "Instead of quitting at ten o'clock, we'd work till midnight."

Tsunami flew for the first time on 17 August 1986. During the next month Hinton put in over forty hours of test-flying. There were problems. He made half a dozen dead-stick landings with the experimental racer. On one flight, *both* magnetos failed, causing the engine to shut down. On another, the oil tank split, dumping all the Merlin engine's oil.

With barely a month's flying behind them, they took *Tsunami* to Reno that September. Hinton qualified at a respectable 435 miles per hour. Then, in the championship Gold race, he was forced to pull out when the specially built Merlin engine developed a glitch. But in the meantime, part of John Sandberg's decade-old ambition had been fulfilled. He'd built his special racer. And he'd taken it to the final proving ground—the pylons at Reno. And for a fresh-out-of-the-box race plane, *Tsunami* had proved it could compete.

In 1987, back at Reno, *Tsunami* grabbed everyone's attention. This time, Hinton blistered around the course, qualifying the little racer at an eyeball-popping 464 miles per hour—faster by a quantum amount than any home built airplane had ever flown. And then, in the Sunday Gold race, the Merlin once again started its hammering and death rattling, and Hinton was forced to pull out.

It was then—in front of a hundred thousand awed spectators— that things *really* went to hell. Hinton brought the racer in for a landing on runway 26. The approach, flare, and touchdown were picture perfect.

And then, after touchdown . . . ever so slowly, as if being played in slow motion, the left landing gear . . . began to *fold! Tsunami* settled onto its left wing. Then it began a veering, metal-bending ground loop—*Screeeee!* The racer came to a stop in a swirl of dirt, concrete scrapings, and broken metal. It was an ignominious second season for Sandberg's hot little flagship.

The problem turned out to be the landing gear, an undersized and capricious piece of hardware taken from a twin-engined Piper Aero Star. It was this skinny and fragile landing gear that would prove to be *Tsunami*'s Achilles' heel.

During the next year, Sandberg kept tinkering with *Tsunami*. He made engineering changes to the airframe, and he fiddled with the temperamental Merlin. He tinkered so much, in fact, that other teams accused him of overengineering his airplane. Every flight was like a test flight on the airplane. With so many changes, something could go wrong.

And, usually, something did.

Sandberg had another idea residing like an amoeba in his head: Wouldn't it be neat if *his* airplane, *Tsunami*, were to capture the world's 3-kilometer speed record for propeller airplanes? And wouldn't it be even neater if such a feat were accomplished not by a test pilot or professional race pilot but by a plain old everyday garden-variety private pilot?

Someone, for example, like himself.

No one tried very hard to talk him out of it. After all, he *was* the boss, and it *was* his airplane. Anyway, talking Jack Sandberg out of something he'd already decided to do was as likely as changing the weather.

The truth was, Sandberg was an accomplished, though self-taught, warbird pilot. And by the summer of 1989 he had already logged several hours flying time in *Tsunami*. He felt ready for the shot at the speed record.

In a way, Sandberg's record attempt was also a race. His arch-rival, Lyle Shelton, had already announced *his* plan to go for the same record, which was still held by Steve Hinton in *Red Baron*. Shelton and his hot Bearcat, *Rare Bear*, were in the middle of a four-year streak of winning at Reno. Shelton was king of the hill, and he intended to capture yet another prize. One of the imponderable rules that governed such records was that any new record had to exceed the old by 15 miles per hour. It meant that the first of the two competitors to break Greenamyer's record had a huge advantage.

They took *Tsunami* out to Salt Lake, to Gary Levitz's facility at an old ex–military field. While Sandberg's crew was still laboring over the racer, getting it ready to make the timed runs over the dry expanse of the salt flat, they received the news from Las Vegas. Shelton had beat them to it. He had flown *Rare Bear* to an unbelievable 528 miles per hour.

It was bad news. To set a new record, *Tsunami* would have to rip through the Utah air at over 540 miles per hour.

Sandberg seemed unfazed. The grin never faded from his big, round Scandinavian face. *Tsunami*, by God, could do it. There to coach him for the attempt was Hinton and several of the diligent crew from Chino, who had put the race plane together. Gary Levitz, savvy race pilot and warbird expert, was on hand, and so were Sandberg's daughters and two of his grandchildren. Sandberg had brought his own cheering section.

Before going for the record, Sandberg wanted one more trial run over the course they'd measured out there on the salt flats. And this time *Tsunami* was *really* cooking. Hinton and the crew, watching from the ground, were already wishing that they'd gone ahead and planned the record shot for today. Never had they heard the Merlin sounding so good. Everything was coming together perfectly.

And then it was time to land. Once again Sandberg plunked the hot little racer down on the runway. It ballooned back into the air, thirty feet above the runway, and Sandberg let the racer plop back down on the concrete.

Clunk! It was another of those scenes from a bad movie. You could see it happening, each dreadful detail of the sequence . . . the spindly landing gear taking the shock of the second touchdown, quivering and wobbling like a wet dog . . . then collapsing. . . .

Scrunch! The left wing settled to the runway. The crew watched in horror, yelling epithets: *Oh, shit, it's doing it again! Head for the hills! Tsunami* was off on another of those high speed, metal-grating, parts-shedding slides toward the boondocks.

Whump! Crunch! The racer went into the boondocks, the big four-bladed propeller gouging through the Utah grit like a Roto-Rooter. A bow wave of dirt, encrusted salt, and malnourished cactus flew over the nose of the racer.

When they got to the wreck, a fine mist of dirt was still tinkling down on the fractured aluminum. Hisses and bubbling noises were coming from inside the cowling. Sandberg was in the cockpit, just sitting there, not bothering to extricate himself from the gurgling mess.

"I'm okay," he said to the first guy who came running up. Sandberg kept sitting there. "It wasn't that bad of a landing," he said, shaking his head. "Was it?"

Reno was less than a week away. The word was out: *Tsunami* was a wreck. Forget Reno this year.

It was one of those moments they still talk about at Reno. They couldn't believe it. It was only minutes before the deadline for the entrants in the 1989 races to arrive and register, and everyone was gazing overhead. It was making that familiar, crackling Merlin sound—the sleek silver shape of none other than . . . *Tsunami*.

How can that be? No way. I heard that it crashed out in Salt Lake.

It was incredible. Only four days earlier, *Tsunami* had been a pile of mangled metal on a flatbed trailer, headed across the salt flats. Everyone figured that if *Tsunami* were ever to fly again, it wouldn't be until next year. Or maybe never. You just had to wonder how much expense and disappointment John Sandberg was willing to bear.

But here it was, like a Phoenix, slipping down through the cool Nevada evening sky, Steve Hinton in the cockpit, chirping down on the runway. *Tsunami* was back.

Tsunami's ground crew pulled up looking hollow-eyed and bedraggled, as if they'd been on a nonstop work binge. In a frenzied, round-the-clock effort in the hangar back there in Utah, they had literally rebuilt the wrecked racer. Every component that was trashed by the excursion into the toolies had been repaired or replaced. They'd replaced the engine, the propeller, the landing gear, the tailwheel assembly, and refabricated a belly scoop. *Tsunami* was reborn.

Hinton took the rebuilt *Tsunami* out on the course at Reno and proceeded to qualify at a near-record speed of 462 miles per hour. The elation in the *Tsunami* pit was only temporary, however. The replacement engine started going sour during the heat races, leaving the crew with no choice except to replace it with the engine they'd pulled off *Tsunami* after the gear collapsed out at the salt flats. On the seventh lap of the Sunday Gold race, that engine also began shaking and hammering. Hinton pulled out and brought the racer back to the pits. *Tsunami* was, officially, a DNF (did not finish).

It didn't matter to John Sandberg. He looked tired and drained from the failed record attempt out in Utah, but you could see the glow in his big Scandinavian face. He was grinning and flashing a thumbs-up to everyone. Just *being* there, seeing *Tsunami* race around the pylons after what happened last week, amounted to a victory. He felt as if he had witnessed, and presided over, a miracle.

From then on, *Tsunami* was on a roll. The next spring, they took the racer to a special Unlimited Race—one of air racing's many attempts to find a new "venue"—out in Sherman, Texas. For the first time, *Tsunami* tasted *real* victory. *Tsunami* beat the entire field, running away with the Gold Trophy.

Next stop. Reno.

But then something happened to Steve Hinton. One summer day in Chino, not long before the race season commenced in Reno, he was test-flying a built-from-scratch replica of a 1930s racer. He'd just gotten airborne in the experimental craft when—*Sput!*—the round engine emitted one terminal chuff and stopped dead as a stone.

Hinton didn't have many options. From four hundred feet, he put the racer into a nearby cornfield. The force of the impact stopped almost all forward momentum, and the racer lurched to a stop in less than a hundred feet.

The racer was totaled, and so was Hinton, at least temporarily. The hard landing caused a back injury that required hospitalization. He would recover, but not in time for the Reno races.

Sandberg had a problem. Hinton was *Tsunami*'s original test pilot and the only one who had ever raced the unique airplane. Sandberg thought they should just stand down for the year and wait for Hinton to mend.

But Hinton didn't want that. *Tsunami* was just beginning to realize its potential, and after what they'd been through, it was unthinkable *not* to enter the championship races at Reno. He urged Sandberg to go find an experienced Unlimited racing pilot. Someone who could slip into an exotic airplane like *Tsunami* and make it a winner. In short, a hired gun.

A guy like Skip Holm.

But Sandberg had a problem with Holm. In his opinion, Holm was the kind of pilot who broke machinery. Airplanes were impersonal objects to him, like dispensable tools. He didn't regard them as love objects, as Sandberg and Hinton regarded *Tsunami*.

Holm admitted as much. "I'm not Steve," he told Sandberg. "If Steve breaks it, he'll stay and fix it. Not me. I just walk away."

Just walk away? That was tough for Sandberg to accept. After you'd worked as long and hard on an airplane as he and his crew had labored on *Tsunami*, the machine metamorphosed into something more than just a collection of cold metal parts. Hell, it *was* a love object. You didn't turn it over to some hired gun who broke it and just walked away.

But Sandberg was also a realist. There was no one out there more qualified to strap on an Unlimited racer than Skip Holm, hired gun or not.

Holm, in fact, had been Sandberg's original choice to fly *Tsunami*

204

back when it was still being developed in the early eighties. Skip was a professional test pilot as well as a successful Unlimited racer. But as the years went by and the project ran behind schedule, Holm had signed on to fly another Unlimited racer, a Mustang named *Stiletto*.

Now they'd come full circle. Holm, the hired gun, would fly *Tsunami*.

"I won't second-guess you, Jack," Holm told him. "I won't tell you how you ought to fix it when it's broke. If nothing's wrong with it or if you fix it, we're gonna get along great."

As it turned out, they did get along great. Even after Holm's second flight in *Tsunami*, when the belly scoop ripped off the airplane. Even after the electrical fire that caused the electronic ignition to fail, which in turn caused the engine to quit, nearly forcing Holm to land on a busy freeway. Two hundred feet above the traffic, with Holm looking for an opening, the engine sputtered back to life, running on one of the two ignition systems.

That autumn of 1990 they went to Reno. In his first outing in *Tsunami*, Holm qualified the racer at 465 miles per hour. That Sunday, he finished the Gold race with an average speed of 462, only seconds behind the winner, Lyle Shelton, in *Rare Bear*, whose speed of 468 miles per hour set a new Reno record.

The next year was even more spectacular.

For the past decade speeds in the Unlimited Division seemed to run up against an invisible barrier. About 460 miles per hour seemed to be as fast as anyone could hope to propel one of these classic racing machines around the 9-mile course at Reno. Beyond that speed, a wall of transonic air swelled like a bow wave that could not be penetrated by piston-engined airplanes.

Or so it seemed until 1991. It was as if some potent nostrum had been poured into the tanks of *all* the top Unlimiteds. Suddenly, lap speeds were going out of sight, nudging toward the magic mark of 500 miles per hour.

Lyle Shelton was in the middle of his reign as the fastest race pilot in the world. He had won the Unlimited Championship in 1988, 1989, and last year, 1990. And he had taken time out to go shatter the 3-kilometer record. And hard on his heels was a new competitor, the Mustang called *Strega,* flown by that feisty little farmer Tiger Destefani.

And now *Tsunami.*

No one had ever seen a race like this Sunday Gold Championship contest. The three front-runners—*Rare Bear, Strega,* and *Tsunami*—roared around the course as if joined in formation. It was an odd-looking cluster—Shelton's barrel-shaped Bearcat, Destefani's trimmed-down Mustang, and the diminutive silver home-built, *Tsunami.*

The winner, again, was *Rare Bear.* Shelton ripped across the finish line with a new Reno racecourse record speed of 481 miles per hour. A heartbeat behind him was *Strega,* which also broke the old record. And tight on *Strega's* wing, less than half a mile an hour slower, was *Tsunami,* also shattering the old mark.

Down in the *Tsunami* pit, there was disappointment—and cheering. They'd done better than they had dared to hope. But this race had been like no other in history. How could you figure? Your airplane runs more than 10 miles per hour faster than the existing world record, *and you come in third!* What more could you do?

Nothing, at least this year. You had to be philosophical about it. You just swallowed your disappointment and recited the old Reno mantra: *Next year . . . Wait till next year . . . We're gonna beat that son of a bitch. . . .*

Such brave talk made the *Tsunami* crew feel better. It would get them through the next year. What they didn't know—and wouldn't know for ten more days—was that there would be no next year.

On Wednesday, 25 September 1991, the propeller blades ticked over, three, four turns; then the engine caught—*chuff, chuff, chuff*—coughing and stirring to life in that distinct Merlin staccato bark. Puffs of sweetish high octane-exhaust wafted back across the cockpit.

Sandberg loved that smell. In the chill morning air he could breathe the intoxicating exhaust, see the vapor streaming like a white contrail down the fuselage and over the tail of *Tsunami*.

Skip Holm had ferried *Tsunami* as far as Casper, Wyoming, then ran into bad weather. He then had to return to California, so Sandberg would now ferry *Tsunami* the rest of the way back to Minnesota. He had plans for the racer when he got it home. As far as he was concerned, *Tsunami* was—and always would be—a work in progress. He had ideas for more airframe cleanups: a different, drag-reducing configuration for the wingtips, better ducting, slicker skin.

Sandberg couldn't stop tinkering with his airplane. He had been taking some flak for doing so from the racing community. He already had a fast airplane, they were saying. Why didn't he leave things well enough alone? It was an obsession with him. His incessant innovations caused almost as many problems as they solved.

One of his innovations was the landing flaps. In its original configuration, *Tsunami* had a slick wing, no flaps—which made for some *very* interesting landings. Hinton liked to joke, but with a certain truthfulness, that *Tsunami* was the only airplane he'd flown that *accelerated* after you landed it. The airplane's attitude was more nose up during the approach to landing than after touchdown. At landing, with all three tiny wheels on the ground, the airplane's attitude flattened. The drag induced by the wings was thus dramatically lessened, and *Tsunami* would shoot down the runway like a scalded jackrabbit.

So Sandberg had devised a set of landing flaps. And they worked, after a fashion, though they didn't help much in lowering *Tsunami*'s hot approach speed. Mainly, they acted as effective speed brakes and shortened the racer's jackrabbit landing roll.

Sam Torvik, Sandberg's engine man, would fly the Mitsubishi chase plane and accompany *Tsunami* on the journey. The plan was to make a fuel stop in Pierre, South Dakota. From there they would press on to their home base in Minneapolis.

It was during the approach to the airport at Pierre that something went wrong. Something broke.

Torvik was flying behind *Tsunami,* watching Sandberg get set up for the landing at Pierre. And then, to his astonishment, *the airplane rolled!* With its gear and flaps out, *Tsunami* went into a roll to the left and *kept* rolling. All the way around, with the nose dropping toward the bluffs short of the runway.

The roll seemed to be stopping—the airplane was nearly upright— and then the nose abruptly pitched up. *Tsunami* snap-rolled—a hard, diving plunge to the right.

Torvik winced. He knew now, with a dreadful certainty, what would happen next.

Tsunami smashed nose down into the steep bluff. Torvik saw a brief geyser of dirt and metal and fire, then nothing.

From the accounts of witnesses on the ground and by the appearance of the failed parts, it seemed likely that Sandberg had lowered the flaps at an excessive airspeed. Extending in a more than 200-mile-per-hour airstream, the flaps had exerted too great a strain on the torque tube that connected to the flap actuator. Something broke. And it killed John Sandberg.

Thus ended the career of the most charismatic air racer of the new generation. *Tsunami* was like a brilliant but troubled young star. When it was good, it was *very* good. But when it was bad, it gave everyone megaton migraines.

The exotic racer had come tantalizingly close to making history. It was—*almost*—the first and only out-of-the-box racing airplane since the prewar Thompson Trophy era to win the Unlimited Championship. During each year of its career, Sandberg's work-in-progress had flown faster. Fast enough to shatter existing speed records but still a hairbreadth shy of the Gold Trophy.

But *Tsunami* wasn't the only radical, built-to-order airplane left in the racing game. There was one left, and this one was even more radical. It was called the *Pond Racer.*

✈ 18 ✈

Pond Racer

Nobody loved the *Pond Racer* except, possibly, Bob Pond, who caused the thing to be constructed. Sure, everyone agreed that sooner or later someone *had* to come up with a machine that would replace the fifty-year-old warbirds they were campaigning at Reno. *Tsunami* had seemed to be such a machine, with its ever-improving speeds and the promise of a lap speed of more than 500 miles per hour. But *Tsunami* and its creator, John Sandberg, were history.

But this plane, the *Pond Racer*, with its two elongated engine housings and center pod for the cockpit, looked like a *Star Wars* rendition of the twin-engined World War II P-38 Lightning. The idea was that an airplane of such diminutive size, with its composite-structured lightness, powered by two high-tech auto-racing engines, ought to rip through the air at something close to 450 miles per hour. And in the late 1980s, such a speed was considered to be Gold Trophy–winning velocity.

Pond commissioned Bert Rutan, the composite-materials pioneer, to design and build his new Unlimited racer. Rutan was the maverick creator of exotic, all-composite airplanes like the Long-Eze and the history-making *Voyager* in which Rutan's brother, Dick, and Jeanna Yeager accomplished the world's first unrefueled, globe-circling flight. Rutan was just the designer to yank Unlimited Air Racing out of its fifty-year-old obsession with ex–military hardware.

Pond laid down three criteria: The new racer had to have two engines; it had to be built around *modern* technology (not a replay of the same old World War II–designed warbirds), which meant composites and computer-based instrumentation; and the most important criterion—the thing had to be safe.

With that mandate, Rutan went to work constructing Pond's racer. As the new airplane took shape, it was clear that Rutan was doing what Pond had ordered: It was new technology, all right. The airplane had a sexy, sinister look, with those P-38-like twin booms and long, pointy nacelles and the slick, white-plastic sheen of an all-composite surface.

The safety of the racer, supposedly, would come from the cockpit's location behind and between the long engine booms. In theory, this would keep the pilot a safe distance from parts-shedding engines and from the inflammable fuel cells. The two Nissan engines were designed to run on both regular gasoline and, for a maximum of twenty minutes during a race, on an exotic custom alcohol fuel.

The *Pond Racer* rolled out of Rutan's Mojave, California, facility in April 1991. Now Bob Pond was looking for a pilot to race his built-from-scratch, experimental airplane. What he needed was an experienced race pilot. A smart guy with guts and good hands. A hired gun like Rick Brickert.

Rick Brickert had an engaging smile and, everyone said, a natural touch with an airplane. He was also a young man in a hurry.

Brickert had been fascinated with air racing ever since he saw his first race at Reno when he was a kid of thirteen. As a teenager, he earned all his ratings—private license, commercial, instrument, certified flight instructor. He ferried airplanes, flew charters, and hauled freight. In his early twenties he went to work as an airline pilot for Western Airlines.

Instead of following the normal progression of professional pilots— college to military training and on to an airline career—Brickert turned the process upside down. As a fully qualified airline pilot, he took a military leave of absence to go through air force pilot training.

A pilot like Brickert, of course, wasn't the average air force flight-training student. He graduated number one in his class and won the Commander's Cup. After receiving his air force wings, he was assigned an Air National Guard slot flying A-7 Corsairs for the 162nd Tactical Fighter Group based in Tucson, Arizona. And he went back to work for Western Airlines.

It was at Western in the late seventies that Brickert met new-hire airline pilot Steve Hinton. When the two found that they had much in common—a love of warbirds and air racing—Hinton invited Brickert to Chino. Though Hinton dropped out of the airline business to become a full-time warbird pilot, he brought Brickert into his little clique of hotshot kids who flew classic fighters.

For Brickert, it was only one short step to Reno. And Unlimited racing. In 1980 and 1981, he flew a stock Mustang in the championship races. Then, in 1983, he received the ultimate job in sport aviation: racing the current Unlimited champion, *Dago Red*, the hot new racer developed by Frank Taylor and Tiger Destefani.

Brickert had arrived. He was now, officially, a hired gun.

Dago Red didn't win in 1983. Brickert was running away with the race when a sudden vibration—it turned out to be a propeller-spinner backplate—forced him to pull out and land. A new entrant, a big silver Sea Fury named *Dreadnought*, took the Gold Trophy.

It was the beginning of a long streak of bad luck for *Dago Red*.

During the Gold Trophy race of 1984, a broken connecting rod came through the engine crankcase, nearly severing the Merlin's crankcase in half.

Brickert called a Mayday and set up for a precautionary landing. On final approach, the shattered engine burst into flames. He fired the on-board Halon bottle, which temporarily snuffed the fire; then it reignited. Brickert sideslipped the Mustang down to the concrete, peering out the side of the now-open cockpit.

It was a masterful performance. The fire streaming back from the engine, over the windshield and into the cockpit, had singed the top of Brickert's helmet and melted the visor. The entire nose section of *Dago Red*, all the way past the cockpit, looked as if it had been roasted on a spit.

Brickert was unscathed, but it had been a narrow escape. Fire in the cockpit—the nightmare scenario guaranteed to strike fear in the heart of every fighter pilot.

Brickert had managed to dodge the bullet. This time.

In 1985, Brickert took third place in the Gold Trophy race, again flying *Dago Red*. Then, in 1986, he was tapped to fly the Sanders family's *Dreadnought;* he raced it to a Gold Trophy finish. Now Rick Brickert had *really* arrived. He was a member of an elite club: the roster of Unlimited Air Racing champions.

For the next several seasons, Brickert raced *Dreadnought*. By the late eighties, it was clear that the big Sea Fury, though still a hard-charging competitor, was outclassed by the superslick new Unlimiteds, like Tiger Destefani's *Strega* and Lyle Shelton's *Rare Bear.* Despite the brute power of *Dreadnought*'s mighty R-4360 engine, the Sea Fury seemed to have reached a limiting speed at which the big, blunt-nosed fighter could be propelled through the atmosphere.

By 1991 Brickert was flying the *Pond Racer* and still getting used to its quirkiness. The most troubling was in the power plants. The *Pond*'s Electromotive Nissans were in-line, liquid-cooled engines with computer-managed fuel controls. They were supposed to put out 1,000 horsepower each, but they weren't even getting 600 at this point. The finicky motors were so tightly housed in their long, skinny cowlings that cooling them became the *Pond Racer's* biggest ongoing problem.

The problem never went away. Whenever the engine crew thought they had the temperatures under control, Brickert would go out and push the throttles up again, and—*Zzzzzt!*—the Nissans would start cooking themselves all over again. It was maddening.

Meanwhile, the sport-aviation media were having a field day. That year, 1991, had been a bad time for hot, new Unlimited racers. John Sandberg had been killed in *Tsunami*. Now this latest attempt at a built-for-racing airplane—the *Pond Racer*—was giving the press great material because it was so obviously flawed.

To put a good face on things, the Pond team was careful to say that their first racing season was a "learning experience." They weren't, you know, really *trying* to win out there on the racecourse. Just taking a first incremental step toward real competitiveness. They had to work all the bugs out first.

The truth was, the *Pond Racer* was scaring the hell out of everyone.

At Reno that year, Brickert managed to qualify the racer with a respectable 400 miles per hour. It was the last time that week the racer finished *anything*. Though it started every heat race, the *Pond* completed a total of only five laps, landing each time with overheated engines, usually with one shut down and the propeller feathered (the blades stopped, in a streamlined angle to the wind).

In the background during all these faltering efforts hovered the imposing presence of Bob Pond. People who worked for Pond both feared and respected him. Pond had dumped cartloads of money from his personal fortune into the racer. It was he who had conceived the project, appointed the best people to build it, and handpicked his pilot to fly it.

Pond was the boss, and not one soul laboring out there on the

Pond Racer had any doubt about what the boss expected: *Make this damned thing fly. Fast.*

But it wasn't going to happen this year. The fact was, the *Pond Racer* hardly flew at all at the 1991 Reno championships, finishing none of its races and coming back each time with sizzling engines. It was an unimpressive first outing for a race plane.

So Pond did what hard-nosed CEOs do: He changed management. He removed the project from the further husbandry of its builders, the Rutans, and transferred the racer to a new headquarters out in the warbird country of Chino, California. The new team manager was Steve Hinton, who now presided over Ed Maloney's Planes of Fame Museum in Chino. The technical adviser was the engineer and racing guru Bruce Boland, who had influenced the design of a dozen hot Reno racers.

Rick Brickert would keep his job as the pilot of the *Pond Racer.*

That winter, the team did some fine-tuning on the racer. A new instrument-panel layout was designed to make critical information more accessible to the pilot. Reverting to some *old* technology, it was decided to install ADI tanks and a water-spray bar, similar to the systems that had been running for years on racing Mustangs. To accommodate the changed center of gravity (due to the new installations going to the aft section of the airplane), the booms and the engines had to be moved forward six inches. The airplane's onboard computers, which had been in the habit of crashing because of their proximity to the engine's turbochargers, were also relocated to the more peaceful zone in the aft section of the booms.

In the hope of correcting the engines' overheating tendencies, the exotic alcohol fuel system was abandoned, and the engines were put back on a special gasoline blend. It was an important change, but it didn't fix the problem.

It was maddening. For the Pond team, the 1992 championship races were turning into a replay of the year before. Those damned Nissan engines were *still* overheating!

On Wednesday, during the qualifications, Brickert had to pull off the course and declare a Mayday. Both engines were frying like sausages on a griddle. But he couldn't make his intentions known because Race Control was involved in a radio conversation with a wandering light airplane that was trespassing into the Stead airport pattern. In the meantime, while Brickert was setting up to make his emergency landing on runway 26, to the west, Lloyd Hamilton was making a routine landing of his Sea Fury on runway 08, in the opposite direction.

A calamity was in the making. As Brickert was coming in nose on with Hamilton, someone on the ramp saw the situation and cut through all the radio chaff: "Clear the runway! An airplane is coming in with an emergency."

Hamilton understood and veered his Sea Fury off into the dirt, breaking some hardware on his landing gear. But it was too late for Brickert. Not liking the situation, he poured the power to his faltering engines and pulled up to make another approach.

Now the *Pond*'s overheated engines were *really* cooking. While Brickert made his long, lonely orbit, lining up for another landing, everyone down in the *Pond*'s pits offered up a silent prayer that the straining, overheated Nissans would . . . just . . . please . . . keep running. Three more minutes.

They did. And the now-familiar Reno scene repeated itself: The *Pond Racer* landed, smoke streaming from the nacelles. As usual, out came the fire trucks, red lights flashing, pursuing the racer down the runway. And in the pits, the weary *Pond* crew again gathered their tools. They had more work to do.

So it went that week. The high-tech Electromotive Nissan engines were behaving like creatures from hell. The turbochargers stalled. The induction temperatures soared off the scale. The horsepower of the Nissans stayed well under what it was supposed to be. To cap off the list of maladies, the *Pond Racer*'s tail wheel failed on landing, causing a shower of sparks and some surface damage to the tail.

Brickert managed to qualify in the twenty-second position with a tepid speed of 358 miles per hour. It was slower than most stock Mustangs. But at least the airplane was running. And it would get him into the Bronze heat race Friday.

But not for long. Five laps into the race, another Mayday. Another set of overheated engines, another emergency landing. Another version of the same old scene: The *Pond Racer* plunking down on the runway, engines streaming smoke and vapor. The fire trucks charging behind, red lights flashing. And in the pits the crew of the *Pond Racer* shaking their heads—*I don't fucking believe it*—and gathering their tools.

Then something astonishing happened. On Sunday, the day of the championship races, Rick Brickert started the Bronze Trophy race with the *Pond Racer. And finished!* Even more astonishingly, not only did he complete the race; he finished in second place.

A minor success, perhaps. But to the dispirited crew of the *Pond Racer*, it was just what they needed. A trophy! And prize money. It wasn't much, really, but it was something they could cheer about. It meant that the *Pond Racer* really *was* a racer.

Now they could boast—just a little. When they came back next year, the competition had better watch out. They were going to kick some serious butt!

Even the owner of the project seemed to approve. Bob Pond bestowed a blessing on his crew: "Keep doing what you're doing," he told them. "It will work. I have faith in you, and I trust you."

Thus encouraged, the *Pond* team went back to work; 1993 would be their year.

On 14 September 1993, driving into Stead Field, you couldn't miss it. It was a big banner stretched across the side of an apartment building, just before you turned onto the access road. Everyone saw it, and they all got the unsubtle joke: *The Pond is a pooch.*

Everyone from the race teams cracked up, seeing the banner. It might be a joke, but hell, it was the truth: The *Pond Racer* really *was* the doggiest $2 million high-tech race plane ever built.

Well, so far. Though no one in the *Pond* team was saying it yet, the consensus about the *Pond Racer* was that it would probably *never* be a serious contender. Even if they resolved all the technical troubles with the overheating Nissan engines, it was doubtful that the airplane would ever go fast enough to compete in the Gold races. With its multiple booms and fins and vanes and connecting planing surfaces, the airplane possessed a high degree of what engineers called *intersection drag*. With all those corners and right angles in the airframe, aerodynamic resistance built up until the *Pond Racer* hit a wall at about 450 miles per hour, beyond which *no* amount of horsepower was going to push it.

It was all still theoretical, of course. As everyone was acutely aware, the *Pond Racer* had never lasted in a real race long enough to be put to the test.

Rick Brickert was back to give it another try. By now it was clear to the other pilots that Bob Pond couldn't have picked a more loyal hired gun than Brickert. Whatever Brickert's misgivings might have been about the *Pond Racer,* he was a young man who understood loyalty. He was Pond's chosen pilot, and nothing that had happened to the *Pond Racer* was going to sway him from his mission. Loyalty, everyone thought, might be Brickert's finest attribute. Some thought it might also be his fatal flaw.

It was the kind of afternoon the Reno Chamber of Commerce liked to depict in the postcards. The sky was an azure blue. For once the wind out at Stead Field was almost calm. The temperature was hanging at an autumnal 75 degrees. A perfect day for racing.

Standing on the ramp, Steve Hinton watched Rick Brickert take off in the *Pond Racer* for a practice session. If everything hung together today, Rick would fly a couple of laps, then call for the timer. They'd have the qualifying out of the way. Then the Pond crew could relax a little and work on getting the racer through the first of the heat races. After two seasons at Reno, the *Pond Racer* had gotten through only *one* entire race—taking second in the Bronze final last year—without pulling up with a Mayday.

Hinton and Brickert were best friends. Hinton knew that Brickert was putting a good face on all the *Pond Racer*'s troubles. To anyone who asked, Rick would tell them the *Pond* was doing just fine. Sure, they had a few problems, but they were working them out. Every new race plane had problems, right? The *Pond* was going to live up to everyone's expectations.

Hinton knew how Brickert really felt. That afternoon, while they were getting the *Pond* ready for the practice session, Brickert told Hinton he was having some bad feelings about the airplane.

"If you don't feel right about it, don't fly it," Hinton said.

Brickert shook his head. "I'm gonna fly it."

Hinton wasn't surprised. Rick had been flying hot airplanes for a lot of years now, almost as long as Hinton. He knew that flying any airplane like the *Pond Racer* entailed risk. But that was Rick Brickert's style. He was young—only thirty-eight—and still building his reputation. He was a guy who accepted risk; he liked the exposure that went with it.

Hinton knew about this, too. In 1979 he'd had the same uneasy feelings about *Red Baron,* that gorgeous scissors-bladed killing machine that had nearly killed *him.* And that was what made Hinton different now from Brickert. Hinton had already been there. He no longer accepted risk in the same old spit-in-the-devil's-eye style he used to. And he didn't care about exposure anymore. He'd had enough exposure. Hinton had already been all the way out to the edge of the Great Abyss and come back. He had the scars to prove it.

The *Pond Racer* was nearly finished with its first lap. Hinton could tell from the data link that the engines *still* weren't putting out. Only about 600 horsepower each, instead of the 1,000 they were designed to produce. Brickert was getting a speed of around 360, which was stock Mustang speed—not at all what their specially designed Unlimited racer ought to be doing in its third season at Reno.

There wasn't a large crowd out there today. The heat races didn't start for two more days. It was only Tuesday, and the sole excitement was in the posting of the qualifying speeds. But still, whenever the *Pond Racer* took to the air, the crews in the pits and the fans wandering over the ramp all stopped to watch.

And that's what they were doing now. Some had field glasses out, following the peculiar, twin-boomed white shape of the *Pond Racer* around the course. The *Pond* made its own distinctive sound— *Eeeeeeeooowwww!*—a high-pitched, frenzied kind of howling, unlike the deep-throated growling of the Mustangs or the basso profundo of the round-engined Sea Furies and Bearcats. The *Pond Racer* sounded more like a pair of airborne, high-revving NASCAR racers, which, in effect, it really was.

Many of the fans had their handheld radios out. They were listening to the race operations frequency, because they knew that's where you could hear what was *really* going on. And they knew now that whenever the *Pond* flew, there was usually something interesting going on.

So it was today.

Close to the finish of the first lap, it happened again. "Mayday!" they heard Brickert call. A Mayday for the *Pond Racer*, of course, was almost a routine procedure. Since its appearance two years earlier, the *Pond Racer* had declared more Maydays than all the other racers together.

They saw the *Pond* pull up in the standard emergency pattern. Brickert was obviously setting up for a right-hand downwind to come around and land to the west, on runway 26.

An observer with field glasses reported what he saw: "One shut down. The prop is stopped."

Which was also standard for the *Pond Racer*, which had made almost as many landings with one engine shut down as it had with both engines running. Bob Pond's original design criterion for his racer—that it have *two engines* for safety reasons—seemed almost a joke now. Having two of the hypersensitive Electromotive Nissans just *doubled* the likelihood of an engine failure.

"His prop's not feathered," reported the observer. The propellers, like those on multiengined transports, were capable of being "feathered," meaning that the blades could be rotated into the airstream, providing almost no resistance and allowing the failed engine to completely stop.

Stopped but not feathered? That was *not* good. It meant that the square-tipped, paddlelike propeller blade was flat to the wind, making it a big asymmetric speed brake. But why was the propeller stopped if it wasn't feathered? Unfeathered propellers normally kept turning from the force of the wind. Was the engine seized, locked up tight? If so, then something had *really* gone to hell with the cantankerous Nissan engine.

Still, they could see that Brickert was in good shape for an emergency landing. His landing gear was down. He was on a high-right downwind, in view of the pits and the stands. All he had to do was make a descending right turn to the runway and he'd be okay. Just your normal engine-out, emergency landing. No sweat. After all, he'd had lots of practice.

Just as he'd done before, Brickert started a descending right turn on to a base leg, going nearly perpendicular to the runway. And down below, just as they'd done before whenever the *Pond Racer* came in with an emergency, the fire trucks headed for the end of the runway.

"Hey, where's he going?"

The *Pond Racer* wasn't headed for the runway. It was turning *away*.

And descending rapidly. Headed out over Lemon Valley.

Headed for the boulder-strewn desert.

"What's going on? What's he doing?"

No one knew. No one except, of course, Rick Brickert, who was confronting a problem only he was privy to. He wasn't talking on the radio.

Instead of slowing to landing speed, the *Pond Racer* appeared to be . . . *accelerating*. Downward . . . aimed like an arrow for the floor of the desert. As though its pilot was in a deadly rush to reach the ground.

No one could quite believe what they were seeing. Now the landing gear was *up* on *Pond Racer!* The pilot was obviously intending a belly landing out there in the sagebrush, boulders, and gullies.

It didn't make sense. Why had he turned away from the runway? And why was he going so damned *fast?* The *Pond Racer* was hauling ass downward as if he were making a strafing pass. It was too fast for any kind of landing, even on a good surface.

Whump! The *Pond* hit the desert at something over 200 miles per hour. It ricocheted back into the air, then hit again—*Whump!*—and bounced, spewing parts and sand and debris.

And hit again—*Whump!*

And erupted in a ball of orange flame. The nearly full tanks of specially blended high-octane gasoline ripped open and ignited like a fuel-air bomb.

A telltale mushroom of oily black smoke gushed into the sky.

And that was all anyone could see. The crash scene was in the valley, below the eastern rim of the airport. Back on the ramp all anyone could see that might have been the *Pond Racer* was an indefinable spot out there on the brown Nevada desert, marked by a column of black smoke.

"The *Pond Racer* is down!"

The news raced across the ramp. Everyone could see the ominous smoke column over there in the east. There was no doubt about what it meant. But no one wanted to guess yet how bad it was.

For the crew in the pits, it was an agonizing wait. Only a few minutes before, they had towed the racer out to the start-up spot on the ramp. As always, they had watched their troubled airplane take to the air, then waited with stopwatches while the *Pond Racer* came howling around the course on its first lap.

Now this. Three years of frustration, unstinting hard labor, unful-filled hopes—all for what? A blackened hole out in the Nevada wastelands?

The helicopter was already *whop-whopping* across the sagebrush, hell-bent for the crash site. The trucks were cranking up, red lights flashing, kicking up plumes of dirt as they headed off down the airport-perimeter road.

It was all over when they got there.

The *Pond Racer* was gone, consumed by fire. Its built-in safety features, including the pod cockpit that was supposed to protect the pilot, turned out to be a myth. The all-composite structure had shattered like an egg crate. And burned.

In the Room of Hard Benches, there wasn't much of the usual cut-ting up and teasing and joking. When the Brethren held their morn-ing briefing, you could *feel* the grimness. The crash of the *Pond* was one of those accidents that left them all feeling twitchy. Brickert had been around the racing scene for years and was highly regarded by his peers. Now, in each pilot's head flitted this troubling little kernel of a thought: If it could happen to a guy like Brickert, it could hap-pen to any of us. *Even me.*

Airmen hate mysteries. What bothered the Brethren most about Brickert's accident was that no one had a satisfying explanation.

The investigation showed that one engine was shut down and not feathered. But the other engine *was* developing power. Why, then, had Brickert aimed the *Pond away* from the airport even though he could have made it to the runway?

The autopsy showed that Brickert had died from the fire. But *what* fire? Had there been a fire *before* he put it down in the desert? A fire in the cockpit? There were indications, not conclusive, that fuel had somehow entered the cockpit. If so, and if he had experi-enced a fire, it might explain his sudden push to get the plane on the ground, even if it meant the floor of the desert and certain calamity.

But if he had a cockpit fire, why hadn't he bailed out? One consideration might have been the fact that the cockpit canopy was equipped with an explosive cord for the purpose of blowing the canopy away from the airplane. Some pilots conjectured that if Brickert, in fact, was experiencing fuel in the cockpit, the presence of the explosive device might have influenced his decision *not* to jettison the canopy and bail out.

Only one fact seemed clear: Whatever Brickert's problem was, it was so urgent that he was unwilling to take the couple of minutes to execute an approach and landing on runway 26. His sudden plunge to the desert was the last-ditch maneuver of a desperate man.

Inevitably, a few of the Brethren, with the unimpeded clarity of hindsight, found targets for their resentment. *Someone*—or something—had to bear the blame for the death of Rick Brickert. For most of the race community, it was convenient to blame the airplane. Or its builders. Or its owner.

"The *Pond Racer* was a killer."

"The thing should never have been allowed to fly here."

"Rick should have walked away from the thing."

Most of the bitter criticism of the *Pond Racer*'s design, of course, came *after* the fact of Brickert's death. What the loss of the *Pond Racer* and the crash of *Tsunami* really meant was that radical new designs for Unlimited racers would be viewed with suspicion.

With no exotic, new built-for-racing machines on the horizon, air racing was still faced with the finite shelf life—and the escalating value—of its half-century-old warbirds. The time was approaching when no one, in good conscience, would be willing to risk an object of such inestimable value as a Mustang or Bearcat in so risky a pursuit as an air race.

Thus was Reno air racing poised to enter its fourth decade. Though top speeds had increased dramatically and purse money had gone up, the cast of racers—Mustangs, Bearcats, Sea Furies, and the odd Yak—hadn't changed.

Nor had the same core group of loyal fans changed. The attendance level—a total of 120,000–150,000 spectators over the three-day race weekend—seemed to be an immutable statistic. As a motorsport Mecca, air racing was like an antediluvian creature threatened on all sides by a hostile environment. But somehow it was still alive.

PART THREE

The Young Turks

The important thing in aeroplanes is that they shall be speedy.
—Baron Manfred von Richthofen,
World War I German ace

⊁ 19 ⊁

The Winter of Discontent

3 February 1998

Tiger Destefani shoved the broom across the hangar floor, moving a wave of water toward the open door. It was something he had to do a few times every day. One whole section of the hangar was under water. Outside, the ramp and the adjacent lot were under water, as was the access road.

The forecast was for *more* damned rain.

Destefani stood there in the hangar doorway, glowering at the darkened skies and the steady drizzle. Minter Field looked like a fish farm. Half the roads were flooded out. Even the interstate south of Bakersfield was under water, and several county roads were washed out.

This had been going on all winter. Every day, Destefani got into his pickup and drove through the drizzle out to Minter Field, in the little town of Shafter, California. He had a constant companion these days—a plumpish faded blonde named Mick Dundee. Mick was one of those big-hearted females, loving, agreeable, undemanding. She was well past her prime now, and all she asked was just to

227

be there, to hang out there in the hangar with Tiger. Occasionally, she liked to have her ears scratched.

Mick was a ten-year-old Queensland Heeler. She had been a Destefani family pet since she was a puppy. Now in her declining years, Mick presided over the hangar like an aging matriarch, greeting visitors and following Tiger around the sprawling floor of the hangar.

The weather phenomenon called El Niño was making a bog out of California. Roads were washing away. Entire neighborhoods were sliding into the Pacific. Californians were blaming El Niño for everything from global warming to road rage. In the High Sierra, record snowfalls were clogging the Donner Pass—the same notch in the mountains that once spelled disaster for westbound settlers of the previous century.

Which was why *Strega* still resided in Reno. The decision had been made to disassemble the racer and take her home on a flatbed. Destefani and his crew had already removed *Strega*'s wings and gotten her ready to travel. But each time they tried to head for Bakersfield, El Niño would kick in and fill the mountain passes with a fresh barrier of snow.

To make Destefani's winter even darker, the pending divorce from Mary was getting *very* nasty. Everything he owned—house, cars, even *Strega*—was up for grabs. His main source of income, the fourteen-hundred-acre family farm he inherited from his father, had been turned into an inland sea by El Niño. This was the time they should be planting and seeding, but the only conveyance they could get into the fields was a rowboat.

Meanwhile, the bills for *Strega* kept coming in. He owed money to the crew, to the engine builder, to the bank. He still didn't know the full cost of the damage done to *Strega* during the calamitous landing last September. He was so far in the hole, he didn't know how—or if—he was going to mount another assault on the Unlimited Championship later this year. Destefani suspected that the only guy who was more broke than he was Lyle Shelton, owner and pilot of *Rare Bear*. Shelton had blown an engine *and* lost the race.

He had to laugh when he thought about it. For the third straight year, he was the National Unlimited Racing champion. It was a joke! The public assumed that the owner of hot racers like *Strega* and *Rare Bear* had to be loaded. How did you win the Unlimited Championship six times unless you had unlimited assets to pour into your race machine?

Destefani knew the truth. Through your own sweat. And sacrifice. And through the sweat and sacrifice of a loyal crew. And even that wasn't enough. You needed the infusion of serious money from sponsorships. Somehow you had to entice brand-name companies to allocate their sponsorship money on your team in exchange for displaying their logo.

And *that* was an exercise in supersalesmanship, because Reno air racing—a once-a-year event—didn't offer advertisers the kind of exposure that justified the big bucks they could just as well spend on, say, a NASCAR team or a television spot during a major sports event.

It was the part of the game that Destefani hated. He disliked the whole business: the cold calls and the hat-in-hand sucking up to the marketing and public-relations guys who knew as much about Unlimited Air Racing as he knew about Keynesian economics. But it just went with the territory. Unless you were a multimillionaire, like Bob Pond or Wiley Sanders, who dabbled in air racing for the general hell of it, you had to get out there and solicit. You had to go begging for sponsorship money.

He'd had bad luck with sponsors. An Internet provider called Bigger.net, whose name adorned the wings of *Strega* this season, was in trouble. Of the total thirty-six thousand dollars they had signed on to provide, only twelve thousand had actually been paid. Now Destefani was looking at a twenty-four-thousand shortfall.

The worst luck, though, had been with the tobacco sponsorship.

Back when Destefani made the deal, it seemed like an advertising coup. There was the famous race pilot, Tiger Destefani, a living advertisement for his sponsor's product, with that gunfighter, *High Noon* swagger, a lump of the sponsor's product under his lip, and with that uncanny ability—*Splooot!*—to nail a target ten feet away. And there was the name of his new sponsor emblazoned right there on the side of his airplane: SKOAL!

It should have been a sponsorship made in heaven. And for the struggling air-racing industry, it might have been a replay of what saved NASCAR back in the late seventies: the entry of big tobacco money. It might have been the rising tide that lifted *all* the racers' boats.

But they hadn't counted on the tobacco-company lawyers. On the eve of the Reno races in which *Strega* would be a 500-mile-per-hour, Gold Trophy–winning billboard for Skoal, they showed up. *What about the company's liability? What if someone gets hurt? What if that damned airplane crashes and takes out half of Nevada? Skoal would be liable for . . .*

Destefani, they said, would have to carry a liability coverage of $10 million on *Strega*.

Which turned out to be an impossible requirement. No one—neither Team *Strega* nor the Reno Air Racing Association—was able or willing to pick up the tab. The premium for such coverage would far exceed the payback from the sponsorship. It was race time, and out there on the ramp of Stead Field, the tobacco-company lawyers were ordering that SKOAL be removed from *Strega*.

And why wasn't Skoal picking up the bill for the insurance? It all came back to the glaring difference between sports like high-visibility NASCAR racing and the desert-rat, low-budget, dirt-grubbing world of air racing. A mundane matter like insurance, which meant nothing to the huge-budgeted sport NASCAR, spelled the difference at Reno between breaking even or going broke.

Now, just to go to Reno in 1998, Destefani needed fifty grand. He needed that much in sponsorship money—*plus* the first-place prize money—just to break even. He had just hooked a deal with the Candlewood Hotel chain that would ease some of the pressure. But a vacuum still existed from the collapsed Bigger.net sponsorship. He was back to doing that which he hated: the cold calls, the letters, the hat-in-hand solicitation for funds like a politician running for reelection.

He still didn't know how expensive *Strega's* engine overhaul would be. Just a routine refresher of the Merlin engine after a week of racing came to a minimum of fifteen thousand dollars. If the damage turned out to be something greater, he'd be in serious trouble. Not until he got the Mustang out of Reno, through the snow-filled Donner Pass and back home to Bakersfield, would he know just how broke he really was.

And then, during the last week of February 1998, El Niño took a siesta. The break was enough to let Destefani's crew rumble through the pass in the High Sierra with *Strega* in tow. The truck rolled out of the mountains, down to the waterlogged valley at Minter Field with the disassembled Mustang on board, wings removed, the fuselage wrapped in a tarpaulin. *Strega* looked less like a race plane than the cadaver of a prehistoric flying lizard.

The first order of business was the engine. They opened up the crankcase. It didn't take long to determine what Destefani had already guessed—and hoped: *Strega's* engine was okay. The cracked nose section was replaceable. No serious damage had been done when the propeller blades chewed up the runway after the 1997 Gold race.

Kerchenfaut was pissed.

Strega had just been delivered to Destefani's hangar at Minter Field. And when Kerchenfaut drove down from Santa Clara to check her out, what did he discover parked inside, in a place of honor on *Strega's* very own hangar floor? *Another damned race plane!*

It was their competitor, *Voodoo Chile*, which was now owned by

Bob Button. *Voodoo* was there in Destefani's hangar getting modified and upgraded to near-*Strega* standard.

To Kerchenfaut, whose devotion to *Strega* bordered on obsession, this amounted to rank disloyalty. Damn! How could you keep faith with your own team, who had been busting their butts to win races, while at the same time you gave comfort and solace to the enemy? It smacked of perfidy.

Of course, Kerchenfaut and Destefani had been all through this before. It came up every time another racer showed up in Tiger's hangar. And as much as it pissed him off, Kerchenfaut knew the reality of air racing. The Unlimited racing community was a small one. Out of necessity, they shared resources and swapped ideas.

For Destefani, it was just a matter of business. Since the seventies, he had been restoring warbirds and upgrading racers in his hangar complex at Minter Field. *Dago Red*, the superfast Mustang, as well as *Strega* and *Voodoo Chile*, had been built up there in Destefani's facility. Now *Dago*, with a new pilot, Bruce Lockwood, was poised to give everyone in the Gold Division a run for their money next year.

To Destefani, that was business. It was how he supported his own racing enterprise. But there was a limit to the business. "Hell, I don't give away *all* our secrets," he kept telling Kerchenfaut. What he was doing now for *Voodoo Chile* was what he had done earlier for *Dago Red*—one of his fastest and toughest rivals—was the no-brainer stuff: Clip the wings, plug the air holes, modify the canopy. Make the Mustang go fast, but not *too* fast. *Strega* still had some critical enhancements that no other race plane possessed.

Nonetheless, it was part of the script they played out every year at this time: Kerchenfaut had to go through the motions of being pissed. *Righteously* pissed. And damn it, it was his *duty* to be pissed! He was the crew chief, and being pissed was a condition that went with his title. Where was it written that pilots were the only ones who could be prima donnas?

. . .

Most of the *Strega* crew was there—Jim Foss, Randy Foster, Mike Wilton—and they were listening to Tiger give them his between-races rah-rah talk: "It's a go, guys. *Strega's* gonna be okay. We're gonna kick some ass in Reno again."

And just as they always did, the guys grinned and cheered and high-fived. It was exactly what they *wanted* to hear, even though the preponderance of evidence told them exactly the opposite.

Standing there in the damp hangar, looking around the place, Kerchenfaut found it hard to believe. *Strega,* still stored in the hangar with its wings removed, looked just as it had when they loaded it off the flatbed from Reno. On the other side of the hangar, in the place of honor—or so it appeared to Kerchenfaut—was that damned *Voodoo Chile.* And Kerchenfaut understood why: Tiger needed money. *Voodoo's* owner, Bob Button, was happy to pay someone like Tiger to make his airplane go fast. Maybe even as fast as *Strega.*

It was understandable, of course. By now everyone knew about Tiger's messy divorce and the *very* bitter squabble he was going through with Mary. And like everyone in Bakersfield, they knew that Tiger had gotten into trouble with the cops for having installed a wiretapping device on his home telephone. Tiger was having a bad year.

Still, they believed Tiger, mostly because they *wanted* to believe. More than any other race pilot or team owner, Tiger was revered by the guys who worked for him. They loved him because he was one of *them,* not one of the high-rolling dilettantes or the blue-blooded test pilots who knew how to fly into orbit but couldn't change a spark plug.

Another thing they loved about Destefani was that he didn't bullshit them, at least excessively and not in a devious way.

Until now. Until they heard him saying things like "It's a go, guys. *Strega's* gonna be okay." To Tiger's crew, this definitely sounded like bullshit.

. . .

That weekend, Tiger was forced to do some rethinking. He drove his pickup out to the alfalfa fields. He got out and stood for a long time there in the muck, gazing at the flooded landscape. It looked like an inland sea. He tried to take a step, but the mud sucked at his boots like quicksand. Everywhere there was water. He could see a few scrawny sprigs of alfalfa trying to squeeze up through the flood, but he knew it was no use. Another crop was wiped out.

Yeah, this was a hell of a year, and it had just begun. Destefani couldn't get over the feeling that this goddamned weather—El Niño—was conspiring with his wife's lawyers to get him. The normal rainfall for this time of year was five inches. So far they'd had fourteen. He was down two hundred thousand dollars this year just on lost alfalfa revenue.

And it was raining again.

He stood in the muck for a while longer, hands thrust into his jeans. Between the divorce and the weather and the lost time and expense of getting *Strega* back to Bakersfield, he was in trouble. Something had to give, and he knew what it would be.

On a Monday night, following the weekend he spent down at Destefani's hangar, Kerchenfaut got the call. "I've changed my mind," he heard Tiger say. "It's not gonna work. We have to stand down for a year."

Kerchenfaut had a hunch it was coming. He had already felt the vibrations. He figured that sooner or later Tiger was going to be hit with a dose of reality. The ante for the divorce was already ratcheting up and off the scale. Fish were breeding in his aquatic alfalfa fields. Tiger was broke.

Kerchenfaut hung up and immediately went into the worst depression he'd felt in years. *Goddamnit, it wasn't right.* For nearly thirty years he'd been associated with winning teams. He had personally managed the metamorphosis of *Strega* from a corroded hulk to the fastest and winningest race plane in history.

234

It took the rest of the evening for him to get over being angry. He was pissed not just because it would be the first racing season in three decades he would sit out. He felt bad for the *Strega* team. Everyone knew that *Strega*'s success had as much to do with the quality of the ground crew as it did with the pilot. In such a time-critical sport as air racing, when a minor glitch in your airplane might take a week to repair, *Strega*'s guys did it overnight. *Strega*, in fact, was the first Mustang to go one-on-one with the radial-engined Bearcats and Sea Furies and beat their socks off half a dozen times.

Tiger was the team's leader, the guy they would have followed into hell. He was the macho-talking gunfighter who backed up all that hardball talk with wins. Six of them so far.

Kerchenfaut had already made plans for how they were going to nail a seventh, tying Darryl Greenamyer's record. He had been planning some alterations to *Strega*—some more aerodynamic cleanups—and he wanted to replace a lot of the original electrical wiring.

Now it didn't matter. They had the whole next year in which to swallow their disappointment.

Yeah, he thought, Tiger was still the gunfighter. Still a hero to his guys. But he was a flawed hero now. Kerchenfaut wondered if it would ever be the same.

✈ 20 ✈

Dago

15 July 1998

Silence. It was a seeping, ominous, evil quietude that pervaded Bill Kerchenfaut's life that summer. The silence was coming from his telephone. The damned thing wasn't ringing.

If early 1998 had been the winter of Tiger Destefani's discontent, then this was the summer of Bill Kerchenfaut's unhappiness. Since the day in April when Destefani telephoned to tell him he'd changed his mind about racing *Strega,* Kerchenfaut had felt like a man without a life. For this season, at least, he wasn't leading a race team at Reno.

Racing was in Kerchenfaut's blood. For the past thirty seasons he had crewed on *somebody's* hot warbird. He'd gotten his start working for Darryl Greenamyer back in the sixties.

Those were heady times, with that cocky little Greenamyer whipping the socks off everyone and rubbing their noses in it. Even though he hadn't worked for Greenamyer for many years now, Kerchenfaut still maintained a devout loyalty to him. Whenever someone in the pits or at the bar would start a Greenamyer-bashing session—*That cocky little egomaniac? The guy who took all the glory and left you holding the tab? The son of a bitch who*—the congenial Kerchenfaut would cut them off.

To Kerchenfaut, who had been a young ex-sergeant fresh out of the air force when he worked for Greenamyer, the guy was a hero. "He was a leader of men," he would tell them. "His guys would follow him into hell."

Which would usually put a damper on the Greenamyer bashing. Everyone knew that Kerchenfaut was a guy who believed in team loyalty. Loyalty was a substance that flowed up and down in a racing crew. If the owner and pilot of a team took care of the guys turning wrenches on his airplane, they would give him a good airplane.

But now Kerchenfaut's sense of loyalty was being tested. Since springtime, the gulf between him and Destefani had become as wide as the gurgling lake that covered Destefani's alfalfa fields. Since the day Tiger changed his mind and said Team *Strega* would stand down, the two men had not talked.

It was an unhappy estrangement. For eleven years Kerchenfaut had worked as *Strega*'s crew chief. He had invested his life and energy and talent in the sleek fighter. He had been there while the derelict Mustang was transformed into a racing airplane. Over the years, *Strega*'s impressive string of victories could be attributed, he knew, in no small part to his efforts. It was he who had orchestrated the efforts of *Strega*'s crew members, running the group like the operating officer of a corporation.

Now it had all gone to hell.

In Kerchenfaut's view, Destefani had let his personal problems interfere with what was important: racing *Strega*. And that business of "sleeping with the enemy . . ." Well, damn it, it was Tiger who had opened his hangar to those guys from Team *Voodoo*. How many *Strega* secrets had been compromised and incorporated in the copycat Mustang? And no matter how much Destefani insisted that he "didn't tell 'em *all* our secrets," Kerchenfaut didn't like the idea that they told those guys *any* of *Strega's* secrets. Kerchenfaut couldn't get over this nagging feeling that the team had been somehow betrayed.

Destefani, for his part, thought Kerchenfaut had suffered a total detachment from reality. This was *business*, for Christ's sake! There were only half a dozen shops in the world where you could get a Mustang converted to an Unlimited racing airplane, and Destefani's hangar at Minter Field happened to be one of them. Kerchenfaut didn't understand the realities of divorce lawyers and federal judges and nonstop El Niños that turned your alfalfa fields into inland seas.

Kerchenfaut was a guy who loved nothing so much as stroking and tweaking a high-spirited racing machine. He liked everything about the business—the wrench turning, the airframe slicking, the spitballing sessions during which a crew bounced ideas around for enhancing their racer.

And that was the part he loved most—the total amalgam of a racing team. In his opinion, a racing team was a sum of all its parts. The parts included a good pilot, a top-notch engine builder, a few gifted mechanics, and a bright avionics guy. And to orchestrate the efforts of all these prima donnas, you had to have a crew chief. Or *team manager*, as Kerchenfaut preferred to be titled.

One day in midsummer, Bill Kerchenfaut's phone started ringing. And then it rang *a lot*.

The first call came from Bob Button, owner of *Voodoo*.

"Would you come down to Shafter and look over *Voodoo?*" Button wanted Kerchenfaut to take over the job of crew chief.

Shafter, California, was the home of Tiger Destefani and *Strega*. It was also where *Voodoo* was being transformed into a *Strega* clone. It was well into July now, time when Unlimited racers ought to have their rosters and schedules for Reno nailed down.

Kerchenfaut drove down to Shafter that weekend. He knew this was going to be awkward. And then, seeing the still-derelict *Strega* sitting in pieces in a corner of the hangar, he couldn't help noticing all the money and energy that was flowing into the upstart racer *Voodoo*. It was the old loyalty thing again. *Sleeping with the enemy.*

Kerchenfaut looked *Voodoo* over. He didn't like what he saw. Too much had been done too fast. Kerchenfaut knew that when you applied so many modifications and tweakings to a temperamental race plane, you were bound to have problems. Unexpected glitches would show up. You had to put the airplane through a rigorous flight-test program, verifying and validating all your specifications.

There wasn't time for that. *Voodoo* was going to race at Reno, and it was going to have problems.

Kerchenfaut turned Button down.

Bob Button, as it turned out, was a guy who didn't like to take no for an answer. He, by God, *wanted* Kerchenfaut to work for Team *Voodoo*. He kept offering. Kerchenfaut kept turning him down.

Kerchenfaut was tempted, of course. Damn it, he *wanted* to race at Reno almost more than anything. But there was more to it than just the vibrations he was getting about the *Voodoo*'s readiness to race. Kerchenfaut was still having trouble separating logic from loyalty.

Back in Santa Clara, the phone was still ringing. Suddenly, Kerchenfaut's services were in demand. But the call that got his attention came from an ancient World War II facility stuck out among the Joshua trees and the fossil landscape of the high desert. It was a place called Mojave, and in July it looked like the surface of Mercury.

Even the name—*Dago Red*—had a spit-in-your-eye, sassy, not-politically-correct nuance. As soon as he saw it sitting there in the arid hangar on the old ex–military field, wearing that famous red, white, and yellow paint scheme, Kerchenfaut knew he had struck gold.

Dago Red looked like a sleek ghost from the past. Which, in a way, it was. Of all the hot Unlimiteds that had ever raced at Reno, few had a more glorious history than *Dago Red*, which was like a veteran Thoroughbred that kept showing up every year in the front of the pack.

Dago had, in fact, been the first of a breed of racing Mustangs that came to life in the hangar of Tiger Destefani out at Minter Field. Owned by Destefani and Frank Taylor, *Dago Red* had burst onto the air-racing scene like a new superstar.

Assembled in 1982, *Dago Red* was built from assorted spare parts and the remains of a wrecked Mustang, registered as N5410V. Destefani and Taylor recruited racing's perennial engineering gurus, Pete Law, Mike Nixon, and Bruce Boland, to build their new racer. *Jeannie*, Wiley Sanders's 1980 and 1981 winning racer, was the role model, but *Dago Red* would go on to possess some refinements not yet seen on *Jeannie* or any other racing Mustang.

It was a monumental task, constructing an Unlimited racer from scratch in one year. Not until two weeks before Reno, 1982, was *Dago* ready for her first test flight. The pilot was Ron Hevle, a talented young guy who had been racing Destefani's stock Mustang, *Mangia Pane*. With only about seven hours total shakedown time, *Dago Red* went to Reno.

She was a sensation, just sitting there on the ramp. *Dago Red* was decked out in a dazzling red, yellow, and white paint job with a swoop down the fuselage, wearing her permanent race number, four, on the tail. With the trimmed-down canopy and the sexy colors, *Dago Red* was a breed apart from all the other stock-looking Mustangs, with their pseudomilitary markings and drab paint schemes. *Dago* was a reminder of the old Thompson Trophy days when racers, by God, *looked* like racers, not artifacts from a war museum.

And then Hevle took her out on the course. During the brief series of test flights, *Dago Red*'s engine had not been pushed beyond a conservative power setting of seventy-five inches manifold pressure. Now it was time to make the hyped-up Merlin produce some *real* horsepower. Hevle would be nudging the throttle up somewhere past a hundred inches. But how much past?

Before *Dago Red*'s first qualification run at Reno, Bruce Boland handed Hevle a slip of paper with a precise combination of rpm and manifold pressure. This was a power setting that Boland calculated would push the racer to a target qualifying speed of around 440 miles per hour.

Boland's mechanical genius was already a matter of legend. But this time the savvy Lockheed flight-test engineer outdid himself. When Hevle competed in his official qualifying lap, he turned in a time of 440.565 miles per hour.

Which also turned out to be the fastest time of the field. It gave Hevle and *Dago Red* a locked-in slot for the Gold race and the pole for the first heat race. And *Dago Red* kept up her stunning performance. In their first official air race that Friday, Hevle flashed across the finish line that Friday in first place, untouched by his main competitor, John Crocker, in his Mustang, *Sumthin' Else.*

In the Saturday race, while again holding the lead, Hevle was forced to throttle back due to a high-induction temperature, coming in second behind Crocker. Back on the ground, Boland quickly traced the problem to an inadequate ADI fluid flow and applied an easy fix in the form of a larger spray nozzle.

Dago Red's moment of glory came on Sunday. Snatching the lead from Crocker on the pace lap, Hevle shot ahead, commanding the race, forcing Crocker to stress his engine to the breaking point. On the fourth lap, it happened. Crocker pulled up with a shattered Merlin engine, trailing fire and smoke, and plunked his racer back down in a prop-bending emergency landing on runway 14.

From then on, the day—and the championship—belonged to *Dago Red*. Hevle could throttle back and cruise to an easy victory. Back in the pits, the *Dago Red* team proceeded to uncork their specially labeled stock of vintage "Dago Red" wine in a nonstop celebration.

It was a Cinderella story. *Dago Red* had come flying into town, new and unknown, and taken Reno by storm. A first-time racer had come here and won all the marbles. From her first time in the air, *Dago Red* had thrown down a gauntlet on her first outing by beating all the qualifiers and then sailed away with the Gold Trophy as if she were a veteran of many seasons.

It looked to everyone, especially the *Dago Red* team, as if they had a long-term lock on the Reno championship. There were few racing airplanes in existence that could match her. It was clear to everyone that the 1982 championship would just be the first in a long string of victories. Team *Dago Red* could look forward to many such celebrations.

But something always went wrong. *Dago Red* didn't win next year. Or the next. Meanwhile, newer, faster airplanes came along. The glorious victory of 1982 seemed a fluke. *Dago Red* was one of those classy also-rans whose number never quite came up again. She seemed like a vintage wine, stored on a shelf to age, waiting for the right moment.

Crews came and went. Old pilots retired; new ones took command. *Dago Red* changed owners several times. She switched stables like an unwanted horse.

And then, in 1996, everything changed. *Dago Red* was back.

It was the second-fastest qualifying time ever recorded at Reno—490.826 miles per hour—flown by *Dago Red*'s owner and pilot, David Price. The 1996 Gold Trophy race was shaping up as a blood battle between *Dago Red* and *Strega,* flown by Tiger Destefani.

But then something happened.

What happened was a moment that would remain etched like an engraving in David Price's memory. It was in 1996, on the day of the Unlimited Gold Trophy race. He was flying *Dago Red,* and he had just flashed across the finish line a full second ahead of Tiger Destefani in *Strega.* He had won the National Unlimited Air Racing Championship.

Or so he thought.

It was a hell of a race. That crafty little bastard Destefani had stayed glued to his tail for the entire race. Approaching the last lap, it looked like Tiger was going to make his move. *Dago Red*'s Merlin engine was already peaked out, pulling more horsepower than anyone thought the engine could sustain. And *still* Destefani was out there, right on his tail, flogging his engine just as hard.

Price's crew chief that year was Bruce Lockwood. From atop the team trailer, Lockwood was watching the tableau unfold. He could see that *Strega* was moving up on *Dago Red*. A second behind. Half a second. The race was coming down to minute differences in power and technique. Lockwood knew that *Dago Red*'s engine was already on the brink of destruction. The oil temperature was nudging into the red scale. It couldn't take much more flogging. But damn, man, this was the championship race!

"Tiger's right on your ass," Lockwood radioed. "You're gonna have to melt it, David."

Melt it. Price knew what that meant. If he pushed the power up any more, the Merlin could turn on him like a bitch from hell. He would be flying a smoking torch. But David Price, as much as anyone who raced at Reno, was possessed by a single overwhelming desire. He was within two laps of becoming the National Unlimited Racing champion.

He nudged the throttle up some more.

Price was a latecomer to air racing. More than forty years ago, back in the 1950s, he had earned his wings as a young navy pilot. He had flown F9F Panthers, then done a stint as an instructor in the training command. In 1957 he left the navy, went to law school, and devoted the next three decades to becoming a successful California lawyer. Along the way he had accumulated considerable wealth, becoming chairman of the American Golf Corporation and covering the California landscape with undulating new golf courses.

One September in the mid-eighties, he went to the races at Reno as a spectator. After taking a ride in the back of John Crocker's Mustang, he had what amounted to an epiphany. He had to have a warbird. And he had to race.

Now Price owned a collection of rare airplanes that he kept on display in the Santa Monica Museum of Flying, of which he was chairman and principal contributor. One of the rare airplanes that had been added to Price's collection was the racing Mustang *Dago Red*.

Since 1989, *Dago Red* had been out of the racing game, relegated to static display duty. But in 1993 they brought her out of retirement. With some 1990's modifications, *Dago Red* came to Reno. By 1995 both Price and *Dago* were becoming competitive. Racing in the Gold against the front-runners, *Strega* and *Rare Bear*, *Dago Red* finished in a respectable third place.

By 1996, the Mustang's transformation from a 1980s racer to a modern speed demon was complete. *Dago* had been fitted with a Dwight Thorn Merlin engine that was at least the match of the power plant in *Strega*. With her new airframe cleanups, some borrowed from Destefani and some invented by her new crew, *Dago Red* had become a challenger to the tiresome *Rare Bear* versus *Strega* act the fans had seen for most of the decade.

Then, in the 1996 Gold race, against *Strega*, *Dago Red's* moment of glory came. Price was nose to nose with the reigning champion, Tiger Destefani.

"You're gonna have to melt it."

Hearing Lockwood's radio call, Price nudged up the throttle, and glanced at the oil-temperature gauge. Sure as hell, it was advancing into the red zone.

In that instant, glancing down in the cockpit as *Dago Red* made the slight left bend around pylon 2, something happened.

He cut inside the pylon.

And although over a hundred thousand people were watching

Dago Red sweep around the pylons, Price's mistake went unnoticed by every one of them—except two. One was the pylon judge standing there in the weeds next to the pylon. The other was Tiger Destefani, flying at nearly 500 miles per hour, one plane length behind Price.

Beneath Destefani's oxygen mask, a broad grin spread over his face. He eased the throttle back on *Strega*. Price's pylon cut—*which Price didn't even know about*—would cost him sixteen seconds, which amounted to nearly a quarter of a lap. Destefani could now loaf along in a trail position and save his laboring engine. All he had to do was stay in the race and finish.

Price roared past the finish line several hundred yards ahead of Destefani. He landed, taxied back to the ramp, and beamed at the cheering crowd. He was in the cockpit, still beaming, when someone came running up to give him the worst news of his aviation career: "David, they say you cut number-two pylon."

Price's grin melted like a cow pie on the concrete.

It was then, after losing the 1996 race, that Price did something he would forever regret. He sold *Dago Red*.

Now it was 1998, and *Dago Red* had everything going for her: the best crew chief in the business, a motivated new owner, and a top-notch crew that included telemetry wizard Jim Foss and Museum of Flying master mechanic Chris Wood.

And a new pilot. His name was Bruce Lockwood.

Lockwood?

Well, as former crew chief he *did* seem an unlikely choice, considering his lack of experience actually flying at high speed around the pylons and the number of Unlimited pilots available this season. But in the cloistered world of air racing, friendship and loyalty counted for a lot. And it was Lockwood's best friend, Bob Hannah, who had brokered the chance for him to fly *Dago Red* in the 1998 championship races.

Lockwood was accustomed to such phone calls from Hannah. He and Hannah went way back, all the way to their years on the moto-cross circuit. Hannah, who had been the national motocross cham-pion, liked to call up and say things like "Lockwood, leave the bike at home this time. Just push the box it came in. It's cheaper, and you won't get hurt."

Hannah was better known than Lockwood, at least outside the air-racing arena. His nickname was "Hurricane," a label that was hung on him back when he was a champion motorcycle racer.

In the bone-crunching world of motocross, Hurricane Hannah was already a legend. Straight out of high school ("a really good twelfth-grade education," he liked to say), he blazed into the record books, winning the national championship an unprecedented seven times. Hannah was a guy who loved high-performance machines. More than that, he loved pushing them right up to the razor-thin edges of their envelopes.

And sometimes beyond. Motocross racing being what it was, Hannah spent a lot of time sailing through the air, glancing like a Frisbee off the hard-packed dirt of motocross courses. He was familiar with the *snap* of shattered collarbones, recognized the sickening misalignment of his own broken ankles and wrists. It was just part of the business. But that was what made Han-nah a winner—a willingness to hang his carcass way out over the abyss. And it was what ultimately drew him to Unlimited Air Racing, a sport even more flamboyant and risk-driven than motocross.

Hannah was flying *Voodoo* this year at Reno. And he happened to be a close friend of Utah businessman Terry Bland, the new owner of *Dago Red*, who needed a pilot.

And Hannah had someone in mind: his old buddy Lockwood.

Lockwood was a tall, lean-faced guy with a dark mustache and a quick smile. He grew up in the warbird business in the same tradition as the Chino kids—Hinton, Brickert, the Maloney boys Jim and John—hanging out at airports, crewing on race teams, turning wrenches, and bumming rides in people's expensive warbirds.

Lockwood came from Lancaster, California, but he learned to fly in Alaska in 1978. That was also where he learned about motorcycles and racing and where, for five seasons, he reigned as the state motocross champion. It was in the blood-and-mud, free-for-all world of motorcycle racing that he became buddies with Hannah. Hannah would be his best friend and his toughest rival. And the rivalry went beyond the world of motorcycles.

During the eighties, Lockwood built his own aerobatic plane, a Christen Eagle. When he began lusting for something hotter, he traded the Eagle, along with some creative financing, for a flyable F-4U Corsair navy fighter. From then on, Lockwood's soul belonged to the high-octane, big-motored world of warbirds.

In California he worked for warbird aficionado Alan Preston, then for David Price at the Santa Monica Museum of Flying. Eventually, Lockwood became the museum's director of restoration and the manager of the race team. Under Preston and Price's tutelage, Lockwood got into racing, beginning with his Corsair, then a Yak. At a vintage warbird race at Phoenix, he qualified a P-47.

When he finally got to fly a Mustang for the first time, in 1986, Price put him in the seat of a famous racer. It was a red, white, and gold P-51 named *Dago Red*.

Chuff! Chuff! Chuff!

One thing about jogging in the summer, at least out there in the desert, was that you didn't sweat much. It was too dry. But it was hot! Anything under 110 degrees in the shade in the Mojave Desert was considered a cold snap.

Lockwood kept on pounding down the dirt road—*Chuff! Chuff! Chuff!*—each step leaving a waffle print in the ancient dirt. Off in the distance he could see the hangars at the airport. They were swelling and squiggling in the heat waves like living creatures on the floor of the desert.

Jogging for Lockwood was a form of discipline, and he was a very disciplined guy. He figured that once you got used to this heat, jogging in the desert was good training. It prepared you for the airless, high-temperature atmosphere of the cockpit when you were cranking around the pylons. Heat exhaustion in the cockpit was as big an enemy as mechanical failure and a lot more insidious. It crept up on you, lowered your tolerance to Gs, made you groggy and unfocused. And it caused you to make mistakes.

Chuff! Chuff! Chuff!

Time to turn around, head back to the hangar. Five miles round trip. Lockwood did this every day during this last couple of weeks before Reno. He believed in fitness. Get the stamina up, the heat tolerance, the ability to handle stress. Air racing was a stressful sport.

Kerchenfaut was in Mojave now, getting *Dago Red* prepared for Reno. He and Lockwood had hit it off immediately. Kerchenfaut liked Lockwood's unflamboyant, focused style. In fact, Kerchenfaut was telling everyone that Lockwood was such a classic all-American kid— Mr. Nice Guy—he ought to have his picture on a Wheaties box. He was so clean-cut and viceless, it made people wonder how he got into a sport like air racing.

Mr. Nice Guy, as Kerchenfaut knew, was not an all-inclusive character description of Unlimited air racers. For reasons no one wanted to examine very closely, air racing over the years had attracted a certain element of . . . rascality. It was something that seemed to go with the territory, whether it was an affinity for high risk or just some neurotic impulse to throw both your money and your life away in a single cast. For whatever reason, several habitués of the Room of Hard Benches had been granted close views of the inner walls of penal institutions. Their various crimes against society covered a wide spectrum, from drug running to money laundering to drunken driving to wiretapping.

When someone like Lockwood—Mr. Nice Guy on the Wheaties box—came along, flying a hot contender like *Dago Red,* it made people wonder: *What was wrong with him?*

Nothing, in fact. Lockwood was exactly what he seemed to be: a clean-cut guy with no blemishes on his record. Even the name—*Bruce Lockwood*—seemed too good to be true. It sounded like a label for a new actor. Or a rock star. Or the hero of an action comic.

⊱ 21 ⊰

Return to Reno

This is one of the last arenas where you can raise hell
with an airplane—short of going to war.
—Alan Preston, Unlimited Racing pilot

13 September 1998

The searing heat of summer had abated just a little. When the sun
dropped behind the high western ridge, you could feel the chill descend over Truckee Meadow.

The migration was under way. At airports in California and Texas
and Florida, just as they did every September, the pilots climbed
into their warbirds. They cranked up the temperamental, high-
strung engines and took off for Reno. Some went solo, but most of
the racers launched in flights of two or three, pointing their long,
rakish noses toward the high desert.

By noon Sunday, down there in the pits at Stead Field, you could
hear them coming. They came skimming in over the mountains
from Van Nuys or Santa Monica or up the southern route via Las
Vegas. Or the long haul from the East, some coming all the way

from Florida. Formations of two and three warbirds at a time converged on Reno like hawks to a nest. All day the air filled with the
staccato growl of Merlins, the deep, radial thunder of the Wrights
and Pratts, the purrs and growls of the incoming Formula Ones and
T-6s and T-28s.

And something different—the Lycoming-engined buzz of the new
sport class. These were the slick production-kit aircraft, limited to
engine sizes of 650 cubic inches. Most sport-class entrants were
all-composite airframes, like the slick Glasair III, Lancair, and the
Questair Venture, and were capable of speeds of over 300 miles per
hour.

Waiting for them down there on the ramp were the pit crews.
The long concrete apron at Reno had been transformed to an eye-
watering sea of color—tents, awnings, eighteen-wheel support trailers. Instead of an old airfield in Nevada, Stead Field looked like a
trade bazaar in the Gobi.

The racers landed, climbed down from the cramped cockpits, and
shook a few hands. Then they did what they always did when they
landed at Reno. They checked out the other pits. *Who was here?*
Who didn't make it? Who were the new guys?

One that *was* here, occupying the most prominent place in the
pits, was *Dago Red*, the gorgeous red Mustang. And conspicuously
missing was the most successful racing Mustang of all time, *Strega*.
In its place was another P-51, the Strega look-alike that had shared
Tiger Destefani's hangar all winter up in Shafterville, *Voodoo Chile*.
Over the winter, the owner, Bob Button, had quietly shortened the
name to simply *Voodoo*, having had enough of hearing the name
pronounced *Voodoo "Chili."*

Even more noticeably absent was the most famous round-
engined racer in Reno history, *Rare Bear*. Like Destefani, Shelton
had "stood down" this year for reasons both financial and personal.

Actually, *Rare Bear* was there but out of sight. The big Bearcat was sitting in the same hangar where it had been shoved after

the destruction derby of the Sunday finals last year. The wrecked R-3350 engine had been removed, and you could see only the bare metal firewall of the Bearcat, the tubes and wires sticking out like severed arteries.

It was depressing, at least to anyone who worried about the downside of this high-rolling, low-paying sport. Seeing *Rare Bear* like this was like watching a champion athlete with a fatal disease. All the forces of economics, politics, and the formidable statutes of the state of Nevada had aligned themselves against the Bear and its owner. Shelton's problems with the string of DUIs, the loss of his flying privileges, had cast a shadow over the racing community. They could talk about it over drinks, deplore it, even make jokes about it. Down deep, however, it bothered the hell out of them.

One of the reasons it disturbed them was because it meant that being a winner here at Reno—taking the Gold and being king of the hill—really didn't count for much. Shelton's photo had been in every aviation magazine. He had signed thousands of programs and posters and endorsements. He had snapped his fingers and gotten tables at the poshest restaurants, consorted with the starriest celebrities, drawn the attention of the highest-rolling sponsors.

Then he lost it.

And this was what bothered them, because Ol' Lyle, for all his contrariness, was *one of them*. He was a pilot's pilot and a hard-charging competitor who had scrawled his initials all over the surface of air racing. He possessed all the same sacred juices that flowed through their veins. The Shelton affair struck home because it was a family matter. One of the family had gone out and made a mess.

Shelton wasn't hanging out in any of the pits, nor did he drop in to the Room of Hard Benches for the briefings. Instead, he had a table set up there in *Rare Bear*'s hangar, and he was taking up donations.

Donations! To any of the Brethren who stopped by to watch this spectacle, it was strange. And disconcerting. Ol' Lyle, who wasn't racing and wasn't likely to *ever* get back in the cockpit, was there signing posters and photos of *Rare Bear* and accepting contributions that would go toward putting the racer back in the air. "*Rare Bear* needs about six thousand mechanic-hours of work to be in racing shape again," Shelton was telling the curious fans.

By now everyone knew about his troubles with the law. The legal mess had taken a toll not only on his finances but on his morale. Shelton's appeal of his most recent DUI was pending, and you could see the worry lines in his face. And his problems went beyond just worrying about flying *Rare Bear* again. He faced a very real prospect of never flying *anything* again and, worse, spending the next part of his life in jail.

Though John Penney, Shelton's backup pilot, had tried valiantly to raise sponsorship money to resurrect *Rare Bear*, nothing had materialized. It was as if Shelton's problems had rubbed off on *Rare Bear*. No one wanted any part of it. Now even Penney was out of sight, having clashed with the race committee over the handling of last year's final races. He had turned over his job as Unlimited Class president to longtime Mustang racer Art Vance.

Shelton wasn't the only racing champion who was in trouble. Destefani was wearing a new pattern of worry lines on his face this season, too. Back in Bakersfield, his scorched-earth divorce was gathering energy like a Pacific storm. And in the heat of the proceeding, Destefani had complicated his life beyond measure by doing something that even he now realized was an egregious error: He installed a *wiretap* on his home telephone.

Which, as he learned after it was discovered and reported to the FBI, was illegal.

Which resulted in his arrest and prosecution.

Which meant that Destefani, like his rival, Shelton, was about to confront an unsmiling judge. He, too, faced the very real prospect of going to jail.

It was almost too bizarre to be true. The two winningest race pilots in modern history—Ol' Lyle and the swaggering Gunfighter—
both contemplating the interior of a cell.

So it was a different atmosphere there in the Room of Hard
Benches. You could feel the climate change, beginning on that first
Sunday when they all came swarming into Reno. There seemed to
be less kibitzing, at least the wiseass, one-line obscenities that Tiger
loved to throw out. Tiger was sitting almost unnoticed at the fringe
of the group, not at his usual place in the center, where he used to
hold court and crack everyone up. He was keeping his mouth shut,
watching the proceedings like a village elder.

Tiger even *looked* different this year. Gone was that grinning
George Raft cockiness. (*I'll tell you what you're gonna see out there:
twenty-three losers—and me!*) Gone, too, was the ass-kicking swagger. These days Tiger was walking and acting just like what he was—
a worried little guy whose life had come unstitched at the seams.

Another pilot who was out of the action this year was Skip Holm,
who, in normal times, could crack jokes as fast as Tiger. Skip was at
the briefings, looking almost as subdued as Tiger.

It was tough for a hired gun like Holm, not being where the action was. This was one of those rare years when no one needed the
services of a fly-for-hire warbird jockey. Tom Dwelle's exotic Sea
Fury, *Critical Mass,* was absent this year, not yet recovered from the
previous season's damage.

Holm had a supporting role in this year's show: He would be flying the A-1 Skyraider, the official pace plane for the new T-28 class.
It wasn't exactly his first choice of jobs, but what the hell? It was
flying.

Tiger, for his part, had put out plenty of feelers that he was available and ready to fly. All he needed was an airplane, and at this point
he wasn't too fussy. A plain vanilla stock Mustang would do.

The sidelining of winners like Destefani and Holm, while less experienced pilots were given the seats of hot racers like *Dago Red* and
Voodoo, seemed a mystery, at least to outsiders. Why would an

owner entrust his million-dollar race plane to an unproven new guy when he could hire Destefani or Holm?

It had more to do with loyalty than with reality. Owners didn't often switch pilots even when a hot stick like Destefani came along. Even if you *knew* he could get a few more miles per hour out of your race plane. It came down to superstition as much as practicality. Of course, if race-plane owners had a grain of practicality in their systems, they would have cashed in their long-snouted killing machines and bought safe and sensible T-bonds.

And even though Tiger knew all this, he was still *very* frustrated. So frustrated, he told everyone after a morning briefing that he was thinking of putting up a sign—Will Fly For—leaving the offer open. Some of the pilots were cracking themselves up suggesting *what* it was that Tiger would fly for.

But it was showtime, and no one was offering their warbird to Destefani. No one except Steve Hinton, who recruited Tiger to ride the backseat of his T-33 pace plane. The idea was that if someone got into serious trouble out there (and, of course, someone *always* got into trouble out there), then they'd have this living natural resource available for airborne advice.

Still, it looked peculiar: the winningest race pilot in modern history a damned *passenger*.

Some of the race pilots thought it was pretty funny. "You gonna let him call the start?" someone asked Hinton.

"You kidding? Tiger? With everyone listening?"

Which got a laugh. Tiger Destefani was a guy who could not utter an entire sentence without inserting an obscenity. It was part of his style, like the wad of dip. They could just hear it over the radio, being relayed by loudspeaker to a hundred thousand eager fans: "Awright, gentlemen, you have a fucking race."

This year, Destefani was hanging out in the *Voodoo* pit. *Voodoo* was the *Strega* clone that had spent the winter in Destefani's hangar. *Voodoo*'s owner, Bob Button, was a trucking-company owner who had poured an endless stream of dollars into the perverse Mustang. And so far he had gotten nothing back for his investment except frustration. And Button was getting pissed. This damned Mustang was like a restive racehorse that could run like hell but always broke a leg. After four seasons, Button had yet to see a real purse.

This year, however, Button and his crew just *knew* it was going to be *Voodoo*'s year. It had all the prerequisites of a super-Mustang: a Dwight Thorn engine, complete with a Merlin-9 supercharger (the most powerful blower you could run on the engine at this density altitude), and all the *Strega* airframe cleanups that made this particular Mustang capable of something in excess of 500 miles per hour.

Also at Reno this year, but staying very much in the shadows, was the winningest racer in Reno history. He didn't drop by the Room of Hard Benches, but you could catch glimpses of him out there in the pits, chatting with old acquaintances, trading a few jibes about past exploits.

Darryl Greenamyer was in his sixties now, graying at the temples, going crinkly around the eyes but still wiry and looking fit. And still grinning that Cheshire-cat grin that told everyone: "Check your six o'clock, pal, because I'm gonna pass you like you were roadkill."

The air-racing community—at least the *old* air-racing community— was still divided over Greenamyer. To a sizable faction, he was a larger-than-life hero who had dared to accomplish what most aviators only dreamed about. To another, equally large faction, Greenamyer's only acknowledgment would come after he was buried and they stood in line to pee on his grave.

For several years now Greenamyer had been working on his comeback racer, an exotic hybrid he called *Shock Wave*. *Shock Wave* was a built-for-racing machine in the tradition of Levitz's *Miss Ashley II*, *Tsunami*, and the *Pond Racer*. With engineering help from Lockheed engineers Bruce Boland and Pete Law, Greenamyer had mated heavily modified Sea Fury outer wing panels to a fuselage designed by Boland. For a power plant he used a mighty Pratt & Whitney R-4360, turning a three-bladed Lockheed Electra prop. *Shock Wave*, according to Greenamyer's calculations, would be capable of 550 miles per hour.

When Greenamyer raced, he liked to be in front.

But several years had gone by, and *Shock Wave* still hadn't raced. Like *Strega* and *Rare Bear*, the racer had fallen on hard times, even before its career began. And for the same reason: The owner was out of money.

Greenamyer's adventures had a way of ending in calamity. There was the F-104 adventure, for example. In 1969 he had gone out and posted a new world speed record for propeller aircraft—483.041 miles per hour—with his hot Bearcat, *Conquest I*. And then, having done that, he decided to go for the absolute speed record, flying his own civilianized jet fighter, a Lockheed F-104 Starfighter, which he stripped down and modified for the record attempt.

That episode ended like several such Greenamyer episodes: dazzling success followed by unmitigated disaster. He *did* shatter the existing closed-course speed record. And then, having made history with his own supersonic fighter, he found that the landing gear would not extend.

Which meant he couldn't land. Without its gear, the Starfighter had the landing characteristics of a mortar shell. He was forced to eject from the jet. Greenamyer's record-setting, highly mortgaged, personal supersonic fighter become another junk pile in the Mojave.

But the *absolute* grimmest calamity of Greenamyer's career happened in the frozen wasteland of Greenland. In the late 1980s, Greenamyer learned about a huge World War II B-29 bomber that supposedly lay somewhere atop the Greenland ice cap, abandoned after an emergency landing half a century ago. He and his crew found the old relic. For two summers they made secret journeys out to the ice, rebuilding the bomber. They replaced each of the four rusty old engines. They repaired the damaged landing gear. They refurbished the control surfaces. Then, when everything was almost ready, they carved out a five-thousand-foot-long runway in the ice.

Greenamyer was going to *fly* the ancient artifact off the ice.

Then came the heartbreaker. With all four engines rumbling, the big bomber ready to fly, the auxiliary power unit developed a fuel leak. A fire ignited in the tail section. While Greenamyer and his crew scrambled out of the bomber, the resurrected warplane erupted in a towering blaze. Within minutes the B-29 was reduced to a charred hulk, sinking onto the arctic ice cap from which it had nearly escaped.

Instead of glory and a huge reward for his bold adventure, Greenamyer found himself enmeshed in litigation. His own fortune, as well as that of his backers, had gone up in the flames of the B-29. The government of Denmark was incensed about the environmental damage. For Greenamyer it was a huge setback, and one of the casualties was *Shock Wave*.

Darryl Greenamyer, the all-time big winner, was walking the pits at Reno. When would *Shock Wave* be flying? Not this year. Perhaps next year. Perhaps never.

Just like last year, three astronauts—Curt Brown, Hoot Gibson, and Bill Anders—were on the card for the Unlimited Races. For the Reno Air Racing Association, it was great public relations—air racing, the sport of the spacemen!—and they were making the most of it. What more palpable evidence did the world need that air racing was a sport not just from the past but of the future? The same pilots who had orbited the planet were now tearing around the pylons at Reno.

For their part, the astronauts were happy to oblige. They dutifully posed for endless photos with race fans, signed countless programs, and shook a thousand hands. For them, it was all part of the drill.

But this year, just like last year, only two of the three made it to Reno. Back again was Gen. Bill Anders, who had been one of the Apollo astronauts, a retired CEO of General Dynamics and now the owner of a stable of exotic warbirds. But Curt Brown, who had flown a stock Sea Fury in last year's races, was missing this season.

Brown, with four shuttle missions in his logbook, was now a senior astronaut. He had not been scheduled for another shuttle flight during the coming season, which left him free to race again in 1998.

But then life suddenly changed for Curt Brown. Back in Washington, a former astronaut and now powerful Democratic senator from Ohio, John Glenn, was making a heavy pitch to NASA administrator Dan Goldin. Glenn wanted to return to space. At age seventy-seven, Glenn wanted to fly as a crew member on the space shuttle. And Glenn had worked up a perfectly sensible rationale for such a mission: NASA could conduct a study of the aging process.

Which drew an instant barrage of hoo-haws and flak from Glenn's detractors. Sending a fossil like Glenn into space to study . . . aging? It amounted to a $100-million boondoggle to give an old guy one last ride around the planet.

But Goldin was, if nothing else, a pragmatic bureaucrat. He could sense which way the political winds were blowing. This was the season of Monica Lewinsky and campaign corruption and antiheroics. And here was good ol' grinning John Glenn, a legitimate American hero, not to mention an influential Democrat, who wanted to do something heroic. An orbital study of the aging process? Well, hell, why not? This was the high frontier! And there was certainly no one better qualified to fill a spacesuit than a legendary frontiersman like John Glenn.

And so it was announced: The old guy would orbit again. The septuagenarian senator was assigned a slot as payload specialist on STS-95, scheduled to launch on 29 October 1998. And then came another decision: Who should command such a high-visibility mission? For such a mission they needed the most experienced of their present cadre of astronauts. The job went to Lt. Col. Curtis Brown.

Thus ended Brown's 1998 air-racing ambitions. He was thrust into NASA's high-intensity prelaunch training schedule, which meant, while in training, he was obliged to observe an inflexible rule: no high-risk activities—skiing, rugby, hang gliding, skydiving, martial arts, or mountain climbing. And no flying hot fighters around pylons.

In Brown's place in the briefing room now was another high-profile astronaut, Capt. Robert "Hoot" Gibson, U.S. Navy (Ret.). Gibson and Brown had the same kind of friendly, kick-the-other-guy's-butt rivalry that existed between Hannah and Lockwood. As NASA's chief astronaut and most experienced shuttle pilot, Gibson had retired from the space program the year before. And though he had planned to race a Sea Fury called _Riff Raff_ last year, a problem with the R-3350 engine had canceled his Reno plans.

Gibson was senior to Brown by a few years and had preceded him in the space program. When Gibson wanted to irk Brown, he would say he "took the kid into space" on his rookie flight. Brown liked to get back at Gibson, who was now retired from the space program, by calling him a has-been.

Gibson was a year over fifty, though he looked about thirty-five. Like Brown, he was a trimly built guy, with brownish hair and mustache and the same kind of Redford-like good looks.

He was a classic airplane-head, meaning that his entire adult life had been consumed by the pursuit of things aeronautical. His life had been a modernized version of Bob Hoover's career, always seeming to place him at the vortex of whatever storm was brewing on the planet. Or _off_. He personified the old dictum of fighter pilots: _Thou shalt go where the action is._

Back in the late sixties and early seventies, when Gibson was graduating from Cal Poly and going into navy flight training, the action was in Southeast Asia. Earning his naval aviator's wings in 1971, Gibson caught the end of the Vietnam War, flying combat missions off Yankee Station in F-4 Phantoms. Selected to join the first squadron to fly the new F-14 Tomcats, he went on to be an instructor in Tomcats and then received the coveted assignment to test-pilot school at Patuxent River.

And then Hoot Gibson's career took off like a rocket. Literally. After a brief tour as a navy test pilot, he was picked in 1978 for NASA's first space-shuttle class. During the next fifteen years, Gibson flew five missions, four of them as shuttle commander, and became NASA's chief astronaut. His moment of greatest glory came on his last flight, when he commanded the first rendezvous with the Russian space station *Mir.*

Along the way Gibson married an astronaut, a surgeon named Rhea Seddan, who came to NASA among the first class of women astronauts. The Gibsons managed to have three children while flying a total of eight shuttle missions.

But there was another facet to Gibson. Aside from the standard Eagle Scout, rule-abiding, flag-waving space voyager in the image of Glenn and Armstrong, Gibson just happened to be a guy who *loved* hauling ass close to the earth in a hot airplane. Any hot airplane! He even owned one—a slick little Cassutt race plane that he built himself and with which he had set an official altitude record for light airplanes.

In fact, it was Gibson's passion for fast airplanes that got him into trouble with NASA back in 1990. It was at a demonstration air race, and Gibson's plane was rammed by another racer. Gibson recovered and landed safely, but the other pilot was killed. The NASA hierarchy reacted like outraged schoolmasters. They grounded Gibson. He would fly no more space missions for a year.

And then, six months later, they ungrounded him. Gibson's experience was needed. NASA wanted Gibson to command the space shuttle's first rendezvous with the Russian space station *Mir.*

After his fifth shuttle mission, Gibson elected to retire. His wife, also retired from the astronaut program, became the deputy chief of medicine at Vanderbilt University, back in her hometown of Murfreesboro, Tennessee. Gibson confounded everyone who expected that an ex-astronaut would become some sort of a gray eminence in the aerospace business, perhaps becoming a corporate chieftain, like Bill Anders, starting his own company, like Eugene Cernan, or going into politics, like Glenn. Gibson did none of these things. He became a pilot for Southwest Airlines.

What? Gibson had always been something of a rebel in the ranks, considering his passion for hot airplanes and setting records. Here was a guy who had every cachet on his record you could get—combat veteran, test pilot, astronaut. Why start all over again at the bottom of a seniority list as a *copilot?*

It was simple. "I want to fly," he told them. That was Gibson's raison d'être: I want to fly. He wanted a cockpit job, not a corporate desk, and a copilot's seat suited him just fine. He could live in Murfreesboro with his astronaut-surgeon wife and their young family, and he had time to indulge himself with private flying activities. Like air racing.

First, of course, he had to deal with the Brethren.

"And let's say hello to another *rookie,* Hoot Gibson."

That's how he was introduced at that first briefing in the Room of Hard Benches. *Another rookie.*

The Brethren applauded politely, and a few shook his hand.

Gibson was used to it. Hell, he *was* a rookie, and he was happy with the label. Still, he could feel it—the same old *coolness* that astronauts, test pilots, and aeronautical celebrities received whenever they encountered a group of airmen as elitist and self-absorbed as the True Brethren of air racing.

The message he was getting there in the Room of Hard Benches was silent and unmistakable: *Forget all that hero-astronaut stuff, pal. Here at Reno you're just another rookie.*

Which was okay with Gibson. One thing he'd learned during all those years as a naval officer and then as an astronaut: Keep your mouth shut and do your job. He hadn't come here to dazzle the Brethren with his record. To hell with that. He was here to race.

Back at Reno, too, was Bill Rheinschild with his family and a formidable crew of mechanics and technicians. Not only was he again flying his fast Mustang, *Risky Business;* Rheinschild had a new mount in his stable—an R-3350-powered Sea Fury he had named *Bad Attitude.*

Another old face at Reno was Gary Levitz. Levitz was back with *Miss Ashley II,* the Scissors Plane he and Bill Rogers had developed. If prizes were awarded for the sexiest-looking racer, *Miss Ashley II* would beat them all.

Levitz's major sponsor, Courtaulds Aerospace, was a manufacturer of aircraft coatings. *Miss Ashley II* was a stunner, sitting there in her pit with a brilliant red-and-white paint scheme, mirror-shined, contrarotating propellers gleaming in the desert sun.

Spectators would stroll past, then do a double take when they first saw *Miss Ashley II.* Yeah, sure enough, the thing had not one but *two* sets of propellers. But that wasn't the only thing. It *looked* like a Mustang—the distinctive belly scoop and general profile—but there was something odd about it.

Miss Ashley II, of course, wasn't really a Mustang. She wasn't even a warbird or anything with a data plate. She was a built-from-scratch race plane in the tradition of the 1930s Thompson Trophy speedsters.

If *Miss Ashley II* were to sweep the Gold this year, it would be on the strength of her aerodynamic superiority, not her excessive horsepower. The hybrid racer had a stock 2,300-horsepower Griffon engine installed, which amounted to a thousand or so fewer horsepower than the top Gold contenders.

And to Levitz's thinking, that wasn't all bad. He had been coming to Reno for twenty years now. And he had flown his share of hand grenades and lighted powder kegs, seen the unleashed violence of a self-destructing Merlin. A good old stock Griffon, cranking out its design horsepower, suited him just fine.

Levitz and Rogers were keenly aware that they were doing something unique. Only two other airplanes in the history of Reno air racing had been constructed as one-off, built-for-racing machines: *Tsunami* and the *Pond Racer.*

Now they had *Miss Ashley II.* The sole survivor.

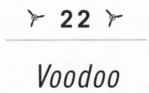

22

Voodoo

Lord knows I'm a voodoo chile!
—*Jimi Hendrix*

14 September 1998

Something was different in the Room of Hard Benches. And it didn't take long to figure out what it was. With the traditional leading men, Destefani and Shelton, sitting this one out, a new bunch—the Young Turks—had taken over. And they had a style of their own.

Actually, they weren't taking over. It was just that a vacuum had been created and the up-and-coming young race pilots were happy to fill up the empty space. This was where the action was, and they had moved to center stage. And for most of the Brethren, who had heard enough bad news about their colleagues going to the slammer, it was refreshing. It was like having a new cast of actors in a tired old sitcom.

Central casting couldn't have chosen two better guys for the roles.

264

Both the new front-runners, Bruce Lockwood and Bob Hannah, had lots of charisma and the *cojones* to jump into a hot Mustang like *Dago Red* or *Voodoo* and fly the hell out of it. They even resembled actors, with Tom Cruise–like good looks and suitably cocky grins. And they were *funny,* which still counted for a lot when things went to hell and the tension at Reno started crackling like summer heat.

Not that Lockwood and Hannah were stars, at least in the sense of having won anything at Reno. Not yet. Nobody seriously believed that they could outfly the likes of Destefani or Shelton or Greenamyer. But none of the former champions were racing this year. Unlike the old-timers, the young guys were *there,* which counted for everything in this, the season of the Vanishing Airmen. And they had a couple of hot airplanes.

By traditional Reno air-racing standards, neither Hannah nor Lockwood qualified as legitimate hell-raisers. Their personal lives were prosaic, at least when compared to the legendary excesses of their predecessors among the Brethren. When they drank, which was seldom, they tended toward light beer, though neither could make a big dent in a six-pack. Their only wild side seemed to be motorcycles.

Motorcycles? Well, it did seem a bit odd to the Brethren, considering how the low-rent world of motocross was several light-years removed from the rarefied heights of the astronauts and the test pilots and the captains of industry. It meant that these guys, Hannah and Lockwood, were basic *wrench turners.* No elite educations, no lofty credentials, no cachet. They were classic examples of the mechanic who got to drive the boss's sports car.

And yet no one could fail to notice that they possessed . . . *something.* They both had a full measure of the old Turner-Greenamyer-Hoover willingness to strap on a red-hot warbird and push the edge of the envelope as far as it would stretch. Without military-funded training, personal wealth, or family backing, each had leapfrogged over his contemporaries and worked his way into the cockpit of one of the two fastest racers at Reno.

Watching them, you could sense that you weren't going to see the unerring accuracy of a Tiger Destefani. Or the savvy Gary Cooper *High Noon* coolness of Ol' Lyle. Not yet, anyway. They were too green, too unexposed to all the nuances of high-speed flight around the pylons. Still, you knew they had *something*, these two young ruffians, grinning and photogenic and cocky as all hell. You just knew they possessed in full measure that vital prerequisite for winning at any motor sport—*balls*.

After his second day of qualifying at Reno this year, the Brethren had hung another name on Hurricane Hannah. It was scrawled up there on the big greaseboard one morning when they came into the briefing room: Captain Mayday.

It started on Monday, the first day of qualification.

Hannah wasn't pushing it, just letting *Voodoo* run hard—but not too hard. The idea was to post a lap time just fast enough to beat the other guys.

That meant Lockwood and *Dago Red*, who presented the only serious competition to *Voodoo*. Lockwood had already been on the course that day and turned in a stately qualifying speed of 443 miles per hour. It wasn't an impressive number, considering last year's speeds in the high 460s posted by *Strega* and *Rare Bear*. Everyone knew that *Dago* had the capability of a 490-mile-per-hour-plus lap. Clearly, Lockwood was playing it cool.

For good reason. No one was willing to blow his engine this early in the game. You pushed it up in increments. The idea was to get qualified, to post a fast enough time to win the pole position. Don't blow anything. Go a little faster next time if you have to. Try to win a heat race but don't flog the machine. Wait for Sunday. Then you could light the fuse.

Hannah was still getting used to *Voodoo*. It seemed that every time he flew the thing, there was another modification he had to learn about. Not just mods on the Dwight Thorn Merlin, which possessed heavier-duty supercharger gears. But *Voodoo*'s crew had added a custom-built composite cowling that was lighter and tighter than the old model. And new wing filets that slicked up the wings' mating to the fuselage.

And things were going wrong. It seemed that for every modification they made, another glitch would appear. Every flight was turning into a damned test flight.

Hannah was glad that Tiger Destefani was around. Tiger had taken a proprietary interest in *Voodoo*, having hosted the racer for two winters in his hangar and supervised the many *Strega*-like mods. And with both Tiger and *Strega* out of the game this year, Team *Voodoo* was getting the benefit of Tiger's paternal counsel. Tiger had done much of the test-flying on *Voodoo* and had coached Hannah on the complex management of the *very* tricked out Merlin engine—running the ADI and the spray bars, monitoring the induction temperature, and matching the rpm to the manifold pressure.

All this tweaking and tuning on *Voodoo* had gone on right up to the last minute before departing for Reno. And it was *still* going on. Sometimes Hannah envied Lockwood, who was flying a tested and proven airplane like *Dago Red*. *Dago Red* sure wasn't a stock Mustang, but over the years most of the major bugs had been worked out.

But today *Voodoo* was humming. And conditions couldn't be sweeter for a fast trip around the pylons. It was one of those classic Nevada days, with gentle winds and puffs of cumulus that looked like sheep's fleece on a blue blanket.

Hannah was ready. "Race Fifty-five, on the clock."

Time to go for it. Post a qualifying time that would make Lockwood's eyes water.

"Roger, Race Fifty-five. On the clock."

Hannah cranked up the power. ADI on, water on, rpm coming up. Manifold pressure a hundred inches, coming up. A hundred and ten. A hundred and twenty.

The Merlin was howling—*WHRRROOOOM*. Jesus, he loved that sound!

Voodoo was hauling ass now. Bending around pylon 3.

It was the perfect time to fly. The air was slick, and you had the course to yourself. You could pick your line, carve a perfect turn around the pylon, not concerned about whoever was out there hiding under your wing.

Rounding pylon 8, down the home stretch past the pits . . . the Merlin still growling like a healthy animal . . . Hannah *knew* he was racking up a hell of a good qualifying lap.

And he was. He flashed past the home pylon.

"Looks like four-fifty-two," said owner Bob Button on their discrete frequency.

Four-fifty-two? *Perfect.* Just enough to take the pole away from Lockwood. Beneath his oxygen mask, Hannah was grinning to himself. This was cool! He was *really* beginning to enjoy himself when—

What the hell? Something—what was it? Pouring into the cockpit . . .

Smoke. Lots of it, clouds of the stuff, acrid, thick, eye-stinging *smoke!* Something was very definitely going to hell up front, something *burning, something on fire!*

Of all the scenarios that stuck raw terror into the hearts of pilots, none was more frightening than the specter of fire.

Hannah hauled the nose of the Mustang skyward.

"Race Fifty-five, Mayday!"

"Roger, Race Fifty-five," said Jack Thomas from the race director's tower. Thomas had his binoculars on the Mustang. He could see the smoke streaming from the cowling. "Wind zero-five-zero at ten. The field's yours."

Yeah, great. The problem was: Where was the goddamn field? The smoke was so thick in Hannah's cockpit, he couldn't see. And it was getting worse.

Voodoo had been fitted with a canopy like the one on *Strega,* the kind you could slide back in order to vent smoke. But opening the canopy had a downside risk: If your engine was *really* on fire, you could suck flames into the cockpit like a blowtorch, turning yourself into a crispy critter.

All this flitted in a microsecond through Bob Hannah's mind as he soared up above the field. Open the canopy and get toasted? Shut the engine down and hope the smoke stops? Or just get rid of the canopy and jump out?

He slid the canopy open. And hunched down in his seat.

Whooof! The 400-mile-an-hour cyclone snatched *everything*—pencils, paper, loose screws, dirt, and *smoke*—from Hannah's cockpit. The flames, wherever they were, stayed inside the cowling.

He could see again.

One and one-half minutes later, the main wheels of the Mustang screeched down on the hard runway at Stead. *Voodoo* was safe.

As the Mustang was still taxiing off the runway, it was obvious what had gone to hell inside the cowling: the cowling itself. The new carbon-fiber cowling was bubbled and blackened like plastic on a stove.

When they opened *Voodoo* up, they found the cause: The tight-fitting new cowling was *too* tight. At sustained high power—something they hadn't put *Voodoo* through until today—the heat from a couple of the exhaust stacks had cooked the composite cowling, creating the curtain of evil, noxious smoke.

Bob Hannah stood there on the ramp gazing at the torched cowling. A thought passed through his mind: *This shit isn't fun.* He hadn't signed up to be a test pilot. *What else is gonna go wrong?*

Plenty. He would find out tomorrow.

It started out to be another gorgeous late-summer day in the High Sierra. But in the middle of the afternoon a squall came blowing down from the mountains and covered Reno with a pall of gray clouds and rain.

Rain meant trouble to a fast-moving fighter. Even a light shower had the feel of machine-gun bullets hammering the thin aluminum skin. And it blurred the flat-plate windshield, making it dangerous as hell skimming the desert at a hundred feet. So they shut down the course for a while and waited for the squall to blow through.

Not until nearly six o'clock did Hannah get back in the air. The cowling was repaired and the necessary adjustments made—he hoped. *Please, don't let this sucker torch off again.*

Whether he liked it or not, today's session was as much a test flight as another shot at improving the qualification time. Bumping *Voodoo*'s qualification speed up a few more miles per hour didn't count for much. Lockwood still hadn't gotten *Dago Red* up to Hannah's speed yesterday.

Still, Hannah *liked* putting the pressure on Lockwood. That's the way it was in the racing business, whether it was motorcycles or Mustangs. *Never let the other guy forget why you're there: to kick his butt.* And with Lockwood it was especially appropriate. He'd been keeping up the pressure on Lockwood for years.

So here he was again, hammering around the pylons. Only this time the sun was low, already sliding down behind the high ridge in the west. It was the kind of flat light over the desert where you had no depth perception. Everything had a muted, dimensionless look. If you weren't careful, you could fly right into the dirt and never see it coming.

Rounding pylon 4, as he pushed the throttle up to 120 inches of manifold pressure, it started.

Rat-a-tat-tat. Rat-a-tat-tat. It was intermittent at first. A vibrating, hammering noise from the engine; then it would go away. The Merlin seemed to be smoothing out.

Then it was vibrating and hammering again. *Rat-a-tat-tat. Rat-a-tat-tat.*

Now what? Hannah tried easing the power back, and it smoothed out. *Good.*

Then it got rough again. *Shit!*

Hannah couldn't figure it out. What was it doing? He wasn't even pushing the engine hard yet. Was this going to be one of those classic parts-shedding, oil-spewing, fire-streaming episodes? Hannah had been lucky so far in his short air-racing career. He hadn't had an engine totally disintegrate on him. For him, that day hadn't yet come.

Rat-a-tat-tat.

Well, maybe today was the day.

"Race Fifty-five, Mayday!" Hannah hauled *Voodoo*'s nose upward, easing off the throttle. If the engine was truly self-destructing, then he would at least be in position to dead-stick the Mustang back to a runway.

And then something astonishing happened. The Merlin, the bitch-mistress of racing engines, *smoothed out.* Just like that. The big V-12 metamorphosed from a rackety, nerve-jangling vibrator to a purring feline.

Hannah set up for a dead-stick landing, anyway, just in case. The Merlin was ticking along like a well-oiled watch. Feeling just a bit foolish, Hannah landed *Voodoo* without further incident. But he knew he hadn't been dreaming. The damned engine *was* running rough!

They opened up the cowling. There was nothing wrong with the engine. The best explanation for the roughness seemed to be the spark plugs, fouled from the heavy dose of the manganese additive in the 145-octane racing fuel. When the capricious Merlins were allowed to run at low power too long before pushing the throttle up, the plugs could sometimes load up with concentrations of manganese. And then, just as capriciously, they would unload again.

So it was with *Voodoo*. And despite the ribbing Hannah took in the briefing room—Captain Mayday—no one was seriously criticizing him for being conservative and coming home with a rough runner. You didn't take chances with a cranky engine, at least not in a qualification lap.

Nevertheless, for a guy with a name like Hurricane to holler Mayday *every* damned time he flew? It was embarrassing.

. . .

Wednesday was the last day of qualifications, and most of the pilots had already posted their qualifying speeds. But then a controversy erupted over the official NAG (National Air-Racing Group) rule that stated: "The best speed from either the first or second timed lap will be used as the qualifying speed. Running of the second timed lap is optional, and not required."

Did that mean your one-lap qualifying time was set in stone? Or did it mean that you were allowed *another* lap, in another qualifying session, if you wanted to try improving your time.

Several Unlimited pilots were insisting that, according to the rule, they had a right to make another one-lap attempt at a better time. Others, pleased with their position in the qualifying lineup, were adamant that once you'd qualified, that was it. You lived with it.

The race officials huddled, then issued a judgment: Yes, by literal interpretation of the rule, the one-lap qualifiers *did* have another shot at qualifying.

Thus began a last-minute flurry of new assaults on time. Back in the air was Levitz in *Miss Ashley II*, and he astounded everyone by zipping around the course at a speed of 437 miles per hour—faster than either he or *Miss Ashley II* had ever flown before. And fast enough to move him all the way up to number-three position in the Gold race lineup.

Rheinschild took off again in *Risky Business* and managed to push his lap speed up to 430 miles per hour, also improving his place in the lineup.

Back in the air, too, was Hannah and *Voodoo*. By now, after two consecutive Maydays, everyone was watching. Down in the pits some hard money was being wagered: Would Captain Mayday get through one full session without declaring an emergency?

Actually, there was no need for *Voodoo* to requalify, since the hot Mustang already had the fastest qualifying speed at 452 miles per hour. But Hannah wanted to run the ante up a bit, just to keep the pressure on Bruce Lockwood and to guarantee his pole position for the Gold race Friday.

There was another reason, of course, although no one was saying it out loud: It would be reassuring to prove that *Voodoo* could get around the pylons at high speed just once *without* a major calamity.

And so it did. Watching the Mustang navigate the course, it was hard to tell whether Hannah was dogging it, playing it cool, or whether *Voodoo* was underperforming. But at the end of Hannah's requalifying attempt, *Voodoo's* speed turned out to be an unimpressive 440 miles per hour. Twelve miles per hour down from the blistering qualification run on Monday.

Neither Hannah nor owner Bob Button was disappointed. What counted for them was that *Voodoo*, for once, did not seem to be hexed. Nothing broke. Nothing caught on fire. No Mayday declared. Down in the *Voodoo* pit, that in itself was a cause for major celebration.

That night at the Pylon Bar, everyone was smiling. All the airplanes in all the classes had survived the qualifications. Despite Hannah's adventures, and not counting a few minor mechanical problems, no one had been in serious jeopardy. Now they could get on with the heat races.

The next morning, a few minutes before ten o'clock, the smiles faded.

As usual, the Unlimited pilots were ambling across the big concrete apron, on their way to the daily briefing. To get to the Room of Hard Benches, they had to thread their way through a pack of parked Formula One race planes. The little race planes were parked all over the ramp and inside the big hangar.

For the most part, the Unlimited pilots showed no interest in these impossibly tiny, home-built Formula Ones. To the high-and-mighty Brethren, it was simply a matter of *class*. Compared to their glamorous, overpowered Mustangs and Sea Furies, these little 100-

horsepower weed whackers were *toys*. Yeah, it was neat that these things could actually go 200 miles per hour. And sure, the guys flying them had a right to go play on the course. But as far as the Unlimited Brethren were concerned, the only real air racing out there was Unlimited. All the other racing classes at Reno, particularly the Formula Ones, were just . . . a *sideshow*.

Which was why, as usual, they were ignoring the Formula One race that was in progress this morning. They could hear the little engines howling like leaf blowers out there on the course, but hell, who could be bothered to actually notice?

But then someone *did* notice. "Hey, look at that."

Half a dozen of the Brethren stopped and peered out there toward the pylons.

"What's he doing?"

"Oh, shit."

It was like glimpsing one of those cinematic vignettes when you *knew*—seeing that impossibly steep nose-down angle and the out-of-control wing wobble—something bad was about to happen.

The little race plane was rolling into a dive. It was heading almost straight down toward the desert. The Brethren stood there on the ramp, transfixed, unable to take their eyes off the horrific scene. The racer disappeared just out of view, at the eastern end of the field.

Ploom! A geyser of dirt and debris shot up, then settled like the aftermath of a depth charge.

"Jesus, what happened?"

"I dunno. Looked like he just lost it . . . went out of control . . ."

There was no way to know. All they could see was an airplane center-punching the floor of the high desert. And they could only surmise, judging from the nearly vertical dive and the ominous geyser of dirt, that a pilot had lost his life.

Stunned, they walked on to the ten o'clock briefing. Inside the Room of Hard Benches, they told the others what happened. And even though the accident didn't involve one of the Unlimited

Brethren, it cast a pall over the morning's briefing. No one felt like cracking jokes.

By noon, the sketchy details of the crash were making the rounds. The Formula One pilot's name was Dick Roberts. He was sixty-three, an inspector for the FAA, and he was flying his own airplane, a homebuilt Cassutt racer named *Miss Maybe*. According to witnesses, he experienced an engine failure while turning on base leg for his approach to runway 26. What happened next seemed to be a classic stall-spin accident. The little racer ran out of airspeed, fell off on a wing, and augered into a suburban backyard, only thirty yards from a house and a barn. The pilot was killed instantly. Already, the local corps of Reno anti-air-race activists were calling for a removal of the National Championship Air Races to a more remote location.

It was the first day of heat racing, and at least for the moment, the joy had gone out of the day.

⊱ **23** ⊰

Friday

Showtime. Here it was. After a season of prepping, tweaking, and testing, the day had come. It was Friday, the first day of heat racing for the Gold racers—*Dago Red, Voodoo, Dreadnought,* and *Miss Ashley II.* Because of their top qualifying times, they had been excused from the Thursday heat races in which the slower racers tried to elevate themselves from Bronze to Silver or Silver to Gold.

Traditionally, Friday was a conservative race, with the hot Unlimiteds babying their engines, playing and dicing with each other, trying to coax the other guy into pushing too hard and straining his engine. The starting order was determined by their qualifying speeds. The only real purpose of the race, other than to provide a show for the fans, was to allow slower qualifiers to bump up in the starting order.

Which was exactly what Bruce Lockwood intended to do today.

Looking over the long snout of *Dago Red,* Lockwood saw his big, four-bladed propeller ticking over, flashing in the late-afternoon

276

light. He had the mixture pulled back as far on the Merlin as he dared, trying to keep the plugs from fouling on the ground. Spark-plug fouling was a problem with the racing Merlins, particularly when they used the manganese additive in the racing fuel.

Ahead of him in the lineup was the T-33 pace plane. Lockwood could see Hinton sitting in the front, Destefani in the backseat. They were peering back at him, waiting for all the Gold Unlimiteds to come trundling out to the starting line.

Also ahead of him in the lineup was the white-painted Mustang *Voodoo*. Bob Hannah was sitting there next to the pace plane, doing his own pretakeoff checks. Hannah had the pole position for today's start. The lineup for this first heat race was determined by qualifying speeds, and Hannah—Captain Mayday!—had captured the pole position with his 452-mile-per-hour qualifying speed on Monday.

Owning the pole at the start was a critical advantage, especially with evenly matched racers like *Voodoo* and *Dago*. Statistically, whoever led at the start—if his engine remained intact—maintained his lead and won the race. That was just the way it worked out. The amount of energy required to overtake the front-runner, passing him on the outside, was usually more than the second-place racer possessed.

The winner of today's race would have the pole position for Saturday's heat. And the winner of Saturday's race, likewise, would lead in Sunday's trophy race, when it really counted. The ante went up with each heat race.

Thus did Lockwood and Kerchenfaut and *Dago Red*'s owner, Terry Bland, decide on an objective for Friday's race. It was simple: *Win this sucker if you can. But don't break the airplane trying.*

That morning, after the ten o'clock briefing, Lockwood had had nothing to do until starting time in the afternoon. He wished he had something to work on, something to keep his mind off the pylons and the race and the image of the desert skimming under him at 500 miles per hour.

He walked down to the *Voodoo* pit and visited Hannah. Hannah looked subdued, not his ebullient self.

"You nervous, Buckwheat?"

"Yeah," said Hannah.

"Me, too."

They laughed. Hell, yes, they were nervous. If you were waiting to climb into a tweaked-out, 4,000-horsepower flying time bomb and go run it at three-quarters the speed of sound fifty feet over the desert and within spitting distance of eight other tweaked-out fighters and you *weren't* nervous, then you were, by definition, some kind of dangerous nutball.

Nervous, sure. But it was a healthy nervousness, a kind of wary respect for a circumstance that could get them snuffed out like a lightbulb.

"Remember the most important rule of racing?"

"Yeah," said Hannah. "Make it back to beer call."

Sitting there in the cockpit of *Dago Red,* waiting to start, it struck him: *This is a dream come true.*

The dream went back almost two decades, back when Lockwood and Hannah used to race motorcycles. In those days, out in some godawful motocross event in the American outback, they'd be sitting around. They would be covered with mud and bruises and bug stains, and they would talk about airplanes. And a different kind of racing.

They would indulge in a little fantasizing. In their dream race they would still be buddies and rivals, going head-to-head. But instead of being astraddle these yowling, biwheeled bone-breakers, they would be *flying.* They'd be flying a couple of really hot airplanes. Like, you know, Mustangs. Hot damned fighters. *You and me, man—just imagine—sitting out there in our cockpits, ready to race around the pylons.*

Yeah, we'd flash each other a thumbs-up.

Yeah!

It was all illusion, of course, the kind of larger-than-life dreams kids have when they still think *anything* is attainable. But out there in the piney woods at the motocross races, they loved talking about it. What the hell, it didn't hurt to dream a little, did it?

The memory came rushing back to Lockwood's consciousness like an electric shock. He felt as if he were dreaming again. *I'm there!* He was sitting in the world's fastest damn propeller-driven fighter. And who was sitting over there, thirty feet away, in the cockpit of that clipped-wing, pointy-nosed killing machine but . . . *Hannah!*

Hannah's oxygen mask was hanging loose. Lockwood could see the big, cocky grin on Hannah's face. He was flashing a thumbs-up.

Voodoo, as expected, jumped into the lead. But Hannah wasn't pushing—*really* pushing. He had the throttle up to only a hundred inches of manifold pressure, enough to set a fast pace. He and Button had already decided on today's strategy. Hannah would just use enough power to stay ahead of Dennis Sanders in *Dreadnought* and thereby lock in the second position on the Saturday start. If Lockwood and the *Dago Red* bunch wanted to win this thing bad enough, they could have it. But they'd have to work for it.

As it turned out, Lockwood didn't have to work too hard. On the fourth lap he nudged the throttle up on *Dago* and sizzled past *Voodoo*. Bob Hannah seemed disinclined to use the horsepower he had available to maintain the number-one spot. *Dago Red* cruised past the checkered flag at the uninspired pace of 430 miles per hour.

But it didn't matter to the fans, who had come to see a race, and as far as they were concerned, that was what they got—the two hottest Mustangs at Reno dueling for first place.

And it didn't matter in the *Dago Red* pit. The team—new owner, pilot, crew chief—had come to Reno and won their first race! So far everything was going according to plan. The uneventful race had served as a tension breaker for the all-new *Dago Red* team. It meant their strategy was working. And it meant, best of all, that *Dago Red* would start Saturday's race in the prime spot—on the pole.

Even Team *Voodoo* was satisfied with the outcome of the Friday race. It didn't much matter to Hannah and Bob Button, *Voodoo's* owner, that they had forfeited the pole. Today's race, for them, amounted to just another damned test flight. The idea was, don't push, don't break anything. Just set the throttle at a nominal power setting and let it run. And—*Hooray!*—it worked. For once *Voodoo* got around the circuit without setting itself on fire or blowing an engine.

Saturday was another matter. On Saturday the ante went up.

So did the level of nervousness, except for Lockwood, for whom any nervousness about going fast, *very* fast, around the pylons was now over. Everyone knew there was a big visual and mental adjustment you had to make to graduate from the Bronze-Class speeds of 360 miles per hour or so up to Gold Trophy velocity of nearly 500. Now he'd been there.

Not that Lockwood hadn't raced fast fighters before. He'd been on the course both at Reno and Phoenix, but always in relatively stock warbirds, tootling around the pylons at a sedate 350 or so, not the scorching upper-400s numbers that *Dago Red* could deliver.

Lockwood knew that some of the veteran racers had their doubts about him. He knew they were saying that it just didn't seem *right* that this guy Lockwood—an inexperienced racer, a *ferry* pilot, really—would get the seat in a top racer like *Dago Red*. This was a season when several of the top pilots—Destefani, Holm, Penney, Price—were not flying Gold racers. With all that talent available to fly your hot racing machine, why pick . . . an amateur?

Such talk just made Lockwood smile. Amateur? To him, it was a joke. Of all the pilots racing at Reno, he probably came the closest to being a *professional* warbird pilot. It was he who had done all the recent developmental test-flying on *Dago Red*. Lockwood's job as director of restoration at the Santa Monica Museum of Flying gave him the chance to fly sometimes half a dozen of the museum's warbirds in a single day. Lockwood calculated that he had more time in *Dago* than the combined flying time of all the other pilots who had ever flown her since she was converted to a racer. Unlike Destefani, who flew *Strega* maybe twenty hours in a year, or John Penney, who climbed into *Rare Bear* half a dozen times a season, Lockwood flew an exotic fighter almost every day.

It was all coming back to him now. Hoot Gibson had raced before, but in the Formula One class with his little 100-horsepower Cassutt. The Formula Ones ran around the pylons at a little more than half the speed he was doing now in *Riff Raff*.

But it was familiar—*that old feeling!* He was out here in the desert, following the same old dictum that had taken him everywhere from combat flying to the fringes of outer space: *Thou shalt go where the action is.*

Well, this was where the action was now. It was the Bronze race, the first Unlimited event on Saturday. Gibson's *Riff Raff* was the only Sea Fury in the heat, racing against three Bearcats, two Yak-11s, and a pair of Mustangs.

Gibson shoved the throttle up, and he liked what he heard. Unlike yesterday's race, when the R-3350 radial engine seemed to be loading up, delivering less than its full complement of horsepower, now the big Wright engine was ticking. Yesterday's miserable performance had gotten him an undistinguished sixth-place finish with a speed of 339 miles per hour.

Gibson was steaming down the chute, number three in the lineup for the Saturday Bronze race. And whatever had plagued the big Wright engine yesterday seemed to be cleared up. *Riff Raff* was running like a Swiss clock. He was getting a speed of nearly 400 miles per hour!

Up ahead Gibson could see the front-runners—Ike Enns in his Mustang, *Miracle Maker;* Howard Pardue in his rare XF8F-1, *Bearcat;* and fellow astronaut Bill Anders, flying his own F8F, *Wampus Cat.*

It didn't take long. Still on the pace lap, Gibson started moving. Sliding up on Pardue's right wing, Gibson waited until the straightaway; then he went out and around.

Now he was behind Ike Enns, another rookie. Enns was down low, leading the pack in *Miracle Maker*. Gibson moved up, staying just to the outside and away from his wake.

Coming up on pylon 4, nudging up close to the wing of *Miracle Maker,* Gibson waited for Enns to go into his nearly vertical bank around the pylon. He went up with him, looking almost straight down at the hard-charging Mustang directly under him. Gibson knew that if he could stay right on the Mustang's wing, keeping the same relative position, he could fly nearly the same line around the pylon and not lose ground by going wide.

And he did. Around the pylon they came, the Mustang low and Gibson's Sea Fury directly above him, the two locked wing to wing. And coming out of the turn, rolling wings level, Gibson made his move.

Down in the grandstands, the crowd was going crazy. Even though this was only a Bronze race, not the high-profile Gold competition, the fans knew they were seeing a real balls-out air race. This was what they came to Reno for! And this guy Gibson—a damned rookie!—was coming up from behind, knocking off the leaders one by one.

Now *Riff Raff* led the pack. Gibson kept the throttle up and widened his lead. *Riff Raff* flashed across the finish line seven seconds ahead of second-place *Miracle Maker*.

Atop the trailer back on the ramp, owner Mike Keenum and the *Riff Raff* crew were ecstatic. Sure, it was only a heat race, not a trophy event, and maybe it was only Bronze, not the rarefied Gold race.

But today's victory bumped Gibson and *Riff Raff* into Sunday's Silver Trophy race. This was *Riff Raff's* first trip to Reno, and they'd already won their first race!

Later, Gibson was back in the pits, grinning and signing programs and basking in the warm glow of victory. A few of the other racers—the Brethren—came by and congratulated him. Gibson was still standing beside *Riff Raff*, chatting and signing a fan's program, when he glanced up and saw someone familiar. A tall, grinning guy with a brown mustache.

It was astronaut Curt Brown, Gibson's old protégé and rival, who had raced here last year. Though Brown was in intensive training for his space shuttle mission with John Glenn next month, he had cut loose for the weekend and come to Reno.

It was the same old Brown. He wasn't cutting Gibson any slack. "Not bad," he said. "For a rookie."

⍟ 24 ⍟

Saturday

The four-stroke engine: That's one stroke for producing power
and three for wearing the engine out.
—Sir Stanley Hooker, Rolls-Royce chief engineer

19 September 1998

Lockwood could see the T-33 pace plane up ahead, trailing air-show
smoke. It was time for the last race of the day, the Gold. Hinton
turned on the smoke after takeoff so that the racers, taking off one
by one, could find him and join. Hinton would fly a wide half-loop
to the south, around the back side of Peavine Mountain, before
leading them down the chute toward the start.

Lockwood liked being the first to take off behind the pace plane.
Since he had the pole position, he would be the first to join the formation. It meant he didn't have to keep sorting out all seven other
racers as they converged like a gaggle of geese on Hinton's jet.

One by one the racers joined up, forming a big, sloppy echelon off
Hinton's right wing—*Dago Red, Voodoo, Dreadnought,* Levitz's radi-
cal new *Miss Ashley II,* Rheinschild in *Risky Business,* and Sherman
Smoot flying the Yak-11 called *Czech Mate.*

Lockwood glanced once over his shoulder. There was *Voodoo*, moving up on his wing. He could see the other warbirds weaving and bobbing in the strung-out formation.

Coming around Peavine Mountain, turning to the left, Hinton called on the radio for his flock to slide into a line-abreast formation off his right wing. The jet's nose dropped, and the formation began accelerating down the chute toward the start.

Lockwood felt his pulse banging. This was it—the adrenaline pumper, the big moment, the most dangerous time of a race. The Unlimited racers were aimed downward in a great, wobbling collection of aluminum, the thunder of the eight engines rolling across the plateau like the sound of an earthquake. Lockwood knew that down there in the grandstands the announcer would be whipping up the crowd: "Smoke's on, ladies and gentlemen, and you can see them coming down the chute."

He could feel the airframe of the Mustang vibrating as they accelerated—300 miles per hour, 350, 380.

"Gentlemen, you're looking good . . ."

Here it comes. Hinton was giving them the kiss-off. Lockwood moved the propeller control forward, up to 3,400 revolutions per minute.

He could see Hinton's head in the T-33 cockpit, thirty feet away. *"Gentlemen, you have—"*

Up with the throttle. Everyone had the same idea—try to bring the power up, drop the hammer!—just as Hinton uttered the last words.

"—a race!"

Vroooom! Lockwood jammed the throttle up to 130 inches of manifold pressure. It was the most power he had ever pulled on the Merlin. *Dago* leaped forward like a quarter horse out of the chute.

This wasn't supposed to be an engine-melting race. That came tomorrow, on Sunday, when you let out all the stops. Still, the Saturday race was one you *wanted* to win, because it locked you into the pole position for the final event tomorrow.

Lockwood knew he had gotten a good start. Over his right shoulder, in his peripheral vision, he caught a glimpse of the all-white shape of *Voodoo.* Hannah! Lockwood knew his buddy was flogging his engine just as hard as he was. Maybe harder.

Ahead, Lockwood could see the first pylon. It was sticking up from the desert like a lighthouse in a harbor. Since he was in the front position, it was important that Lockwood fly a straight line for the pylon, aiming just to the easterly, outer corner. Already a raging argument had erupted back in the briefing room over the problem of the lead race plane aiming *inside* the pylon, then realizing that he was about to cut it, correcting back hard to the right. He would be turning directly *into* the pack of race planes clustered just off his right wing. The effect was like firing a shotgun into a covey of quail.

Lockwood had a good line on the pylon today. On this line he would pass to the outside of the pylon, rolling up on his left wing, grunting under the four Gs, and make the 30-degree turn toward pylon 4. On this first pace lap, with the speed advantage gained on that diving charge down the chute, *Dago* would be hitting over 500 miles per hour. Not until they'd flown one full race lap would the average speed settle down to the middle 400s.

It was a critical time for all the race planes. With the power freshly shoved up on the engines, the desert air ripping across the aluminum airframes at three-quarters the speed of sound, all the normal parameters of flying safety had been thrown out the window. If ever there was a time when something *calamitous* might happen to someone's engine or airframe or set of controls, this was that time.

And it was. Something happened.

I'm gonna beat that son of a bitch!

It was Hurricane Hannah's mission statement, pure and uncomplicated, embedded like an ecclesiastical code in his brain. It was a variation of the same ancient single-combat-warrior dictum that had been applied over the ages to Roman chariots, motorcycles, and Mustangs: *Beat that son of a bitch!*

Which was exactly what he was about to do. He shoved *Voodoo*'s throttle up to *145 inches* of manifold pressure, the rpms to 3,500. It was the highest power setting he had ever demanded of *Voodoo*.

And he could feel it. The Mustang was humming and vibrating like a tuning fork, hurtling toward pylon 4 at something over 500 miles per hour.

Ahead and below, only a few yards in front, he could see the trim silhouette of *Dago Red*. Hannah was flying a high line, 150 feet above Lockwood. When the time was right, he would trade his altitude advantage for energy. Which meant airspeed. Drop the nose, gain a few knots, *and pass his ass!*

But not yet. Not on the first turn—pylon 4. That was too dangerous, with all the racers still sorting themselves out. He'd make his play after pylon 5.

Rounding the corner, coming up on pylon 5. Hannah was moving up now . . . feeling the Gs as he cranked into the turn. Ahead and to the left, he could see pylon 6.

Now. Drop the nose a little, convert altitude to energy, slide past Lockwood's wing.

Whump!

And that was the last thing Hannah remembered.

"Race Five, are you declaring a Mayday?"

It was Steve Hinton, who, having led the racers down the chute, was just entering his guardian-angel orbit over the racecourse.

Hannah, in *Voodoo,* had just pulled off the course. And for once Captain Mayday wasn't declaring a Mayday. He wasn't declaring anything.

Hinton and Tiger Destefani were watching from the T-33 pace plane. What the hell was going on with Hannah? It was very peculiar. *Voodoo* had been charging along a plane length or so behind

Dago, looking as if he were going to make a move. Then he abruptly pulled straight up, going nearly vertical. Now Hannah was up there over the course at eight or nine thousand feet.

Hinton was about to aim the T-33 upward, to go join *Voodoo* in case he needed help. But just then he saw *another* fighter pulling up from the racecourse.

"Race Eighty-six, Mayday!"

It was Sherman Smoot, flying *Czech Mate,* the slick Yak-11. And Smoot's Mayday was for real. Hinton could see an evil-looking trail of gray smoke streaming behind the Yak. Hinton shoved the throttle forward on the jet and headed toward the smoking fighter. Hannah's problem, whatever it was, would have to wait.

This was Smoot's first season in *Czech Mate.* The Yak-11 had been developed as a racer by the late Bob Yancey. Despite the paucity of horsepower in its Pratt & Whitney R-2800 radial, the trimmed down, highly polished, Czech-built fighter had become a serious contender at Reno.

Smoot was a veteran racer with experience in everything from T-6s to the hottest Unlimiteds. He was the pilot who had stepped in to fly *Voodoo* last year when Hannah abruptly left Reno to attend a friend's funeral in Idaho. Bob Button had hung a name on Smoot: "Sherwood Smooth."

Now Sherwood Smooth was in trouble.

And even from the ground it was easy to see why. *Czech Mate* had soared to a couple of thousand feet above the course. Without binoculars, everyone—the fans in the grandstands, Jack Thomas's controllers in the tower, *Czech Mate's* pit crew—could see the ghastly orange flames billowing from the engine compartment. It looked as if the Yak's engine had blown up.

In fact, it had. The pumped-up R-2800 engine had thrown a connecting rod through a cylinder. What followed was a total disintegration of the big twin-row radial—shattered parts and spewing oil and flailing hunks of metal.

And fire. *Czech Mate* looked like a flaming comet. It was the pilot's worst nightmare.

You could see Smoot up there, a tiny figure in the cockpit, trying to get the burning fighter back on the runway. *Any* damned runway. Smoke billowed from the engine compartment. It billowed into the cockpit. Smoot had the canopy rolled back, trying to see through the dense cloud of smoke.

The situation had gone critical. If Smoot couldn't see, he couldn't land the fighter. If the fire didn't go out or spread any further, he would have to jump out. And with the engine shut down, the Yak was coming back to earth in ninety seconds, with or without Sherwood Smooth in the cockpit.

Time and altitude were running out for Smoot. *"Is he gonna jump?"*

Climbing out of a tightly confined cockpit, even one that was filled with noxious smoke, and launching yourself into the thin desert air was an option no race pilot really favored. The only pilot in recent race history to have done this—Kevin Eldridge bailing out of *Super Corsair*—had crunched himself into the horizontal stabilizer on the way out. Bailing out was a last resort.

Smoot had already discharged the Halon fire extinguisher installed in the cowling. Now there was more smoke than fire. The flames still licked and spat from the cowling like a sputtering barbecue.

The Halon seemed to be working. The ugly orange flames were dissipating, but the smoke continued to billow from the nose of the Yak. Smoot was making wide S-turns, trying to get lined up to the southeast, on runway 14.

He had the Yak coming down steep and fast. He knew he had a substantial tail wind, which would make it even harder to get down and stop. But it didn't matter. When you're on fire, *nothing* matters so much as getting the damned airplane back to terra firma. Fast.

He was committed now. He was too low to bail out. And he didn't have the altitude to make a circle to get onto a proper approach to the runway. And he could see now, with the tailwind and the too-high approach, he would land about a third of the way down the runway.

Which was *too* far. And too fast.

Smoke still poured from the shattered engine. Smoot banged the fighter down on the runway. And stood on the brakes. He had a ground speed of over 170 miles per hour. *Czech Mate* was hauling ass.

And at that instant every spectator on the field—even those without a flea speck of knowledge about applied physics or coefficients of friction or the efficacy of disk brakes—knew with absolute certainty what was going to happen: Sherman Smoot was going into the boondocks.

The boondocks off the end of runway 14 were particularly dangerous. Most sinister was the precipice that waited less than a hundred yards from the edge of the concrete. If you were unlucky enough to run your fighter off the concrete at the end of 14, you had the length of *one lousy football field* before you plunged off a sheer precipice.

All this went rushing through Sherman Smoot's mind now as his Yak galloped down the runway like a runaway gazelle. Damn, the concrete was going by in a hell of a hurry! Smoot was standing on the brakes as hard as he could. Smoke was still billowing from the cowling, still coming into the cockpit, making it hard to see. He was still clicking along at over 100 miles per hour, and even with full braking applied, the two miserable little main tires on the Yak weren't getting much bite on the cement.

These same thoughts were occurring to Steve Hinton, who was spiraling down from overhead in the T-33. He could see that from where Smoot touched down, going at such a hellacious speed, he had as much chance of stopping the Yak as he did of halting an avalanche.

"Two thousand feet left, Sherm."

The Yak was gobbling up the concrete.

"A thousand feet."

Smoot jammed down even harder on the toe brakes. The Yak didn't seem to be slowing.

"Five hundred."

Smoot knew he was in for a hell of a ride. The edge of the concrete was rushing toward him like a videotape in fast forward.

Running off the end of runway 14, of course, was nothing new. Over the years the feat had been demonstrated by several air-race pilots, including David Price, when he trashed his beautiful stock Mustang, *Cottonmouth*.

Now it was Sherman Smoot's turn.

The lip of the concrete passed under him. *Clumpetyclumpetyclump!* He felt as if he were riding an all-terrain vehicle on an obstacle course. *Clumpetyclumpetyclump!*

"Ground-loop—now!"

It was Hinton; he could see the edge of the precipice about to gobble the Yak.

Smoot hated doing this—such an unnatural act, *deliberately* ground-looping your airplane. He stomped on the right rudder. *Hard.*

The Yak's tail kicked around, swinging like a pendulum in a great arc around the left side of the fighter. Smoot felt the Yak lurching sideways through the sandy earth.

He was getting away with it. *This thing's gonna hold together.* The gear wasn't collapsing.

Whang! Whump! Wrong. It wasn't holding together.

The left gear snapped. The Yak teetered over on its left wing.

Whang! Crunch! The right gear collapsed.

Now the Yak was bouncing along like a washtub on its slick belly. A huge geyser of Nevada dirt erupted around the Yak. *Clumpetyclump!*

The Yak slid to a stop. As he scrambled out of the cockpit, Smoot felt the fine rain of dirt and debris pattering down on the Yak.

Whooooom! The T-33 flashed overhead. Hinton could see that Smoot had gotten stopped. He'd avoided the great fighter-eating abyss out there in the desert.

Okay, that took care of Smoot. Now, what the hell was going on with Hannah?

Sandpaper?

Hannah couldn't figure it out. Something wasn't right. It felt as if his hands and his face were being jammed down on something gritty. Something rough. Like sandpaper.

He tried to lift his head from the rough surface. Damn, it *was* sandpaper! In fact, it looked like the sandpapered, nonskid floor of the Mustang's cockpit! Hannah's upper body was jammed down on the *floor* of the cockpit!

Why was he down here on the floor of the cockpit?

It was very peculiar. On the first lap of the Gold race, he had just released his shoulder straps so he could better reach the switches on the panel. He had been flying this 500-mile-per-hour, stubby-winged racing machine at weed-top level over Nevada, *and he was on the floor.* In the periphery of his right eyeball, he could see the control stick jutting up from the floorboard.

This angle—it felt vertical, as if the Mustang were going up. Straight up. And the engine was still howling at full Dwight Thorn–racing Merlin power, up around 130 inches of manifold pressure. It felt as if the Mustang were soaring up, and with all this power and all these Gs pressing him down on the floor, it would go on over the top, into some kind of loop . . . and head back down again. Sooner or later the Mustang was going to point its long nose back toward that hard, unyielding mother of a desert floor. *Voodoo* was going to impact Nevada like an unguided Scud missile.

Hannah managed to lift his head up from the gritty floor. He snaked his left hand up to the throttle quadrant, then crooked his wrist around the throttle and pulled it back. The maniacal howl of the Merlin quieted to a lower-pitched growl. The steep climbing angle of the Mustang—it was coming down. Hannah felt the nose lowering from that impossibly steep angle.

And the G forces—that terrific acceleration or *whatever* the hell it was that stuffed him like a laundry bag into the floor of the cockpit—were gone. Hannah hauled his head, his upper body, back into the pilot's seat.

Now he could see, more or less. He felt woozy. Down below—*way* down below—he could see the cluster of race planes flying around the circuit. And then he remembered. Oh, yeah. *He was supposed to be in that race.* Well, hell, man, get back to work. You've got a job to do. From here, all he had to do was shove the nose down and get back in the action.

Wait a minute. His head still felt funny. He still had to figure something out. How he got up here and how his face got plastered against that goddamned sandpaper floor. Something wasn't exactly right with this sucker.

"You okay, Bob?"

Who was that? Hinton? Thomas in the tower?

"Yeah, this thing just popped big time," Hannah replied.

"You want a Mayday?"

"Not yet," Hannah called. Christ, if he declared *another* Mayday, his third of the week, they would consign him to the funny farm. Captain Mayday! And what about *Voodoo*'s owner, Bob Button? The thought flashed through Hannah's fuzzed-up brain: *Button's gonna be pissed.*

On the other hand, something was definitely wrong with *Voodoo*. Something, for that matter, was definitely wrong with *him*. It just wasn't natural to be flying this thing from the floor of the cockpit.

Hannah considered his situation, then made the call: "Yeah, better make that a Mayday."

Out of another damned race. All he had to do was get the Mustang back on the runway.

It seemed to be flying all right. Everything worked—gear, flaps. No engine problems. He had no elevator trim control, which seemed odd. It gave him a still-fuzzy thought: Could the inoperative trim control have anything to do with his going straight up like a homesick angel?

He rolled the Mustang's main wheels back onto runway 08. Not a bad landing, he thought, considering how goofy he felt. He taxied back up the ramp, over to where Button and his crew waited for him to shut down and climb out of the cockpit and tell them what had gone to hell out there.

And then Hannah climbed out of the cockpit. Not until he saw the tail section of the Mustang did he understand what had happened to him.

Hannah was woozy, all right. Later, they figured out that he had *ten Gs* applied to him when *Voodoo* pitched up. Instantly. It happened just after he had released the shoulder straps. The force of the pull-up doubled him over, implanting his face into the sandpapered floor of *Voodoo*.

On the first lap he was close on Lockwood's tail, hammering through some low-altitude turbulence. In the bright afternoon sun, thermals were rising off the sun-fried floor of the desert, causing bumps that felt like potholes on a parkway. *Wham! Wham! Voodoo* was slamming through the potholes when suddenly *Kerthunk!* Something broke.

Voodoo's nose pitched violently upward. So violently, it smacked Hannah's head into the floor like a grapefruit thrown against a wall. He had blacked out both from the force of the Gs and the impact of hitting the floor.

Standing there on the ramp now, looking at *Voodoo*, you could see what it was that broke. The elevator trim tab, a control surface about two feet long by six inches wide, was gone—*ripped* from the aft section of the elevator. The only thing left was an ugly rectangular void where the tab had been.

The elevator was the movable horizontal surface on the tail of the airplane. Controlled by the pilot's stick in the cockpit, it gave the racer its nose-up and nose-down movement. The elevator trim tab, mounted on the trailing edge of the elevator, was a balancing surface, like a smaller, secondary elevator. Moving this trim tab allowed the pilot to neutralize the aerodynamic force on the elevator. Without the balancing force of the trim tab at high speed, the elevator would seek a severe nose-up position.

Which was exactly what it did with Bob Hannah. The untrimmed elevator had snatched *Voodoo*'s nose up like a puppet on a string. Hannah was just along for the ride.

Gradually, the significance of what happened—or what *almost* happened—settled over the *Voodoo* camp. What if the nose had pitched downward? *Voodoo* would have struck the desert like a meteor. What if Hannah, who was an extraordinarily athletic and conditioned young man, had not come to his senses when he did? *Voodoo* would have zoomed upward—and back downward—like an artillery shell.

It was damned discouraging. *Voodoo*'s crew had labored for most of a year to get the racer ready to win here at Reno. Bob Button had poured an unconscionable amount of money into the Mustang. In five flights at Reno, Bob Hannah had experienced three emergencies, including a fire and a loss of control.

Now they didn't know how much damage had been inflicted on *Voodoo*'s airframe by the uncommanded ten-G pull-up. The elevator torque tube, the member connecting the left and right elevators, was obviously damaged. Was the horizontal stabilizer also overstressed? Were the wing spars damaged? A complete airframe inspection would take dozens of man-hours removing panels, applying penetrant dye, inspecting structural members for tiny cracks.

The Gold Trophy race was less than twenty-four hours away.

Tiger Destefani, who had overseen the transformation of *Voodoo* into a world-class race plane, was urging Button to fix the airplane and get back in the competition. They could fly back to Destefani's hangar in Shafter that evening and remove the elevators from *Strega.* It might take all night to get them installed and properly checked on *Voodoo,* but hell, that's what Unlimited Racing was all about. *Voodoo* could still win the Gold Trophy.

Everyone knew air racing was a risky enterprise. But the *Voodoo* crew was losing its taste for risk. They'd used up more luck than they should have been allotted. Having a Mayday nearly every time you flew was a bad sign. It was as if someone were trying to tell them something. No one had forgotten the almost routine Maydays of Rick Brickert back when he was flying the *Pond Racer.* Every landing in the experimental racer was an emergency. They'd gotten so used to seeing the fire trucks chasing him down the runway, it was almost a joke: *"Here comes the* Pond Racer, *and there go the fire trucks."* Until the last flight, when the *Pond Racer* didn't make it back to the runway.

So Button made a decision. *Voodoo* was out. Too much had happened these past five days. *Voodoo* was coming too close to what its name implied—that the airplane was somehow cursed, beset by some sort of evil spell. With *Voodoo,* you never knew what surprise was coming up next.

"*Voodoo* is out!" The word spread like a brushfire around the racing camps there at Reno. It was a controversial call, the kind of development that would fuel arguments in race bars for seasons to come. Depending on where you stood on the scale of risk taking, Button's choice was either imminently rational, reflecting good judgment and a respect for the laws of probability, or it was the pinnacle of wimpishness, the antithesis of the air-racing ethic: *Thou shalt go where the action is.* If you had a flyable airplane at Reno, you raced.

After Button's decision, a feeling of gloom descended over the

Voodoo pit. It was the disappointment felt by a highly trained athlete who suffers a disqualifying injury on the eve of the Olympics. Sure, it was the smart decision, the safe choice, the methodical way to operate. But, damn it, it wasn't fair!

The truth was, Button's passion for Unlimited Air Racing had hit bottom. The next morning, the thousands of race fans strolling through the pits got a glimpse of Button's true feelings. From *Voodoo*'s propeller hung a large sign: *Family Sacrifice Ends! For Sale or Trade.*

Bruce Lockwood was the winner of the Saturday Gold, which surprised no one after *Voodoo* dropped from the race. That made two for two for *Dago Red*. Twice out, twice the winner. In fact, he had throttled back to a hundred inches of manifold pressure—just enough to stay ahead of Dennis Sanders back there in *Dreadnought,* the big Sea Fury.

Lockwood felt bad for Hannah and the guys over in the *Voodoo* pit. Much as he wanted to beat Hannah, he didn't want to do it by default. He wanted to do it in a real race, mano a mano. As they used to do back in their motocross days.

The *Dago Red* team had a lot to be happy about. Their beautiful red, white, and gold racer was purring happily. Unlike *Voodoo,* they had experienced no serious problems. All they had to do now was keep running through one more race.

⊁ 25 ⊁

The Guy on the Wheaties Box

"The only lap that matters to me," Kerchenfaut was telling everyone at Reno this year, "is the last lap on Sunday."

That was the way Kerchenfaut saw it. Reno was a survival contest. You had to survive the qualifications. Then you had to get through the preliminary heat races. None of it counted for anything if you trashed your engine and put yourself out of the trophy race on Sunday. The idea was to pamper your engine, preserve it as much as possible, keep an even strain until the last day. Then you had to survive every lap of the last race.

A hundred yards away was the *Voodoo* pit. Kerchenfaut understood their disappointment, and he made a point of passing on his sympathy to the *Voodoo* crew. And out there on the open ramp, it was impossible not to run into Tiger Destefani, who had been counseling the *Voodoo* team. Now the two men nodded, acknowledging each other, all with a glacial politeness. One thing was clear to everyone: The old *Strega* team would never be together again.

That Saturday evening, Kerchenfaut and his crew went completely over *Dago Red*. More than ever, Kerchenfaut was being the fussy, finicky team manager. As always, he was a compact, bald-headed blur of motion, checking this, inspecting that, insisting that something be checked that had already been checked a dozen times. Check it again. Survive one more race. No one was arguing with Kerchenfaut. He had thirty years of campaigning behind him, and his racers had won here at Reno more than anyone's.

One problem Kerchenfaut wanted no more of was that damned spark-plug fouling that came with the manganese fuel additive. Earlier in the week he had issued an edict: He wanted a new set of spark plugs installed every time *Dago Red* flew. That meant two of the team mechanics, Doug Gallant and Eric Hoffman, stayed busy gapping, testing, and installing *240* new Champion spark plugs.

With *Voodoo* definitely out of the Sunday championship race, the Gold Trophy was now *Dago Red*'s to lose. How fast would *Dago* have to run? It was like the old joke about running away from a bear. "If you and your buddy are running away from a bear, how fast do you have to run?" The answer: "Faster than your buddy."

The "buddy" in this case was *Dago*'s next-fastest competitor, *Dreadnought*. The blunt-nosed Sea Fury, with its R-4360 Pratt & Whitney corncob engine, ran into a wall of air at about 450 miles per hour, which was a speed well below *Dago Red*'s top end. In theory, Lockwood could run *Dago* at a leisurely pace and still win.

But only in theory. What *Dreadnought* lacked in top-end velocity, it made up for in endurance. "To finish first, first you gotta finish," said Dennis Sanders, *Dreadnought*'s pilot.

Over the years, the strategy had worked splendidly. Twice it had won—flown by Neil Anderson in 1983 and by Rick Brickert in 1986—when the outlast-your-adversary strategy paid off and the front-runner self-destructed.

Now Dennis and his brother, Brian, alternated years racing *Dreadnought* at Reno. For twelve straight years they had campaigned *Dreadnought* in the Unlimited Gold without a pull-up or a DNF.

This year, Dennis Sanders's strategy was the same: "I'm gonna let

Dago run right out in front—until he breaks. I'm gonna be right behind him to clean up. And keep him honest."

The race-association members were ecstatic. Sunday, the day of the championship races, was one of those picture-postcard days—a deep blue sky dotted with cumulus puffs, gentle breeze from the west, temperature in the low seventies. It was cool enough to wear a sweater.

They were ecstatic not because it meant perfect flying conditions for the racers today. What it meant was that the stands were overflowing. Nearly a hundred thousand fans, groupies, spectators, tourists, airplane freaks, and thrill seekers were jammed onto the tarmac at Stead Field.

The Gold racers were assembling out at the end of runway 26. From the stands you could see the sun glinting off the silver propellers in the late-afternoon sun. It was a perfect day for air racing.

On such a glorious afternoon it was hard to remember those other afternoons—the days from hell when the demon winds howled down from the High Sierra, the dust devils ripping through the sagebrush and the dwarf trees, the sand scouring the paint off your airplane. A day such as this was benign. It was hard to believe that anything bad could happen on a day like this.

It happened before the race even started, on the initial takeoff. Hinton, flying the T-33 pace plane, was getting a thumbs-up from all his racers. Jack Thomas, up in the operations tower, gave the signal: "Pace plane, the runway's yours. Wind two-five-zero at six; you're cleared for takeoff on runway two-six."

Off they went, Hinton leading in the jet, followed a few seconds later by the pole-position flyer, Lockwood in *Dago Red,* and then Dennis Sanders in *Dreadnought.*

For the fans, this was the perfect way to start a race. Because the wind was from the west, the active runway was 26, allowing all the racers to take off on the runway directly in front of the grandstands. The spectators could see each of the big fighters rolling down the concrete. They were close enough to hear—to *feel*—the big, beefy growls coming from each of the fifty-year-old piston engines.

The third racer in the lineup, Howard Pardue in *Fury*, was rolling now. The Sea Fury had its tail up, rolling on the main mounts, the big Wright R-3350 radial bellowing like a happy animal.

And then just after liftoff, with the gear still coming up, something happened that chilled the blood of a hundred thousand spectators. The great bass bellowing of the radial engine . . . *stopped*.

Just like that. Nothing. Not a peep. The stillness swelled across the ramp and into the grandstands like a shock wave.

To the race fans watching in horror, the deathly silence pouring from Howard Pardue's engine was . . . simply . . . *not real*. It couldn't be. That big camo-painted, British-built fighter with the elliptical wings and blunt nose was soaring through the air, three hundred feet above the runway, like an apparition.

The Sea Fury had already used up two-thirds of the concrete, and from its present height there was no way it could land again on what was left of the runway. Ahead lay the great pocked, boulder-strewn deathscape of the Truckee Meadow.

And then sounds of life. *Chuff! Chuff! Kapocketapocketapocketa. Chuff! Chuff! Pocketapocketapocketa.*

Not that Pardue's engine was roaring back to life. It sounded more like a stricken rhinoceros, choking on something too big to swallow. *Chuff! Chuff! Pocketapocketapocketa.*

In the packed grandstand, a hundred thousand watchers were in the grip of a mass paralysis. Not one breath was being drawn. Not an eyelid blinked. Not a word was uttered. Every eyeball was riveted on the apparition out there above the runway, chuffing and wheezing, struggling to stay aloft.

The Sea Fury's engine was running intermittently. In short bursts, the R-3350 growled, chuffed, wheezed, quit again. All the runway was behind the Sea Fury now. The fighter was clawing through the air like a sick bird, clinging to its measly three hundred feet of altitude. Beneath and ahead and to the right lay the waiting desert. To the left were buildings and hangars and barracks and suburbs.

In one collective thought, the crowd wondered: *Where's he gonna go?*

Over there. To the left. Over the buildings, where, if the Sea Fury's engine packed it in for good, it was certain to create a spectacular suburban inferno.

The engine was belching and chuffing. The fighter made a slow, painful turn over the buildings, back to—where? *What the hell is he doing? Will he make it back to the runway?*

The engine kept cranking out power, enough at least to keep the Sea Fury flying. Pardue kept the left turn going, back around until he was perpendicular to the runway he had just left.

Which looked *very* peculiar. The watchers knew they were about to witness an aerial calamity. From the Sea Fury's nearly impossible position, going crosswise to the runway, halfway down—*and with a goddamned tailwind*—Pardue was going to try to put it back down.

The gear came down. The right wing dropped, and the Sea Fury cranked around in a hard 90-degree turn, aligning with runway 8, going in the opposite direction from which he had taken off.

It looked impossible. The Sea Fury rolled wings level, lined up with the runway, and—*Squawk! Squawk!*—plunked down on the concrete. Less than three thousand feet of the eight-thousand-foot runway remained. You could see Pardue going through his bag of tricks—getting the tail down so he had all three wheels on the concrete, getting the flaps up to put maximum weight on the gear. You could see the propeller swing to a stop, indicating that he had shut the engine down to remove *all* residual thrust from the propeller. Or else the engine died of its own accord.

And he was stomping on the brakes. Hard. *Chirp! Squawk!* The end of the runway was rumbling toward him.

The inefficient original brakes on Pardue's Sea Fury had been replaced by more powerful brakes from a T-33 jet. Which was evident, for you could see streams of smoke and burned rubber pouring from each main wheel as the powerful brake pucks clamped down on the disks.

The runway end rushed toward him. Fifteen hundred feet remaining. The same thought was on everyone's mind: *Was he going to run off the end and ground-loop as Smoot had done yesterday?*

A thousand feet. The Sea Fury was slowing, gray smoke streaming from each wheel.

Five hundred.

The Sea Fury lurched to a stop. Still on the runway.

In one collective gulp, the crowd in the grandstands resumed breathing. It seemed a miracle had been wrought. Only by divine intervention could that gasping, coughing Sea Fury have stayed aloft, gotten turned around and plunked back on the runway—going in the *opposite* damned direction—and have survived. Oh, yes, that guy in the Sea Fury was one very lucky pilot, right?

Not really.

What only a few of the more informed watchers of the incident could know was that the Sea Fury's pilot—the old, amiable ostrich Howard Pardue—was as cool as snow water. Since back in his Marine Corps fighter-pilot days, Pardue had dealt with every imaginable cockpit calamity, including off-field emergency landings (putting his F-4U Corsair into the boondocks after an engine failure). *Engine failure? Well, hell, you just put the thing back where it belongs.*

It hadn't been a miracle that saved Pardue's hide. Pardue had saved himself.

Lockwood, with the other Unlimiteds, was joining on the T-33, unaware of the drama playing out back there on the runway behind him. He slid *Dago Red* into a tight-right echelon formation on the pace plane. Half a minute later, he saw in his peripheral vision the gray blunt-nosed shape of *Dreadnought* forming up twenty feet from his right wing.

As usual, Hinton led the gaggle around the backside of Peavine Mountain, in a great left-handed sweep across the brown desert-scape, then back to the north, toward the pylons.

Lockwood slid his Mustang forward, up to a line-abreast position off Hinton's right wing. He could feel the speed building up. The entire gaggle was heading downhill now, accelerating down the chute.

This was the busiest time of the flight. He had to fly formation on Hinton. And he had to manage the Mustang's intricate engine enhancements. Like a punchboard operator, he was flipping switches, setting levers, monitoring gauges:

Spray bar—ON. The spray bar squirted massive doses of water across the coolant radiator, keeping the temperature from going off the scale.

ADI—ON. ADI fluid was sprayed directly into the intake manifold, increasing the density of the fuel-air mixture while suppressing its tendency to preexplode.

Propeller control—SET, 3,400 revolutions per minute.

His left hand was steadily advancing the throttle to stay up with Hinton. Sixty inches of manifold pressure, seventy inches, eighty. The gaggle was accelerating, getting up to race speed. Lockwood could feel *Dago*'s airframe humming, vibrating, the airstream noise increasing in pitch: 300 miles per hour, 350, 380.

"Gentlemen, you're looking good. Gentlemen, you—"

Lockwood started forward with the throttle.

"—have a race!"

Varoooom! In one firm shove, Lockwood pushed the throttle all the way up to 130 inches of manifold pressure.

Dago Red responded. One hundred thirty inches of manifold pressure, combined with the engine's 3,400 rpm, equated to 3,800 horsepower—*nearly twice* the stock Merlin's maximum horsepower.

And—*Wow!*—Lockwood could feel it. The thrust was shoving him back in the seat. The Mustang felt like a drag racer heading down the track.

This was a critical moment in the race. *Grab the lead. Get a jump on the others.*

And so he had. In the right side of his canopy, he could see *Dreadnought* moving back. Up high, off to the right, Bill Rheinschild, in *Risky Business,* was coming down, trying to gain a speed advantage in the descent.

He'd gotten a good start. He was in front. Now he just had to stay there.

"*Dago* plus three seconds," Kerchenfaut said on the discrete frequency.

Three seconds. It was a big lead. It amounted to several plane lengths. It meant that in only one lap Lockwood had opened up a big lead on *Dreadnought.*

Kerchenfaut was standing on top of the team trailer, holding a stopwatch and monitoring the race. He sent periodic updates to Lockwood about his position. "Plus three seconds" meant he was that many seconds ahead of number two.

Kerchenfaut could also see how *Dago* was holding together. All the engine and performance numbers were being data-linked right on to Kerchenfaut's computer screen: manifold pressure, rpm, oil temperature, airspeed. The idea was that the crew chief could relay all the engine readings back to the pilot so that he wouldn't have to keep moving his scan from outside—the racecourse and the pylons—back to the inside to read gauges.

Three seconds was good. It was plenty of lead. Now Kerchenfaut wanted Lockwood to ease the power back a bit. Buy some survival insurance.

Lockwood eased the throttle back to a hundred inches. That ought to be enough, he guessed, to stay ahead of *Dreadnought.*

And at that moment he heard and felt a *whooom!*

It was a hell of a noise. A whistling, howling air noise. And he knew what it was.

The canopy—the damned canopy—*was coming open!*

An open canopy at 500 miles per hour was bad news. A long-ago thought flashed through Lockwood's brain. He remembered the same thing happening to Alan Preston, who had been flying *Dago* several years back. The canopy came open—all the way open. And it had nearly taken Preston's head off.

Lockwood suddenly hunkered down like a turtle. With his left hand he reached up to the canopy lock and tried to close it. The canopy wouldn't shut again. But it was only open about half an inch. And it seemed firm in that position.

Okay. No big deal. Never mind the noise. Back to racing.

The whole incident—the partly opened canopy and the time to check the mechanism—took Lockwood no more than fifteen seconds. And in that time, unnoticed by him, the throttle had crept back from its setting of a hundred inches of manifold pressure to eighty.

Which slowed *Dago Red*'s pace around the pylons by a few scant miles per hour. And which went unnoticed for several seconds by almost everyone—Lockwood, Kerchenfaut, the *Dago Red* crew watching from the trailer, the fifty thousand fans in the grandstands.

But not by Dennis Sanders in *Dreadnought*. He was moving up on *Dago*'s backside like a bear chasing a burro.

"*Dago* plus three," Kerchenfaut called.

"*Dago* plus two." Kerchenfaut's voice was taking on an urgency.

"He's making a move!"

Sure enough, he was. Too late, Lockwood saw it happening. *Dreadnought* was catching and *passing* him. Above his right shoulder he saw the big, blunt gray shape steaming by him. Jesus, he was hauling ass! *Dreadnought* had a speed advantage of at least 30 miles per hour over *Dago Red*.

Lockwood and Kerchenfaut realized at the same instant what had happened. The friction lock was loose on the throttle. When Lockwood had taken his hand off the throttle to work on the canopy, the throttle had crept back. The slight power change had been enough to let Dennis Sanders in *Dreadnought* make his move. *(I'm gonna be right behind him to clean up.)*

Lockwood shoved the throttle back up where it belonged. But his problems weren't over. At the low power setting of eighty inches, the big Merlin's racing engine had loaded up and fouled its spark plugs. Now the Merlin was rattling like a tin lizzie. The fouled plugs were causing it to misfire.

Great, thought Lockwood. The *Dago Red* crew was never going to forgive him if he let *Dreadnought* have this race because he *let the damned throttle slip back.*

And down in the grandstands—and in the pits—the fans were going wild! This Gold race had started out looking like a runaway for *Dago Red*, which was clearly the fastest racer at Reno. But now— Hell, man, this was a race! Either *Dreadnought* had found some extra propellant to zip past *Dago Red*, or *Dago* was losing its potency. Whatever the reason, watching two high-performance warbirds duking it out around the pylons was like old times.

Dago Red's engine was smoothing out again. Lockwood could ease the throttle forward in increments, and the Merlin was taking it. He was starting to move up on *Dreadnought*. He knew Dennis Sanders *liked* being out in front. He wasn't going to cut Lockwood any slack if he tried to retake the lead.

Closer. *Dago* was moving closer to *Dreadnought*'s tail. They still had four laps to go. Plenty of time to take him. Lockwood nudged the power up some more. He could see that Sanders was *really* flogging the Sea Fury, doing everything possible to hang on to his lead.

Rounding pylon 2, Lockwood rolled into a nearly vertical bank, feeling his guts and his eyeballs sag as the force of four and one-half Gs pressed him down in the seat. Just ahead was *Dreadnought,* in an identical hard left turn. *Dago Red* was flying almost directly behind *Dreadnought* now when—

Wham! Something grabbed *Dago Red's* left wing, shoved it down hard, past the vertical. It felt like a giant hand snatching at him. Lockwood jammed the stick to the right. He was rolling inverted, headed for the dirt, out of control!

He kicked the right rudder and planted the stick in the right corner of the cockpit.

Dago popped up and over to the right like a jackrabbit. Wings level, free of the giant hand. But now Lockwood was headed off to the north, away from the race!

He zoomed up in a high left turn, then eased back down, back in pursuit of *Dreadnought*.

It happened in the space of a heartbeat. He had nearly caromed right into the desert. And he knew exactly why: *Prop wash.* He had flown into the wake behind *Dreadnought*—a narrow maelstrom of turbulent air that had nearly spun him right into the hard floor of Truckee Meadow.

Now he had lost all the ground he had gained in catching up to *Dreadnought*. And he had not only scared the stuffing out of himself; he had startled every one of the spectators down there on the concrete. For an instant it looked as if *Dago Red* were going to be an oil stain on the high desert.

In the *Dago Red* skybox, Kerchenfaut's heart resumed beating.

"Well, that was . . . exciting," he heard Lockwood say on the radio.

Kerchenfaut removed his baseball hat and wiped his bald pate. Yeah, exciting. He had had enough of such excitement. He wanted this race over with and in the record book.

In the grandstands, the fans were on their feet. This had turned into a hell of a race! No one could remember seeing such a contest, at least in the Gold Division, with the leaders trading places, flying through each other's prop wash. Every eyeball at Stead Field was trained on the pair of fighters dueling out there over the desert. Sandy Sanders, the announcer, was giving them the numbers: *Dreadnought* had just turned a lap that was 20 miles per hour faster than its qualifying time last Monday. Where had all this speed come from? Why wasn't *Dago Red* catching up?

Actually, *Dago Red was* catching up. But slowly. Painfully. In such tiny increments you couldn't see it from the ground. Both Kerchenfaut and Lockwood knew what had to be done, and Lockwood was doing it. He had the throttle at full power. Forget pampering the engine. Forget survival. Just being faster than the Sea Fury no longer mattered. He had to *catch* the damned Sea Fury before he could outrun it.

It was time to pour on everything *Dago* had. *Melt it.*

Four laps to go. *Dago* was closing the gap, averaging 470 miles per hour on each lap.

And Sanders was using up all of *Dreadnought*'s reserves.

Around the pylons they went, *Dago Red* closing the gap on *Dreadnought*'s tail. On lap five, Lockwood pulled alongside Sanders, taking a high, outside line. Now you could see the top-speed difference between the two fighters. It was clear that *Dreadnought* was going flat out, exceeding all its previous lap speeds. But it wasn't enough. *Dago Red* had a 20-knot advantage now. With 4,000 howling horsepower at work, *Dago Red* went skimming past *Dreadnought*'s right wing like a Ferrari overtaking a dump truck.

And the fans went crazy. Two passes between the front-runners—in a Gold Trophy race! It was the best race anyone had seen at Reno for a decade.

Once again, the championship was *Dago*'s to lose. And as Lockwood and Kerchenfaut—and Sanders, for that matter—well knew, everything rode now on *Dago Red*'s high-strung Merlin—the bitch-mistress of engines that could still turn on him like a fury from hell.

Lockwood pulled the throttle back a tiny increment. Buy a little insurance. But that was all, just an increment. He didn't want to have to explain to Kerchenfaut, Terry Bland, or anyone else how he sat there and *twice* let *Dreadnought* overhaul him because he didn't give *Dago* enough throttle.

"White flag," announced the race director on the radio.

One more lap. *Hang together, baby.* All he had to do was stay in the race now. He was maintaining a solid three-second lead over Sanders.

Up ahead was a traffic jam. Lockwood was about to lap the slowest-moving Sea Fury—Matt Jackson in *Bad Attitude.* Now he had to pass Jackson in order to stay ahead of *Dreadnought.*

Lockwood took a high, wide line. He went zipping past Jackson with a speed advantage of over 100 miles per hour, being careful this time to avoid the Sea Fury's wake. And being careful—*really* careful—not to nip a pylon or cross the dead line in front of the ramp and the stands. Don't make the mistake that David Price made two years ago and lose the race because of a damned pylon cut.

Down the long western leg—the Valley of Speed. A hard four and one-half G turn around pylon 5—*Don't cut it close!*—turning, turning. *Don't nip the dead line!*—down the home stretch in front of the grandstands . . . all alone . . . still three seconds ahead . . . all alone . . .

"Checkered flag!"

Lockwood pointed *Dago Red*'s nose upward, to the cool-down orbit over the field, while he let the Merlin gradually shed its load.

He knew he ought to be feeling something like exhilaration. He'd won this thing! He'd flown *Dago Red* across the finish line in first place. But he couldn't celebrate yet. Still on his mind was what happened to David Price in 1996, who was still sitting in his cockpit on the ramp after beating *Strega* across the finish line when he learned that he'd been bumped back to second place for a pylon cut.

Now Lockwood had to wait and worry. Had he flown a clean race—no pylon cuts, no dead-line excursions?

He was the first to land. And as he taxied up the ramp, to his parking spot in front of the grandstands, he could see Kerchenfaut's face. He was grinning like a baboon. All the guys on the crew were grinning, waving their arms, flashing the thumbs-up. They looked as if they had just won the Super Bowl. Or the World Series. Or the National Championship Air Race.

Lockwood shut down the big Merlin and waited for the blades to tick to a stop. He pulled his helmet off and let the cool breeze waft over him. The guys from his crew were swarming up the leading edge of the wing. Everyone was grinning, cheering, hands clasped together.

Okay, thought Lockwood. There it is. We won.

Dusk descended like a curtain over Truckee Meadow. At the very instant the sun dipped behind the High Sierra, you could feel the arctic coldness spreading over the desert. The stands at Stead Field were mostly empty now, and the long columns of vehicles still clogged the two-lane access road. The lights of the bumper-to-bumper traffic snaked up the interstate all the way into Reno. The thirty-fifth running of the National Championship Air Races at Reno was over.

Only the pits were busy, still filled with the movement of trucks and tugs and golf carts. Beneath awnings and under the wings of still-crackling, hissing race planes, impromptu parties sprang up. By now everyone was pulling on flight jackets and parkas and down vests. Some of the parties were transient, rolling from pit to pit, trading booze and jibes and promises to come back next year and blow everyone's doors off.

The noisiest celebration, not surprisingly, was up front, in the big eighteen-wheel pit complex of the *Dago Red* team. The champagne was flowing, and each of the red-and-white-jacketed *Dago Red* team members was wearing a goofy, king-of-the-world grin.

They were a happy bunch. *Numero uno!* They had come to Reno to win this thing, kick some butt, by God, and that's exactly what they did! *We beat that son of a bitch!*

Bruce Lockwood, for his part, was still the guy on the Wheaties box, grinning and shaking hands and making sure all the crew got credit for the victory. For the Unlimited Gold Trophy winner to be a real-life Mr. Nice Guy was a hell of a change. In fact, it was enough to make a few old-timers grumble that this kid might be behaving *too* damned modestly. It was embarrassing! Air-racing champions, for Christ's sake, were supposed to be *flamboyant*. They should be swashbucklers like Roscoe Turner, hotshots like Darryl Greenamyer, Skip Holm, or spit-in-your-eye Tiger Destefani. Or even ol' High Noon himself, Lyle Shelton. Instead, they got an Eagle Scout.

That night, in the big hangar that formerly housed the Formula One airplanes, they held the annual racers' banquet. "Banquet," of course, was a colloquialism at Reno, meaning they crammed about five hundred pilots, crew, family, friends, and groupies onto narrow bench tables and fed them ribs and beans and corn, served on plastic plates, the whole mess washed down with gallons of draft Coors and wine coolers.

After dinner, the race-committee chairman, Jack Walther, took the stand and delivered the standard homilies, praising the officials, thanking the pilots, and observing a moment of respect for the Formula One racer Dick Roberts, who had lost his life on Thursday. All in all, it had been an eventful and, for the Reno Air Racing Association, a profitable race week.

Then they summoned the winners and near winners of each class, one after the other, and let them gush a little for the crowd. The new Unlimited champion, the all-American kid Bruce Lockwood, shuffled up to the stage. He gave the crowd that big poster-boy grin and proceeded to thank his crew; *Dago Red*'s owner, Terry Bland; his buddy Bob Hannah; his wife, his kids—everyone in the Northern Hemisphere—for making it possible for him to, you know, *win* this nice trophy.

The crowd applauded, but not with the same old whistling, cheering, raised-fist, foot-stomping gusto they used to display when one of their flinty-eyed hell-raisers took the championship. It just wasn't the same. This guy Lockwood was carrying on as if he had won the damned sixth-grade spelling bee.

Out of sight and ignored by the crowd and the photographers and the race reporters was last year's Unlimited Air Racing champion. He was gumming a wad of dip the size of a Ping-Pong ball.

The Gunfighter . . . he was leaning against a pillar, arms crossed, squinting at the stage like a cat watching a birdbath. *I'll tell you what you're gonna see out there: twenty-three losers—and me.*

"Whaddya think, Tiger?" someone asked. "You gonna race *Strega* next year?"

"Bet your ass."

"Think you can beat those guys?"

Tiger Destefani looked at the guy as if he had just landed from Uranus. He didn't answer right away. He launched a glob of dip— *Sploot!*—in a perfect six-foot arc across the hangar floor.

Then he put on the old squint-eyed, kick-ass Gunfighter grin. "I'm gonna thrash 'em like a stepchild."

UNLIMITED CHAMPIONS
1964–1998

Year	Winner		MPH
1964	Mira Slovak		376.84
1965	Darryl Greenamyer	#1 *Greenamyer Bearcat*	375.10
1966	Darryl Greenamyer	#1 *Smirnoff*	396.22
1967	Darryl Greenamyer	#1 *Smirnoff*	392.62
1968	Darryl Greenamyer	#1 *Greenamyer Bearcat*	388.65
1969	Darryl Greenamyer	#1 *Conquest 1*	412.63
1970	Clay Lacy	#64 *Miss Van Nuys*	387.34
1971	Darryl Greenamyer	#1 *Conquest 1*	413.99
1972	Gunther Balz	#5 *Roto-Finish Special*	416.16
1973	Lyle Shelton	#77 *7¼% Special*	428.16
1974	Ken Burnstine	#33 *Miss Suzi Q*	381.48
1975	Lyle Shelton	#77 *Aircraft Cylinder Special*	429.92
1976	Lefty Gardner	#25 *Thunderbird*	379.61
1977	Darryl Greenamyer	#5 *Red Baron*	430.70
1978	Steve Hinton	#5 *Red Baron*	415.46
1979	John Crocker	#6 *Sumthin' Else*	422.30
1980	Mac McClain	#69 *Jeannie*	433.01
1981	Skip Holm	#69 *Jeannie*	431.29
1982	Ron Helve	#4 *Dago Red*	405.09
1983	Neil Anderson	#8 *Dreadnought*	425.24
1984	Skip Holm	#84 *Stiletto*	437.621
1985	Steve Hinton	#1 *Super Corsair*	438.186
1986	Rick Brickert	#8 *Dreadnought*	434.488
1987	Bill Destefani	#7 *Strega*	452.559
1988	Lyle Shelton	#77 *Rare Bear*	456.821
1989	Lyle Shelton	#77 *Rare Bear*	450.910
1990	Lyle Shelton	#77 *Rare Bear*	468.620
1991	Lyle Shelton	#77 *Rare Bear* (Race Record)	481.618
1992	Bill Destefani	#7 *Strega*	450.835
1993	Bill Destefani	#7 *Strega*	455.380
1994	John Penney	#77 *Rare Bear* (Super Gold)	424.407
1995	Bill Destefani	#7 *Strega*	469.029
1996	Bill Destefani	#7 *Strega*	469.948
1997	Bill Destefani	#7 *Strega*	453.130
1998	Bruce Lockwood	#4 *Dago Red*	450.599

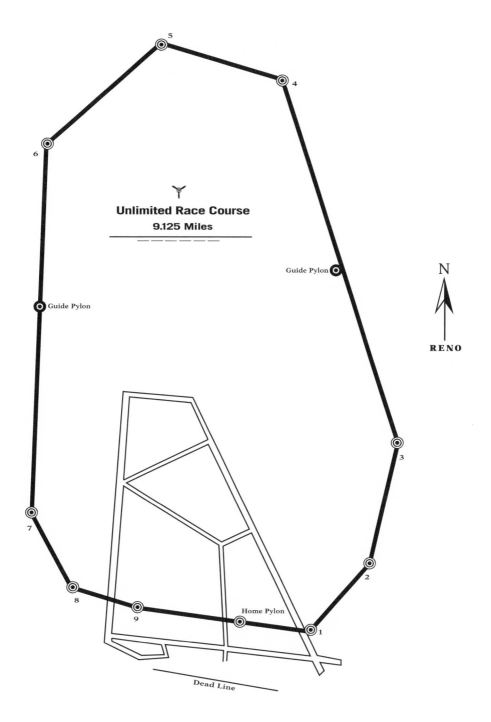

Unlimited Race Course
9.125 Miles

N

RENO

5

4

6

Guide Pylon

Guide Pylon

3

7

2

8

9

Home Pylon

1

Dead Line